To Jack   Birthday 1996

From Ron & Betty

BEHOLD YOUR KING

BEHOLD YOUR KING

by

J. C. MACAULAY

MOODY PRESS

CHICAGO

Library of Congress Cataloging in Publication Data

Macaulay, J. C. (Joseph Cordner), 1900-
  Behold your King.

  1. Bible. N.T. Matthew—Commentaries. 2. Jesus Christ—
Royal office. I. Title.

BS2575.3.M26   226'.207   81-22580

ISBN 0-8024-2417-1   AACR2

CONTENTS

PREFACE

THIS WORK DIFFERS from my previous commentaries (John, Acts, and Hebrews) in that it is not based on preached sermons, but is the product of the study. At the same time I have sought to fit the expositions to the needs of Christian people at various stages of spiritual development. That difference will reflect more in organization than in substance. Perhaps others will add the homiletic touch.

If I were to give a title to this volume, I should doubtless suggest *Behold Your King*, for one can hardly contest the regal character of Matthew's gospel.

As in former works, I have not confined myself to any one version of the text, but have used what seemed most appropriate in each situation.

I gladly acknowledge my debt to those who have gone before, leaving to us a heritage of rich study. They are wellsprings from which we draw, both for our own refreshment and for the blessing of others. My thanks are due also to those who have contributed to this work in practical ways—typing, correcting, and offering suggestions. Above all, I offer thanks to the Lord for the enabling of the Holy Spirit and pray that the distribution of the work will redound to the honor of the King.

9

INTRODUCTION

AUTHORSHIP

FROM EARLIEST TIMES the church has held that the gospel that bears the name of Matthew was written by the apostle of that name, the former tax collector. Eusebius quotes Papias (who belongs to the end of the first Christian century and part of the second) as saying, "Matthew, therefore, composed the oracles in the Hebrew tongue, and every one interpreted them as he was able." There can be no doubt that this early writer was referring to the apostle, and so Origen, Cyril of Jerusalem, and Jerome understood it.

If the statement attributed to Papias is correct, the question then arises: Who translated the Hebrew document into the Greek? Jerome, who made the Latin Vulgate, held that there was no certain answer to that question. We still do not have the answer. There is no good reason why Matthew himself may not have made the Greek version that survived, whereas others, like the original Hebrew autograph, were lost. Of course the evidence for such a Hebrew original is not compelling, and the whole matter carries more academic interest than devotional value.

SOURCES

From what sources did Matthew draw his material? Before we deal with that question, let us be clear in our minds that the use of sources does not negate divine inspiration. The Old Testament contains many references to source material, and Luke frankly affirms that he tracked down original sources of information so that Theophilus might have an unshakeable certainty concerning the contents of the gospel. That is clearly brought out in the revised renderings of Luke 1:1-4.

There are three possible types of sources: literary, traditional, and original.

Many believe that Mark's gospel was the first one written and that its material and order form the hard core of Matthew's and Luke's gospels. That is part of the attempt to answer the "synoptic problem," namely the similarities and the dissimilarities of the first three of our gospels.

But Matthew contains large sections of our Lord's teaching that are either omitted from Mark's gospel or passed over lightly. Where did they come from? It has been suggested that Matthew had written a previous work on the *Logia* (sayings) of Jesus Christ, which he then incorporated into his gospel, or that he utilized such a work written by someone else.

Still there are portions of Matthew's gospel that could not be accounted for in those ways. To fill the gap, a document has been imagined and given the designation Q. It is quite hypothetical, but many, even some outstanding conservative writers, have accepted it as a possible answer. Some critics regard the *Logia* and Q as one and the same. There are, of course, other completely divergent theories.

Those, then, are the suggested literary sources for Matthew's gospel. In addition, there were numerous oral traditions. They could be traced and tested by careful investigators. If Luke used that reservoir of information, certainly Matthew did.

Let us not forget that Matthew was an eyewitness of a great portion of our Lord's ministry, of which he could write firsthand. I personally feel that many writers on the subject have not given sufficient weight to that aspect of it. Matthew was a constant companion of Christ from the moment of his call to the end of our Lord's earthly ministry, and he must have had sufficient personal acquaintance with Him before that crisis day to prepare him for the revolutionary step of leaving all to follow Jesus.

We may ask, Did Matthew need Mark's gospel as a source of basic information? Even if Mark's gospel were written first, which is widely though not universally accepted, Matthew had actually more immediate access to the basic material than Mark who, if tradition speaks truly, must have depended on Peter as his guide. With all that in mind, I suggest that Matthew's own eyewitness testimony may be the prior source for his gospel, with tested oral tradition a good second, and literary sources an uncertain quantity. If the same Holy Spirit guides the evangelists to record the same general story, we shall expect similarities. If He directs them to different emphases, we shall expect dissimilarities. That may not sound as scholarly as the Markan, *Logia,* and *Q* hypotheses, but it seems simpler and more natural.

DATE

Matthew did not append a date to his work, and we have no way of fixing it exactly. His gospel undoubtedly was written before the destruction of Jerusalem by Titus in A.D. 70. If that event were history at the time of Matthew's writing, we should expect a clearer distinction between it and the eschatological events envisioned in chapter 24. The suggestion that our first gospel was produced between 60 and 65 seems reasonable, but that is all we can say.

PURPOSE

Two of the evangelists state their purpose clearly. Luke declares that he wrote to give Theophilus (and therefore all readers) a certainty in his belief (Luke 1:4), whereas John affirms his objective, "that ye might believe that Jesus is the Christ, the Son of God, and that believing ye might have life through his name" (John 20:31). Matthew has no such categorical statement of purpose, but his method indicates his aim. Throughout his gospel, he keeps presenting the various incidents in the life of Jesus as fulfillments of messianic prophecies, so that we have a cumulative demonstration that Jesus is the Messiah foretold in the Old Testament. That does not confine the relevance of Matthew's testimony to the Jews. We remember that messianic prophecy presents the Messiah as "a light to lighten the Gentiles" as well as "the glory of thy people Israel" (Luke 2:32).

VIEWPOINT

It is evident that the four gospels present our Lord in different lights, thus giving us a fourfold portrait. Those have been variously stated. For instance, the four gospels have been likened to the four heads in Ezekiel's symbolic presentation of the cherubim as follows:

Matthew portrays Christ under the aspect of the lion;
Mark portrays Christ under the aspect of the ox;
Luke portrays Christ under the aspect of the man;
John portrays Christ under the aspect of the eagle.

Following that symbolism, we see the King in Matthew, the servant in Mark, the Son of man in Luke, and the Son of God in John.

The justification of that analysis is a study of considerable magnitude, and beyond our purpose here. I am satisfied it is a valid distinction, so long as it is not pressed to extremes. For that reason, I adopt in this study the suggestion that Matthew presents Christ, the King.

OUTLINE

Matthew's gospel falls very naturally into four divisions:

1. Presenting the King in His preparations (1:1—4:11)
2. Presenting the King in His procedures (4:12—16:20)
3. Presenting the King in His passion (16:21—27:66)
4. Presenting the King in His power (28:1-20)

PART ONE

The King in His Preparations

(1:1—4:11)

1

THE GENEALOGY

(1:1-17)

GENEALOGY IS NOT AN IMPORTANT FACTOR in the hiring of a servant, but it is a primary consideration in the accession of a king. The gospel of the King, therefore, gives the family tree, with particular emphasis to Abraham, the father of the Hebrew race, and David, progenitor of the royal line.

It is frequently stated that this genealogy establishes Christ's right to the throne of David. But is that completely true? For one thing, it is the line of Joseph, and Jesus was not the son of Joseph, save in an adoptive sense. In the second place, this line traces through Jeconiah, of whom Jeremiah said: "Thus saith the LORD, Write ye this man child-less, a man that shall not prosper in his days: for no man of his seed shall prosper, sitting upon the throne of David, and ruling any more in Judah" (Jeremiah 22:30). If Jesus is a descendant of Jeconiah, He is barred from the throne by that curse. To qualify, He must be descended from David, but He must bypass Jeconiah. How is that done? By the virgin birth. If Matthew 1:16 read, "Jacob begat Joseph the husband of Mary, and Joseph begat Jesus, who is called Christ," then the curse of Jeconiah would rob Him of all claim to the Davidic title. But now, being free from that curse through being born of the virgin, He secures double title to the throne, being of the seed of David through Mary. We can see, then, how important is the change of phrasing in verse 16.

Many have drawn attention to the women in this messianic line. Why these five should be mentioned, to the exclusion of all others, is probably beyond us to answer, but as we look at them they surely remind us of the grace of God. Tamar (see Genesis 38) played the harlot with her father-in-law, Judah. Of course Judah's guilt was just as great. Rahab (Joshua 2 and 6) was the harlot of Jericho who learned the fear of the Lord and put her trust in Him so that she became a mother in Israel. Ruth was the Moabitess, a member of a cursed nation, who nevertheless showed herself an example of virtue and faithfulness, was honorably married to Boaz, and became the great-grandmother of David. Bathsheba was the woman who beguiled David by too freely displaying her person at her ablutions and involved the king in the double sin of adultery and murder. Mary was a modest village girl whom God chose for the most blessed child-bearing in all the history of our race and whom Elizabeth called "the mother of my Lord." So in those women we see the sordid and the noble, the base and the pure. In all of them we see God stooping down to lift the fallen, the humble, to places of high honor.

It should be pointed out that the three equal divisions of the genealogy are obtained by certain omissions. Between Joram and Uzziah (v. 8) three are omitted—Ahaziah, Joash, and Amaziah. Jehoiakim is omitted between Josiah and Jeconiah (v. 11). The reason for those omissions cannot be certainly known. Both were periods of apostasy, when the nation was in eclipse.

2

THE NATIVITY

(1:18-25)

MATTHEW RELATES THE STORY of the nativity from Joseph's point of view, whereas Luke describes it as it affected Mary.

It should be remembered that the engagement of a couple was just as binding among the Jews as the actual marriage, so that the laws of marriage with respect to faithfulness applied from the day of betrothal. When it was reported that Mary was pregnant during the days of the betrothal, Joseph's sense of justice came into conflict with his kindly disposition. He had every right to haul her before the court of the synagogue and have the terms of Jewish law enforced so far as Roman dominion allowed, but he could not bring himself to expose her to public shame, even though the stoning would have been omitted. Yet his personal honor would not permit him to go through with the engagement. What should he do? The contract must be voided without public scandal. Perhaps she could be sent off somewhere until the issue was resolved. I sometimes wonder if that had something to do with Mary's visit to Elizabeth, related by Luke.

Gabriel had visited Mary when she was wide awake, but the angel came to Joseph in a dream, as he slept. Why the difference? Was Joseph too preoccupied in his waking hours to entertain an angel visitant? Is disturbing our slumbers the only way heaven can break through to us? At any rate, it was comforting news the angel brought to distraught Joseph. But it was faith-testing news. Joseph was asked to believe that the pregnancy of Mary was not the result of unfaithfulness, but was a miraculous, divine operation—the work of the Holy Spirit. In addition, he was asked to believe that the child to be born was God's appointed Savior. So far from being the fruit of sin, He was to be the great deliverer from sin.

The angel helped Joseph's faith by referring to the great prophecy of Isaiah concerning the virgin's child, whose name was to be Immanuel, "God with us." Both the angel and Joseph apparently regarded the passage in Isaiah 7:14 as speaking of a true virgin. So Gabriel interpreted it, and so Joseph accepted it. In the light of that ancient Scripture, it was easier for Joseph's faith to grasp the announcement of the angel. Then, believing the miraculous nature of the conception that had taken place, he could more readily accept the divine mission of the child.

Without further question, Joseph threw the protection of marriage around Mary and fulfilled the part of father to the child when He was born, giving Him the name announced by the angel—Jesus, or Jehoshua, Savior.

3

THE INFANCY

(2:1-23)

WHO WERE THE WISE MEN, or magi, who came to worship the infant Christ? Our Christmas song, "We Three Kings of Orient Are," depends on legend. It is more likely that they were priests of the monotheistic faith of Zoroaster, a cult that had taken root in Persia. They were students of the stars, but their astronomy was considerably mixed with astrology, which holds that the movements of the heavenly bodies have some connection with events on earth.

Nevertheless, I am convinced that the magi of our story had something more than their astrology to go by. There is no reason why those scholars could not have had access to the ancient Jewish literature, including the sacred literature of the Old Testament. Genesis 1:14 states that the lights in the firmament of heaven should be for signs, and Balaam's wonderful prophecy, given in Numbers 24:17, speaks of the rise of Israel's Prince in terms of the coming forth of a star.

Notice the four instruments of guidance used by the magi. First there was the star, with the support of an ancient prophecy. Then there was reason. They naturally reasoned that the King should be born in the capital city, Jerusalem, and in the house of the ruling monarch, Herod. Next there was the guidance of the holy Scriptures. The scribes were able to tell Herod, on the basis of Micah 5:2, that Christ was to be born in Bethlehem. Finally there was the dream, warning them not to return to Jerusalem or go near Herod. Now which of those instruments of guidance led them wrong? It may be humiliating to admit it, but it was reason that got them off the track. We had better submit our reason to the corrective of divine revelation.

The prophet Micah specified which Bethlehem was to be the birthplace of the King. There was a Bethlehem in Zebulun, so to keep the record clear, the district was named along with the village. Ephrathah was a section of Judah, just south of Jerusalem.

Matthew has been called the Jewish gospel, as over against Mark's Roman gospel, Luke's Greek gospel, and John's universal gospel. Those distinctions must not be pressed too hard. Certainly Matthew is the most Hebraic of the four, but is it not interesting that this very Jewish gospel opens with the coming of the Gentiles to worship the newborn King and ends with the command to go to all the nations with the good news?

We do not know how old Jesus was when the magi came. Certainly they did not come the night of His birth when the shepherds paid their visit. By the time the Eastern visitors arrived, the little family had moved into a house (2:11). When Herod sent out his soldiers to the slaughter of the infants, he ordered all in the district "from two years old and under" to be slain. That he did on the basis of his enquiry of the magi as to the time of the appearing of the star. The actual number of infants killed could not have been great in a small village and the immediate surroundings, but the wickedness of the deed does not depend on the number slain.

The motive of Herod's atrocity could be only fear for his own regal state and that of his heirs. The infant Jesus was a rival who must be got rid of at all costs, and the sooner the better.

It is strange that men with a lust for power fail to reckon with God. Herod ought to have realized that One whose birth had been predicted in the sacred oracles and was heralded by such a remarkable heavenly sign, bringing those oriental philosophers to worship the infant King, would be under the protection of the hand of God. Yet he thought he could thwart God's purposes, that he could catch God unaware and get through the divine defenses. How foolish men can become!

Jesus Christ is the true Israel. It will not be surprising, then, if analogies appear between the nation and its prototype. The infant nation found shelter in Egypt in a time of need and then was brought out of Egypt by the mighty hand of God to begin its national history. Hosea sums that up in the statement: "When Israel was a child, then I loved him, and called my son out of Egypt" (Hosea 11:1). Matthew, by the Holy Spirit, sees that as more than a historic statement. It reaches forward, prophetically embracing Christ, whose sojourn in Egypt was another point of union with those He came to save.

Apparently Joseph intended to settle permanently in Bethlehem, where he had set up house after the birth of Jesus. On the return from Egypt, the news that Archelaus had succeeded his father on the throne made Joseph fear that Bethlehem might not be safe territory for them. Once more he was given divine direction through a dream, and returned to Nazareth. That meant facing the gossips and trying to rebuild a carpentry business he had given up when he went to the enrolling in Bethlehem. There was divine fulfillment in that also. The holy child was destined to bear the name of scorn and reproach before He should be given the "name which is above every name" (Philippians 2:9). Nazarene was a name of scorn among the Jews. "Can any good thing come out of Nazareth?" was one of their proverbs. There are always meaning, purpose, and fulfillment in God's leadings. And that supports Luke's simple statement, "They returned into Galilee, to their own city Nazareth" (Luke 2:39).

4

THE FORERUNNER

(3:1-12)

NONE OF THE EVANGELISTS gives John the Baptist's complete message. Only Matthew announces his text as herald of the King—a call to repentance on the ground that "the kingdom of heaven is at hand." There has been much discussion whether the term *kingdom* is to be understood in the sense of rule or realm, the exercise of authority, or the sphere of sovereignty. Actually there was nothing new in the idea of the rule of the heavens being at hand. Back in the time of Daniel, King Nebuchadnezzar was severely disciplined to teach him that very truth, "that the heavens do rule" (Daniel 4:26). What John the Baptist announced was a new breaking in of the rule of the heavens upon the earthly scene, a new operation of the divine sovereignty. The King was about to appear. His very presence would be a call, first to Israel, then to all men, to submit to the divine rule. The principles of the heavenly kingdom would be presented, not only in definition, but in living demonstration. The basis of citizenship would be clearly established.

For all his remarkable insight into the dignity of the person of Jesus, His messiahship and His saviorhood, John could not see all that was involved in his statement, "The kingdom of heaven is at hand" (3:2). He did know, however, that it had ethical implications. The only proper preparation for that encounter with the kingdom of heaven was repentance. The kingdom that was drawing near in the person of the King was a kingdom of righteousness. To enter it, men must leave their sins behind them. The putting away of sin that the King, as the Lamb of God, was to effect, would not rule out the necessity of repentance. It would open the way into the kingdom of God for repentant people.

With that call to repentance, John fulfilled his mission of preparation. Living an ascetic life, he drew to his preaching and baptism great crowds, some sincerely confessing and turning from their sins, some hypocritically joining the parade without any heart-searching. John, discerning the hypocrisy and pride of the Pharisees and Sadducees, members of the religious orders of the day, challenged them to substantiate their professed repentance, assuring them that the coming of the kingdom would draw a clear line of demarcation between the good trees and the bad, between the wheat and the chaff. John's baptism was preparatory and symbolic, but the baptism administered by the King would be inward, mystical, spiritual, and decisive, by which one would become a partaker of the Holy Spirit. The approach of the King reveals what men are and seals their destiny. Whether our end be the heavenly garner or the unquenchable fire depends on what we do with Him.

5

THE BAPTISM

(3:13-17)

JOHN DID NOT KNOW until he had baptized Jesus, and the Spirit in the form of a dove had come upon Him, that the applicant for baptism was none other than the Son of God (John 1:29-34). Why, then, did he hesitate to baptize Him, saying, "I have need to be baptized of thee" (3:14)? Those two men, with only six months between their ages, were kinsmen, and their mothers were close and understanding friends. No doubt they knew each other "after the flesh," and John sensed the moral grandeur of his Galilean cousin. Perhaps he even weighed the possibility of Jesus' being the One he was sent to proclaim, but could not know till the sign was given.

If, then, the baptism of John was a baptism of repentance, calling for a confession of sin, why was Jesus baptized? He had no sin to confess, a fact that John vaguely felt, and certainly there is no consciousness of sin suggested in our Lord's answer to John's objection. But He did say that even for Him baptism was an act of righteousness. John was a man sent from God, with a message from God that included the call to baptism. Being made under the law, Jesus regarded obedience to every ordinance of God as obligatory. He would not stand aloof, claiming an exemption that might prove a stumbling block to others.

But besides being an act of righteousness, baptism was for Jesus an act of identification. The apostle Paul speaks of our baptism as an identification with Christ, but we should remember that His baptism was an identification with us, first with His people of Israel, but also with the Gentiles whom He came to save. Before He was associated with the transgressors on the cross, He associated Himself with them in the act of baptism.

Baptism was an act of committal. It takes more than the waters of baptism to wash away sin, but in baptism, which was associated with confession and repentance, the sinless one committed Himself in a dramatic fashion to the work of sin-bearing. He later spoke of His cross as a baptism (Luke 12:50; Matthew 20:23). The baptism in water at the beginning was a token and symbol of the baptism of blood at the end.

The answer to that act of righteousness, identification, and committal was the opening heaven, the descending dove, and the approving voice. The three times that the voice from heaven came to Jesus during His earthly ministry were occasions when He definitely committed Himself to the cross. The theme of conversation on the Mount of Transfiguration was "his decease which he should accomplish at Jerusalem" (Luke 9:31). Then came the word of approval (v. 35). Again, the voice from heaven at the time of the coming of the Greeks followed His acceptance of the hour of suffering (John 12:27-28). And we should remember that it is the Christ of the cross, or in other words, the Lamb, who is worshiped in heaven (Revelation 5:9-10, 13).

With the commendation came the anointing, an anointing that had been prophetically announced. "The spirit of the Lord God is upon me; because the LORD hath anointed me to preach" (Isaiah 61:1). So wrote the prophet Isaiah, and in the synagogue of Nazareth the Lord Jesus took up that word and added, "This day is this scripture fulfilled in your ears" (Luke 4:21). But when did that anointing take place? Surely at the time of His baptism, when the Holy Spirit in the form of a dove descended upon Him.

The anointing of kings and priests in the Old Testament had double signification. It was part of the act of consecration to the appointed task, and it signified an enduement of divine grace for the conducting of the high office. What was symbol for them was transmitted into divine reality for Jesus, as Peter so clearly stated later in the home of Cornelius the Roman: "God anointed Jesus of Nazareth with the Holy Ghost and with power: who went about doing good" (Acts 10:38). If we are to serve effectively, it must be by the same anointing.

6

THE TESTING

(4:1-11)

DOES THE TEMPTATION OF JESUS seem inappropriate? Further thought should convince us that, on the contrary, it was exceedingly appropriate.

The first Adam was tempted and failed. The last Adam was put to the test, not to see whether He would fail, but to show that He would not fail. The task for which He had come into the world called for a demonstration of fitness.

We mostly fall into temptation when we are neglectful of the leading of the Holy Spirit or resist His leading. Jesus was led by the Spirit to the place of temptation. There was divine purpose in His temptation. He was qualifying for the priesthood (Hebrews 4:15).

Our Lord was tempted directly by Satan. That was to be expected. Satan's princedom was being challenged by the Lord from heaven, and who should meet the challenge but the prince of this world himself? Jesus had come to champion fallen man and to recover lost territory for the kingdom of heaven. That was no little local quarrel. The whole kingdom of Satan was at stake. He certainly would not entrust that encounter to a lieutenant.

The tactics of the attack should be noted. The adversary struck at a weak point, then at a strong point, then at the vital point. The physical, the spiritual, and the vocational all came under fire.

The forty days of fasting had certainly weakened the Savior's body, and the need of food was urgent. The suggestion to use His powers and prerogatives as the Son of God to meet the need was surely legitimate—or so it seemed on the surface. But see what was involved. First, the temptation predicates the priority of the physical in man. Second, it pointed to a line of action without reference to the will of

God. Third, turning stones into bread to satisfy His own hunger would be abandoning the path of complete trust in the Father. Fourth, it would be counter to the principle of the incarnation that He should lay aside the independent exercise of His own divine attributes as Son of God in order to live as man, in full obedience to and dependence upon God. So, in answer to Satan's "if thou be the Son of God," He affirms His humanity and accepts man's place, while stoutly rejecting the priority of the physical.

Having failed in a frontal attack on the weak point, that of physical hunger induced by a fast of forty days, the tempter tried a subtle attack on the strong point—our Lord's faith in God and in God's Word. Satan knows that the strong point is often the least guarded, just because it seems to need less guarding, and so our strength is turned into weakness. In the second temptation, Jesus was challenged to demonstrate His confidence in the Father's promises by doing something that would require the Father to do what He had said. Casting Himself down from the wing of the Temple would show how utterly He trusted God's promise to send angels to His rescue and would also prove that God was true to His Word. There was just one flaw. Satan omitted the phrase "in all thy ways" which sets boundaries to the area in which such angelic intervention may be expected. Be suspicious when God's adversaries begin to quote Scripture. Our Lord answered a wrong use of Scripture with a right use of Scripture, quoting a great principle from Deuteronomy 6:16, which is capable of wide application. God's promises will be operative when circumstances call for them, but He will not permit us to create artificial situations just to test whether His promise will be made good. "Thou shalt not tempt (put on trial) the Lord thy God" (4:7).

The third temptation hit the vital spot of Christ's mission. In Psalm 2 God calls Him "my king," and in Psalm 110 He is invited to sit at God's right hand until His enemies are made His footstool. Here, then, is God's King, the Messiah, about to set in motion that operation that would wrest the kingdom of this world from the hands of its rebel prince. But it was to be a costly victory. Between Jesus and the throne loomed the cross. Now the prince of this world suggested a compromise. Jesus could have what He came for, the kingdoms of this world, without going the way of the cross. Just one act of homage, of worship, and all would be His. Of course that one act of homage would be an acknowledgment of Satan as overlord, and so would establish Satan's position permanently, with the Son of God as his vassal. A subtle scheme indeed! In answer, Jesus imperiously dismissed Satan from His presence, again supporting His position with a word of holy Scripture. He will not grant to any the worship that belongs to God alone. He will have the kingdom, but only by means of the Father's appointing.

PART TWO

The King in His Procedures

(4:12—16:20)

7

THE START

(4:12-25)

MATTHEW INTRODUCES US directly to the great Galilean ministry of Christ. For what preceded that we must apply to John's gospel. Again, Matthew is silent on the matter of Nazareth's rejection of its own Son. Luke has preserved that record for us (Luke 4:16-30).

Jesus left Judaea to allow the rumor about His baptizing more disciples than John to die down (John 4:1-3). He completed the journey into Galilee when He heard that Herod had imprisoned John. Why that turn of events should affect the course of our Lord's ministry is a question we cannot answer. It does indicate that our Lord was deeply moved by it and attached great significance to it.

His rejection in Nazareth gave Capernaum its supreme opportunity. He made that town on the north shore of the Sea of Galilee His headquarters, so affording it, and the region around, the spiritual privileges predicted by Isaiah (Isaiah 9:1-2). But Capernaum did not rise to its privilege, and the blessing turned into a curse (Matthew 11:23-24).

Our Lord took up John the Baptist's text, with its call to repentance in view of the breaking in of the kingdom of heaven upon the earthly scene. In whatever setting the kingdom of heaven is announced, it calls for repentance on the part of sinful men. Whether the term has special reference to the earthly, messianic kingdom, or whether it embraces "the word of the truth of the gospel," it commands repentance. "Except ye repent, ye shall all likewise perish" (Luke 13:3, 5).

If the anonymous companion of Andrew (John 1:35-42) that day when they left John the Baptist to follow Jesus was, as many believe, John the brother of James, three of the four whom Jesus called from their fishing by the Sea of Galilee had already met Him. That doubtless accounts for their readiness to leave their fish, their nets, and their boats to accept the new occupation of fishing for men at His command. It was appropriate that He should use the figure of fishing when calling those fishermen, but the time would come when He could change His figure and speak in terms of tending sheep. The shepherd heart had to be developed in those Galileans. It was a chastened fisherman who accepted the commission to "feed my sheep" (John 21:17).

Teaching, preaching, healing. That set the pattern for the whole ministry. What Matthew calls "the gospel of the kingdom," Mark calls "the gospel of God." It is both, and it is a gospel of wholeness, of deliverance. The physical healings are certainly symbolic of that "cure of souls" that Christ came to effect in all who came to Him, and promise of the redemption of the body, when "this corruptible shall have put on incorruption, and this mortal shall have put on immortality" (1 Corinthians 15:54).

8

THE PRINCIPLES OF THE KINGDOM

(5:1–7:29)

WE CALL IT THE SERMON ON THE MOUNT, and the opening phrases of Matthew 5 justify the designation. It was addressed to His "disciples," a larger company than the "apostles" and from whom the apostles were drawn. No doubt the multitudes were within hearing range, and how many of them became disciples while they listened to those wonderful words of life we cannot tell.

To some the Sermon on the Mount is of purely academic interest, since they regard it as pertaining to the millennial kingdom and not to the present age. According to that view it was of force until our Lord withdrew His offer of the kingdom to Israel, or until Paul turned to the Gentiles, when it was nullified until the kingdom is again introduced by the return of the Lord to reign from Jerusalem over all the earth.

I do not believe, however, that the Lord would confuse us by presenting an ethic that would be valid only for a few months, or a few years at most, and then be withdrawn for two millennia. I am satisfied that we have here a definitive standard of conduct for the Christian, and if those who think otherwise challenge me to practice it (as they have a right to do), I simply answer that my failure does not alter the standard. To remove the standard to the academic shelf may make reading the Sermon on the Mount more comfortable, but I believe the sermon was given to make us very uncomfortable. The attainment is another question, and a living one at that.

THE NEW HAPPINESS (5:3-12)

The Beatitudes are divisible into two groups—beatitudes of character (5:3-9), and beatitudes of conflict (5:10-12). In the first group happiness comes from the inner springs, from what a man has come to be, or from his inner reactions. The popular virtues and the popular vices are equally conspicuous by their absence from this catalogue of happiness. What men admire in their fellows is omitted, and what men ordinarily despise is made a beatitude. How much room does society make for "the poor in spirit" or for the meek? They will be pushed to the wall every time. But consider: "Theirs is the kingdom of heaven"; "they shall inherit the earth." In terms of the ultimate, the self-reliant and those who hit back are fools.

The world pays formal tribute to mercy, but apart from the sentimental appeals that bombard us from many quarters, little of it is shown. The man of the world may be moved to give a pint of blood, but he will take his full pound of flesh in business. A war-weary world is looking for peacemakers to save it from extinction, but its heroes are still the warmakers—its Alexanders and Caesars and Napoleons.

Every virtue has its own benediction, except that the poor in spirit and the persecuted have the same reward (5:3, 10). That surely tells us that the "poor in spirit" are no craven chickens. They can "take" persecution, can stand up to it and overcome it, and they receive the same recognition as the army of the martyrs. What, then, makes them "poor in spirit"? They are not self-confident braggarts, full of their own importance, but place their reliance on God and give glory to Him.

Those are spiritual laws that operate with the same consistency as the laws of nature. Inheriting the earth is not just an arbitrary reward for meekness. It is to meekness as effect is to cause. Seeing God is not an arbitrary reward for purity of heart. It is the efficient cause of seeing God. The less evident ones are just as truly laws of the heavenly kingdom.

There is no suggestion of salvation by good works. We are dealing with the laws that operate within the kingdom of heaven, not with the requisite for entrance.

The second group of beatitudes has to do with conflict. There is another kingdom, the kingdom of this world, which is at enmity with the kingdom of heaven and all who belong to it. Whoever casts in his lot with the heavenly realm becomes a target for the powers of darkness, who use the citizens of this present evil world to harass the citizens of heaven. Persecution of various sorts, including reviling and malicious reports, is to be expected, and should be accepted, not as a great misfortune, but as a privilege. Our Lord affirms that it is an occasion for rejoicing, not only because of the recompense assured, but also because of the noble fellowship into which it brings us. We become companions of the prophets. Rejoicing in affliction now is practicing for the greater joys above. (1 Peter 4:12-13).

THE NEW RESPONSIBILITY (5:13-16)

Salt and light. What connection is there between the two? How can we be both? Our Lord looks for a quality in His people that will do in the moral and spiritual realm what salt and light do in the material realm. Salt stays corruption, and light chases darkness.

We have heard of our pioneers "salting down the bacon." In the days before refrigeration plants pork would not long stay fresh and usable without such a process. Despite the optimism of the early 1900s, the twentieth century has not witnessed much moral and spiritual advance. We are a race of sinners, and society tends to corruption as meat tends to spoil. When the church of Jesus Christ is fulfilling its mission in the power of the Holy Spirit, the process of corruption is slowed down and in some measure reversed. The Wesleyan revival challenged all that was cruel and vulgar and debauched in English society, and went far to restore it to decency.

Why is today's society sinking ever deeper into the mire of corruption, with one in two marriages ending in the divorce court, with a terrifying increase in illegitimately conceived babies, with the crime rate skyrocketing, with moral standards being held up to ridicule by so many intellectuals, with the very idea of authority being laughed out of court? Has the church lost its savor, and so become helpless to stem the tide? So it would seem. The church has become worldly, pompous, "at ease in Zion," sensuous, or else it has become censorious, critical, quarrelsome, ever finding new issues over which to create new divisions. The testimony is lost in the complacency, in the luxury, or in the noise of beating drums. The individual Christian and each local church must take up the challenge of the responsibility to see that sin is rebuked by a living witness.

"The light of the knowledge of the glory of God in the face of Jesus

Christ" (2 Corinthians 4:6) is not given us to be shut up in the safety deposit box of our own heart. It is given to us to become a beacon shining in this world's darkness. That light shines out, not chiefly in word, but in deed. The life we live in the home, in the office, in the factory, in the school, tells whether we belong to Christ and either confirms our vocal testimony or gives it the lie. "If therefore the light that is in thee be darkness, how great is that darkness" (6:23). Perhaps much of our fear to speak for the Lord arises out of the realization that our conduct speaks against Him. Men are walking in darkness, groping for light. Our lives should be the lights that lead them to the Light.

THE NEW BEHAVIOR (5:17-48)

Jesus Christ did not come into the world to lower the standards of morality as an accommodation to men who neither wanted nor were able to keep God's holy law. He did not suggest that although the law was all right for the days of Moses, it was outmoded in the advanced world of Greek and Roman culture. He did not put a relative value on the great moral precepts of the Old Testament, but insisted on their absoluteness and their undying authority. A broken law is not an abrogated law. Our Lord's championship of the law took various forms. By His death on the cross, he paid the debt due to the broken law, and so repaired the breach. He honored the law of God in His own life, while ignoring many of the traditions that had grown up around it. He reaffirmed the authority of the law for His own and all generations. He revealed the inwardness of the law, thus giving it new depth and power. He provided a new means of realizing the righteous demands of the law, with freedom from its curse (see Romans 8:1-4). Some time after the return from the Babylonian captivity, the sect of the Pharisees had arisen as champions of the law, to stem the tide of carelessness that was observable in the nation. But that movement had degenerated into punctilious observance of the ceremonial law, with little attention to "the weightier matters of the law, judgment, mercy, and faith" (23:23). Jesus restored the law to its proper dignity and gave it an interpretation that goes far beyond outward action.

There is no contradiction of the law in Christ's repeated statement, "But I say unto you." In every case He throws His authority into support of the law, reveals its true intent, and sweeps away the excrescences that had gathered around it. Take the commandment against murder. It stands, but embraces far more than the fatal act of violence. According to Jesus Christ, anger directed against a person is incipient murder. Scornful and malicious language is as much a weapon of murder as dagger or poison, and its use calls for judgment. Our Lord draws His figures here from contemporary Jewish practices in law to make clear the seriousness of all offenses against human life and personality.

God will not accept an offering of worship from one whose heart is defiled with enmity against a brother/man, to say nothing of a fellow Christian or a kinsman. That being so, I wonder how much of our Sunday "worship" is just a meaningless formula, rejected by the Most High. We need to have many of our services interrupted or suspended while Christian men and women get right with each other. All those ugly names we have called one another need to be confessed and hearts knit in the love of Christ if our worship is going to be valid. Perhaps we think we can get away with our wrongdoing, but our Lord warns us that if we are obdurate and refuse to make things right, we shall ultimately face up to it and pay the full price of our stubbornness.

There is certainly no weakening of the commandment against adultery. In that area there is total war between the new behavior expounded by our Lord and the new morality so widely embraced today. Not only is the old law reiterated as an absolute, but it is here indicated that the sin of adultery does not wait for the overt act, but is committed in the heart where lust is permitted to reside. To allow the heart to run after the eyes is sin. We live in a sex-saturated society, exposed to the lure of sin. Discipline is a necessity if we are to keep pure. That discipline extends to all our members, eyes as well as hands. Even the extremest discipline is a small price to pay for purity and for deliverance from ultimate destruction. Yet there is a better way than mutilation of the body. It is our privilege to be united with Christ in His death and to be sharers of His risen life, with consequent victory over "the lust of the flesh and the lust of the eyes and the pride of life." To submit to that participation in His death brings our members into new relation to Him as instruments of righteousness and not of sin.

Adultery may be committed legally. One may secure the sanction of law to divorce his wife, but if she follows a woman's natural desire and remarries she is an adulteress, and the husband who divorced her must bear the responsibility of making her so. Likewise the man who marries the divorcee is an adulterer. If, however, the reason for the divorce was unchastity, the woman was already adulterous; she had broken the marriage bond by her behavior, and the husband could not be held accountable. In chapter 19 our Lord adds that the divorcing husband who remarries is also an adulterer. That is the divine standard, and therefore the standard by which Christians must judge such matters. So an act may be legal and still be sinful.

It is noticeable that nothing is here said about a woman divorcing her husband. The culture of that day was very different from ours. The equal rights of women were not yet established. Today, when a woman has the same recourse to law as a man, we certainly would have to apply those principles in reverse.

Our Lord, having supported the sanctity of human life and personality and the sacredness of the marriage bond, now contends for the dignity of speech. The ancient law held a man to his oath. Perjury in any form was condemned. An oath in its own place is a good thing, impressing upon men the solemnity of the situation in which it is called for. God Himself has used the oath, not as a means of strengthening His word (for what can be stronger than the word of God?), but for our sakes, as we learn in Hebrews 6:13-20. But men have abused the oath, using it to cover falsehood, whether in giving witness or in making promises. In many cases, oaths are used to add spice to one's vocabulary. The Lord Jesus not only condemns all such false uses of the oath, but actually recommends the abandonment of its use, at least on an individual basis. Unless we have control over those objects by which we swear, we have no right to swear by them. Why should we degrade the throne of God, or the footstool of God, or the city of the great King, by making them serve as supports for our shaky statements and promises? There is a better way—the dignity of a straight yes or no.

How that affects official oaths has been much disputed. The Quakers believe that the teaching of our Lord allows no exceptions, so that with them it is a matter of conscience. Fortunately they have so demonstrated the reliability of their plain affirmation that in a court of law, and in other official situations, they are excused from the oath. When my wife was applying for a visa to enter the United States, the consul who interviewed her was a Quaker. When it came to the point of swearing to the truth of all statements in the application he said, "If you are a Quaker you will affirm; if you are a Baptist you will swear!" We cannot but admire a group whose integrity has won for them that confidence from their fellows. At the same time we remember that our Lord Himself was put on oath by Caiaphas the high priest, and He did not refuse to reply on that basis (Matthew 26:63-64). The apostle Paul's statement in Romans 9:1-2 is very close to an oath. At any rate, if there are to be oaths at all, they should be reserved for very solemn occasions. To pepper one's speech with oaths is not only to destroy the dignity of the oath, but to destroy the dignity of speech itself.

Another mark of Christian conduct is not to insist on what the law allows. The law is based on equity, not on grace. Under the terms of the law, then, we are entitled to demand "an eye for an eye, and a tooth for a tooth." But there is a more excellent way than requiring our "pound of flesh." It is the way of love, leading to nonresistance, to returning good for evil, to going the second mile, and to generous dealing with the needy. That is our Lord's recipe for turning enemies into friends. Yet whether or not they respond, such conduct on His children's part is well pleasing to the Father, and ultimately that is more important than the friendship of men.

Some of those instructions are couched in the language of the culture of that day. For instance, a Roman soldier was permitted to coerce a non-Roman civilian to carry his pack for one mile. The Christian answer was to do it with a smile and go farther. That second, voluntary mile would give him his opportunity to witness for Jesus. The cultural setting has changed, but we still have our bullies giving expression to their inward frustrations and our petty bosses trying to show their authority. The weapons of the kingdom of heaven—refusal to retaliate, going the second mile, and the like—are more likely to win them than insistence on our privilege under law.

I am sure that verse 42 does not counsel indiscriminate giving and lending. There are many situations where withholding is the greater kindness, when giving would only be encouraging dissipation and lending would aggravate an already bad financial condition. David Bentley-Taylor, describing one who used his Christian baptismal certificate to impose on unsuspecting people, adds this comment: "I was convinced that the scriptural injunctions about giving and lending were not to be applied indiscriminately to deceivers and crooks, for to do so only encouraged lying and crime by making it successful."[1] On the other hand, we can be so calculating in our charity as to drain all the love out of life. Better to take the occasional loss than to protect our own interests at the expense of lovingkindness.

The climax of our Lord's ethical teaching is reached in the last paragraph of chapter 5. What He quotes there is partly from the law and partly a rabbinic corollary. The law He accepts, but the corollary He rejects. Love your neighbor?—Yes! Hate your enemy?—No! Far from allowing that unworthy corollary, Jesus brings our enemies and our neighbors into a common category, as those whom we are to love. By refusing to accept His standard we nullify any claim to sonship with God, whose overflowing bounty sets the pattern for us. When He begins to withhold His rain and sunshine from the ungodly, then may we begin to withhold beneficence from our enemies. Of course that is not the standard of the world. But surely we are not going to degrade the Christian standard to the level of the world. It is the extra that counts. The world of sinners knows how to give love for love. But the Christian is to give love for hate. That is the perfection of God to which we must aspire.

THE NEW WORSHIP (6:1-18)

Three acts of worship are treated here: almsgiving, prayer, and fasting. In each case Jesus calls for an abandonment of that ostentation so characteristic of the Pharisees in all their exercises of devotion.

The word translated *alms* in the first verse (KJV) is the usual term for "righteousness." In the Jewish mind righteousness was so closely associated with almsgiving, or charity, that the terms were used interchangeably. Whether or not the reference to sounding a trumpet is to be taken literally, the phrase aptly describes the theatrical performances of the religious hypocrites whose motive in their almsgiving was to receive the plaudits of men. They had doubtless secured much of their wealth by unscrupulous means (see Mark 12:40), and their charities were both a salve to their consciences and a method of redeeming their image before the public. Such pompous giving was called "giving with both hands." Doubtless our Lord had that in mind when He so picturesquely said, "Let not thy left hand know what thy right hand doeth" (6:3). The reward of theatrical giving would end with the admiration so greedily sought, but quiet, unostentatious giving would win heaven's notice and by no means go unrewarded.

The same principles hold in the matter of prayer. Religious showmen would strive to be at a busy intersection or at a well-traversed part of the synagogue when the hour of prayer struck. There they would "strike a pose" and display their prayer techniques before an admiring crowd of lesser lights. There is a place for public prayer, as when Solomon prayed at the dedication of the Temple, but as soon as public prayer becomes a display of form and rhetoric, it comes under the anathema of God. Our own personal prayer life should be conducted as far from the curious eye as possible, in the secret place.

Rosaries and prayer wheels doubtless come into the category of "vain repetitions" condemned by the Lord, but so would many of our boasted free prayers. We think we have to browbeat God into granting our request. We remember how Elijah mocked the heathenish prayers of the prophets of Baal (1 Kings 18:25-29). Perhaps some of our prayers are in the same class. Do we pray as if our God were asleep or on a journey?

Here our Lord gives us the model prayer. I am very sure it was not intended simply as a form of prayer for congregational recitation. That is indeed one legitimate use, provided those who thus repeat it understand what they are saying and mean it in their hearts. But surely we have here a pattern, a mold by which to formulate and express our own private prayers. In order to use it in that way, we shall have to study it, discover its spiritual lessons, and then translate it into life as well as into prayer. Without such discipline, we shall fall into the snare of vain repetition from which the prayer was intended to save us.

An exposition of the Lord's Prayer calls for a separate book. Here are a few general thoughts:

1. It is a prayer for the disciples of Christ, who by reason of their acceptance of Him have the right to call God Father. It does not apply to others.

2. In that prayer our Lord teaches us to put first things first. Thy name, Thy kingdom, Thy will, all come before our daily bread or even our forgiveness.

3. Full recognition is given to our physical and temporal needs as well as to our spiritual needs.

4. Some have ruled the prayer invalid for us because of the condition attached to forgiveness. Ephesians 4:32 is pointed to as the order for this day of grace. I would suggest that there is a difference between the forgiveness of a sinner unto salvation and the forgiveness of a child of God unto restoration and maintenance of fellowship. The forgiveness referred to in the prayer is forgiveness within the family. Where fraternal forgiveness is refused, the paternal forgiveness will be withheld until discipline has accomplished its task.

There were three serious faults in fasting as it was practiced in our Lord's day. In the first place, it had degenerated into another form of religious showmanship, calculated to increase one's reputation for piety. In the second place, it was considered a means of heaping up merit with God as a form of righteousness. One of the self-laudations of the Pharisee in the parable of the Pharisee and the publican was, "I fast twice a week." Then the fast was used as an instrument of pressure on God to secure favors, just as it is used today to bring pressure on government and the like. Thus it had lost its spiritual value. Jesus called for a new kind of fasting that would have no outward marks but would be a matter of sacred confidence between the soul and God. It is true that with most of us the body is too much in the ascendency, and while we pamper the body the spirit is starved. That needs to be corrected, and some discipline of the body may be necessary in order to give undistracted attention to the things of God. Such discipline does not call for the abuse of the body by scourgings, long continued starvings, or other extreme measures. Whatever the form of the discipline, it should be healthful and even joyous, not advertising the fast, but making for fuller expression of the inner life. To be more conformed to the image of Christ is the recompense of true fasting.

THE NEW OBJECTIVE (6:19-34)

Christ offers two reasons for our laying up treasure in heaven rather than on earth. In the first place, "treasures upon earth" are not a safe investment. The great estates of the English aristocracy, once such reliable sources of income, are in many cases today a burden to the owners. Some are turning their ancestral palaces into showplaces to make ends meet. Many of those palaces betray signs of moth and rust, while crushing taxes, the cost of upkeep, and spiraling wages of a whole retinue of servants are among the thieves that break through and steal. But even if a man can keep hold of his treasures while he lives, the thief death suddenly and finally sweeps everything from his grasp. It is not so with heavenly treasure. What we deposit in heaven, by our prayers and our witness and our sacrificial giving and our kindnesses wrought in Jesus' name, will be ours in eternal possession. Time, money, and effort poured into the kingdom of God are a safe investment.

The second reason for investing in heavenly things rather than in the treasures of earth is the effect upon ourselves. The heart goes with our treasures. If, therefore, we concentrate on earthly things, our hearts become earth-bound and we take on the characteristics of this world—selfish, grasping, hard, harried, feverish, and anxious. We lose taste for the things of God. We become "of the earth, earthy." On the other hand, when we "seek those things which are above, where Christ sitteth on the right hand of God" (Col. 3:1), then our affections are set on things above, and we ourselves are more and more patterned after the heavenly order, "changed into the same image from glory to glory" (2 Corinthians 3:18). Focusing our vision upon heavenly things makes way for heaven's beams to flood all our inward parts with light. Turning our eyes upon worldly aims means eclipse and darkness.

One cannot be a bondservant to two people. A man may indeed carry two jobs if the two bosses want his services at different hours. But a bondservant knows nothing of an eight-hour day or a job description. He must be available twenty-four hours a day for any task required. Therefore, any attempt at serving two men will end in conflict and confusion, and the more so if they have opposite and contradictory desires and purposes. God and mammon are just such opposites. We cannot love both, nor serve both. In measure as we try to, we turn life into a bundle of frustrations and contradictions. Our Lord would have us realize that life is something more meaningful than physical existence, and that the body is not an end in itself, to be pampered and indulged. To see life in the higher perspective will save us from fretting about the temporal things or according them more importance than they deserve. Undue concern over what we shall eat and drink and wear is an admission of the priority of those things in our thoughts and affections. In our theology, hymns, and devotions we acclaim the preeminence of Christ, but in our daily walk and in our fixed attitudes, we deny His supremacy and give first place to the physical. Christ would lift us from such groveling to sit in the heavenlies with Himself.

All that does not mean that God has no care for our bodily needs. He cares for the birds and the flowers, and theirs are purely material wants. He feeds the birds and clothes the lilies. In our case He requires effort in the form of sowing, reaping, garnering, and spinning, but His providing for the lower creatures without such effort is assurance that He will bless our work to the end that we shall be fed and clothed. Our superiority over birds and beasts and flowers is in the fact that they belong only to the kingdom of matter, while we belong to two realms, the material and the spiritual. Should we, then, neglect that which raises us infinitely above the beasts and live on their level by making material interests our first and dominant concern? That is a denial, not only of our own spiritual nature, but of God's fatherly care for His children. "Gentiles," men of the world who are "alienated from the life of God," may pursue an increase of material good, for they have no further objective, no higher aim. It must not be so with us who have been received into the family of God, and for whom our heavenly Father has prepared a glorious and eternal destiny. For us the kingdom of God must hold prior place over every other pursuit. Jesus assured us that, as we press loftier interests, the lesser needs will be cared for by our Father, who invites us to ask, yet knows what things we have need of before we ask. As someone has well said, "If we make God's business ours, He will make our business His." And God has not yet failed in business.

All that could be summed up in two brief precepts: do not covet more than you need, and do not worry about what you need.

THE NEW DISCERNMENT (7:1-23)

Our Lord introduces this section of the sermon with a categorical command: "Judge not" (7:1). What does that mean? It cannot mean that we are not to exercise the faculty of judgment, for that we are as clearly taught to do. In this very chapter we are exhorted to recognize men whom the Lord designates as "dogs" and "swine." We are to distinguish between "false prophets" and true. The apostle Paul not only claimed the right to pass judgment on evildoers, but commanded the church to do so as well (1 Corinthians 5:1-5, 12-13), and also called for a church court to try matters of dispute between fellow believers (1 Corinthians 6:1-5). So when Jesus says, "Judge not," it does not mean that we are to be blind to false doctrine or to evil practices, or to whatever is contrary to the Scripture of truth.

But there are areas where our right judgment ceases. Motive is one of those areas. We are so prone to impute motives when we have no basis for our judgment. In such cases our judgment is far from charitable, attributing men's actions to jealousy, to self-seeking, to cowardice, and the like. By such tactics we make men's good deeds bad and their bad deeds worse. But what about our own motives in doing so? Does it give us a malicious pleasure to detract from our neighbor's goodness or to aggravate his fault? Or is that our way of exalting ourselves? It will be better to examine ourselves than to judge others.

But ultimately the judging here forbidden is that final adjudication of another's life and conduct that belongs to God alone. He is a bold man who assumes the divine prerogative, yet we do it so much. In a court of law at least an attempt is made to secure all the facts relevant to the case. Those are correlated, and a judgment made on that basis. Despite such care, there are miscarriages of justice. Yet we, with no effort to gather evidence, draw conclusions and pronounce judgments that seriously damage our neighbors. We show no mercy, make no allowances, but pass the heaviest possible judgment. Beware, says our Lord, for such a course is a boomerang. By so judging we are exposing ourselves to judgment. Our judgments of others will not turn to our justification, but to our own condemnation.

That judging is generally indulged in by those least qualified to do it, for they are condemning in another what is present in themselves in much larger measure. Our Lord presents that fact in caricature. Can you see the grotesque figure of one man with a log in his eye squinting and straining to find and remove a speck from another's eye? In more theological terms the apostle Paul describes the same situation: "Therefore thou art without excuse, O man, whosoever thou art that judgest: for wherein thou judgest another, thou condemnest thyself; for thou that judgest doest the same things" (Romans 2:1). Now it is noticeable that our Lord does not deny the presence of the "mote" in our brother's eye, but He does indicate that we are not qualified to deal with another's need until we have judged ourselves and rid ourselves of that evil that negates our testimony.

Having told us not to judge others, our Lord now gives us a directive that necessitates judging. If we are not to give the precious and holy things of our faith to the dogs, nor cast them before swine, we must know who are the dogs and the swine from whom we are to withhold them. And the only way we shall know them is by spiritual discernment. Now the "dogs" here referred to were the pariah dogs, the village scavengers, half wild and vicious. The "swine" were, to the Jew, unclean according to the Mosaic law. There are men, then, whose minds feed on moral garbage, who are utterly polluted in their thinking, and whose reaction to the holy things of God would be only to tear them apart, trample upon them, and blaspheme the sacred name. When the apostle Paul came upon such men, he withdrew from them and presented his treasure to others. That does not mean that we are not to preach to sinners, else we should never preach. But it calls for differentiating between men and men, and it may also call for distinguishing between truth and truth in order to know what would be appropriate for this man and that man. So we must use our faculty of judgment, not for condemnation, but for discernment.

Now we are invited to exercise discernment in another area—that of prayer. Our Lord begins here with a general principle that could very well be adopted into the book of worldly wisdom. In general this is a true maxim: "Ask, and it shall be given you; seek, and ye shall find; knock, and it shall be opened unto you" (7:7). A jingle that I heard from a successful insurance executive is to the same effect:

> All things come to those who wait,
> But here's a way that's slicker—
> The fellow who runs after things
> Will get them all the quicker.

But, then, our Lord was not giving us just a general maxim. He was instructing us in the way of prayer. A like difference exists in the matter of faith. The world says, "You must have faith." Jesus tells us to have faith in God.

Some things are had for the asking. Some things must be sought out. Some things call for persistent knocking. All that is in the realm of prayer, prayer that anticipates an answer.

A child in my congregation was eagerly anticipating the Christmas program, in which she was to have a good part. Midday found her with a sore throat, a temperature, and every indication that she would be unable to participate. She suggested prayer, and her mother was in a dilemma, not wishing to discourage the child's faith, but afraid of the effects of a disappointment. The child went into another room for a few seconds and returned, announcing that she had prayed and would be in her place that evening. Her mother suggested that she had not prayed very long, to which the child replied, "You don't have to waste words when you are talking to God." It was as simple as that. She asked, she received, and she recited her piece, with no ill effects.

But some things call for seeking. For instance, knowing the will of God in certain situations may involve much heart searching, much study of all factors involved, much waiting upon God. Or light on some passage of Scripture may not come just for the asking. That may require consulting the original, weighing opinions, comparing Scripture with Scripture.

Then there is the knocking. God has laid some project on your heart, but the obstacles are many and great. Human effort cannot move them, but God can, and you keep knocking at heaven's door for the operation of divine providence. One by one the barriers fall, and you move in to possess the land.

Of one thing we may be sure—our heavenly Father will give us only what is good. If we ask for what is good, He will not substitute something hurtful. But suppose we ask for something hurtful, thinking in our folly that it is good. In that case He will do us good by withholding what we sought. Of course if we are insistent, He may give us our desire and allow us to suffer the consequences, as He did in the case of Israel in the wilderness (Psalm 106:15). Even that is to teach us to rely upon His goodness and wisdom and to accept His refusals with glad submission.

Sometimes what our Father gives us in response to our prayer for bread and fish may seem like a stone or a serpent, but the fact that we would not so treat our children should be enough to assure us that He will not so treat us. Then let us accept what He sends, and we shall soon discover that the seeming "stone" is the finest bread, and the seeming "serpent" is the best fish. How many of us have passed through times of trial such as we thought we could not endure, to say when it was passed, "I would not have missed it for the world," for the affliction was the basket in which the Lord brought to us His precious things. So here again we must exercise discernment, and learn to say as we see the lion approach, "Here comes honey!" (Judges 14:5-9).

There are two gates leading to two ways and two destinies. The two ends are destruction and eternal life. The gateway to destruction does not advertise the end, but only the "delights" of the way, just as the liquor advertisements do not show the wreckages for which their wares are responsible. On the other hand, neither the entrance to the way of life nor the way of life itself is attractive to seekers after pleasure, wealth, or power. It all looks too costly and calls for too much effort to enter the strait gate. It is so much easier to drift with the crowd through the wide gate on to the broad, popular way. So it comes to pass that many who are very astute and discerning in the business of the world are completely lacking in judgment when it comes to the biggest decision that a man is called upon to make. How foolish it is to judge by outward appearances instead of inner realities, by immediate returns instead of ultimate ends. Even if the Scotsman's estimate of conversion were correct—"Here goes for a miserable life and heaven at the end"—it would be worth it. But the narrow way is not as miserable as many imagine. It is there that we know "the peace of God, which passeth all understanding" (Philippians 4:7), and the "joy unspeakable and full of glory" (1 Peter 1:8).

Now the wide gate and the broad way have their prophets, many of whom dress like prophets of the strait gate and the narrow way. We are warned by our Lord to exercise discernment in this matter— and it is neither easy nor popular. It is not easy, because we have to see beneath the sheep's clothing that hides the fanged wolf. It is not popular, for we are supposed to be broad enough to embrace anything that calls itself Christian. Yet it is the Lord Jesus Christ Himself who is warning us, and we neglect the warning at the peril of our souls.

In Israel there were two classes of false prophets. In days of declension there were prophets of Baal and of other false deities. They did not hide their identity nor pretend to be anything other than they were. We remember how Elijah dealt with them in his day. But there were also those who claimed to be prophets of Jehovah and spoke in God's name, although He had not sent them and they had not received their message from Him. Jeremiah had his trials with those prophets. They dealt lightly and indulgently with sin and raised false hopes in the people without a clear call to repentance. It is the latter class that our Lord had in mind. If a preacher of Islam comes to us, or a blatant infidel, we shall have no difficulty recognizing him. But if one comes professing Christianity, filling a Christian pulpit, using a good deal of our Christian terminology, simple souls, untaught in the Word, can easily be deceived. Is there a test we can apply? Of course we have doctrinal standards by which we may gauge a man's orthodoxy, and that is far more important than many are willing to admit today, when doctrine is being downgraded. But Jesus says, "Ye shall know them by their fruits." The thorns and thistles of falsehood are not going to produce the grapes and figs of righteousness. There is a mold of doctrine that shapes the believer into the likeness of Christ. The application of sound teaching tends to "fruit unto holiness, and the end everlasting life" (Romans 6:22). Christian fruit is "the fruit of the Spirit," and that is "love, joy, peace, longsuffering, gentleness, goodness, faith, meekness, temperance" (Galatians 5:22-23). He is a false prophet, then, who dilutes doctrine, who makes light of sin, who softens the call to repentance, who confuses the saving gospel, and whose message does not issue in the transformation of sinners.

Mind you, false prophets are not necessarily conscious hypocrites, deliberately perverting the gospel and plotting to lead souls astray. Many of them are where they are because of tradition and training and sincerely think that they are serving God. They call Jesus Lord, but fail to give the title its full New Testament content. They will be found corrupters in the final assize.

THE NEW CRITERION (7:24-27)

The final paragraph of the Sermon on the Mount is climactic in its claim to ultimate authority. Throughout the discourse Jesus has been speaking "as one having authority"—authority to set aside the traditions of men, to interpret unerringly the law of God, revealing its true content. But now He claims that His words are determinative. How a man reacts to His words both reveals what that man is and determines his destiny. The figure our Lord uses is a striking one. For every man is a builder, and life is a building. The foundation is of first importance. Two things are required of a foundation. It must bear the superstructure, and it must endure the elements. Lacking that, both the superstructure and the foundation are doomed to destruction. Now our Lord tells us what foundation will stand up against the wildest storm and sustain the building of life. The rock foundation is hearing His Word and doing it. Hearing is not enough. Admiring it as beautiful literature or noble ethics is not enough. Studying it as an academic pursuit is not enough. We are building on it only as we obey it. "Be ye doers of the word, and not hearers only, deceiving your own selves" (James 1:22). That is the practical aspect of faith, as laid down for us by James, and it is in perfect keeping with this parable of our Lord.

Notice that both houses were exposed to the same tests. It was not the severity of the test that destroyed the one, nor the lightness of the test that spared the other. Nor was it that one superstructure was stronger or weaker than the other. The vital matter was the foundation. What about our foundation? Are we hearing the Word of the Lord and doing it? Then, whatever the test, the structure will stand.

Men may not admire the building we erect, but it will receive the Master's commendation, "Well done, good and faithful servant," and it will endure unto life everlasting.

NOTES

1. David Bentley-Taylor, *The Great Volcano* (Robesonia, Penn.: OMF Books, 1965), p. 140.

9

DEMONSTRATIONS

(8:1-34)

HAVING LAID DOWN THE PRINCIPLES of the kingdom, the King now proceeds to demonstrate, by deeds of divine power, that it was no false or shallow authority that echoed in His words. There is indeed no fanfare about those demonstrations, no braggart showmanship. He did not call down fire from heaven, nor offer displays of magical skill. Instead He looked upon the pains and distresses of many of His subjects, and, moved with compassion, ministered to their needs with quiet but kingly dignity and power. In many cases He discouraged any reporting of His deeds of mercy. Nevertheless the evidential value of the miracles is beyond dispute. They validate His claims and enforce His teachings.

Matthew gives us three groups of miracles. The three groups are separated by two interludes, both of which have to do with disciples and discipleship. They serve to show the impact being made upon others by the life and works of Jesus.

GROUP 1 (8:1-22)

Three individual cases are singled out; then the statement is made that many were delivered from demon possession and many were healed of diseases of varied sorts. That makes it clear that the healings included in the sacred record are but representative. There must have been a vast number healed in those days.

It is interesting to notice the varying degrees and expressions of faith on the part of those who came to Jesus and how He responded to faith. The leper's faith granted Jesus' ability to heal, but hesitated on the point of His willingness. Jesus responded to such faith as was present and helped it to reach a farther stage. The touch of compas-

57

sion and the word of power united in the healing of that man who probably had not known the touch of a human hand for many a long day because of his uncleanness.

Our Lord regarded the faith of the Roman centurion as extraordinary, beyond anything He had seen among His own people, who ought to have been in the front rank of believers. Luke gives us some enlightening details. The servant referred to was a bondservant—in other words, a slave. But he was dear, or precious, to his master, who spoke of him as "my boy." There was evidently a very real attachment between those two. Luke also mentions the fact that the servant was "at the point of death," which made the centurion's plea the more urgent. Again Luke informs us that the centurion himself did not come to Jesus, but, moved by a sense of unworthiness, sent a Jewish delegation to present his request. That is no contradiction of Matthew's statement. We speak of an architect building a structure although he did not lift a hammer, or of a general fighting a battle when he did not fire a shot. It was the centurion's doing, although carried out by representatives. The soldier's humility and reverence were further seen in his sense of unworthiness to have Jesus enter his house. But that feeling of unworthiness did not quench his faith. It rather pushed it to new heights. He considered that if he, within the limits of his prescribed authority, could have his word of command obeyed, a word from Jesus was enough within the vast orbit of His authority. It was the reasoning of faith, and the Lord responded accordingly. I suppose Jesus might have insisted on going to the Roman's house and laying His hand on the sick boy, but that would not have been honoring the centurion's superior faith. Jesus did not allow the incident to pass without using it as a rebuke to the unbelief of the Jews, and as a promise of the place of Gentiles in the kingdom of heaven.

The healing of Peter's mother-in-law was of a still different pattern. Again we go to Dr. Luke for a detail not found in Matthew or Mark. The fever that had fastened upon the good woman was a "great fever." That coming from a physician means not only that it was a high temperature, but that it was associated with a serious illness such as typhoid. It was not just a "touch of flu." There is no mention of faith on the part of the sick woman. She was probably too sick to realize that Jesus was there. But Mark's account tells us that those present told Jesus of the illness, while Luke goes farther and states that "they besought him for her." It was apparently a case of vicarious faith, and again Jesus responded with a healing so immediate and complete that she rose up and started operations to serve dinner to the whole party. Not only the ailment itself, but its debilitating effects as well, were dealt with by that tender, mighty touch.

I have no doubt that the physical miracles of Christ were intended to have spiritual application. Perhaps we should not press it too hard, but surely those three cases of healing, grouped together as they are, remind us that Christ is the great physician of the soul, dealing with all the aspects and expressions of sin that afflict us. Leprosy, regarded remember that "the blood of Jesus Christ his Son cleanseth us from all sin" (1 John 1:7). Paralysis is a disease that renders one helpless—and so is sin. Jesus restores the functions of the soul and renews our strength. Fever may speak of the hot passions of sin. The heat of evil in Israel as an uncleanness, speaks of the defilement of sin, and we desire is quenched by a touch from Him.

That had been a full day, and the evening was destined to be even more full. What a procession that must have been—people afflicted with all kinds of sickness of body and mind, besides many whose personality had been brought under the sway of demons. Bent bodies, haggard faces, wild eyes—see them come, led by loved ones half hoping, half fearing. And Jesus poured Himself out for them all. That, says our evangelist, was in fulfillment of Isaiah 53:4. Yes, there is a variation here. The Isaiah text says that He "hath borne our griefs, and carried our sorrows," while Matthew says, "Himself took our infirmities, and bare our sicknesses" (8:17). But are not our infirmities and our diseases a large part of our griefs and our sorrows? Listen to the prayer requests in any live prayer meeting, and you will know how true that is. But whence our griefs and sorrows and infirmities and diseases? Are they not the heritage of a sinful race? The sin of the race is the root of the sorrow of the race and the sickness of the race. And when it is written that He bore our griefs and sorrows and infirmities and diseases, it is a reminder of the terrible reality of His sin-bearing. When He took our sin, He took to Himself all that sin has imposed on the human race. So just as forgiving a sinner is costly, healing the sick and comforting the sorrowing are also costly. He can forgive no sin that He has not borne, and He can heal no sickness that He has not taken to Himself. "With his stripes we are healed" (Isaiah 53:5).

Here we have the first interlude, and it concerns two men. One of them was a volunteer, and the other was commissioned.

What Jesus had been speaking and doing had been making its impression on the scribe. He saw in Jesus the potential leader of a religious order that could outstrip the Pharisees and the Sadducees. It was an inviting prospect to participate in the formation and promotion of such an order. So he came forward and offered himself as a disciple. Now a scribe surely would be a useful disciple. Besides being a learner, he could be a reporter, an amanuensis, keeping official records for future generations and generally doing the writing for the group. There was just one thing wrong with him—he had not counted the cost. In a few colorful words Jesus laid the situation before him. It was not a picture of palaces and luxury and grandeur but of poverty, homelessness, and rejection. That is the last we hear of him.

The other man was already a disciple in the sense of being a believer, but not in the classical sense of accompanying the teacher continually. To him Jesus said, "Follow me." Notice, he was not a volunteer, but under command. Now, while the volunteer was clamoring to go, the man under orders was squirming to get out of the assignment. "Suffer me first to go and bury my father" (8:21), he pleaded. That does not mean that his father was dead, but that he wanted to stay home as long as his father was alive. He argued that his first duty was to his father, and, that duty fulfilled, he would be free to follow Christ. His difficulty was that he had his priorities confused. Our Lord on another occasion distinctly said, "He that loveth father or mother more than me is not worthy of me" (10:37). Indeed He expressed it even more strongly: "If any man come to me, and hate not his father, and mother, and wife, and children, and brethren, and sisters, yea, and his own life also, he cannot be my disciple" (Luke 14:26). We know that He who taught us to love our enemies is not bidding us to harbor bitter feelings toward our dearest kinsfolk. It is a matter of priorities, and there must be no doubt, no hesitating, no compromise in the matter. He is Lord. He has first claim upon our lives, our loyalty, and our dedication. So He refused to release His halting disciple, but reiterated the command to follow Him. There were others, not so commissioned, capable of caring for domestic and family interests.

Does our Lord mean, then, that Christians are not to participate in home duties, but are rather to show callous disregard for the needs of parents, children, and other loved ones? By no means. We remember how He condemned the wretched system of corban, which released a man from supporting his parents by simply declaring his goods "devoted." The whole point is that where there is a conflict of interest, He must be given first place in our obedience. We shall find that within the compass of that obedience our duty to others will not lack fulfillment.

Group 2 (8:23–9:17)

The second group consists of three miraculous actions on the part of the Savior, followed by the second interlude bearing on the subject of discipleship.

The command to "depart unto the other side" of the lake was now implemented. Jesus left the navigating to the men of the sea, while He sought recuperation from His strenuous labors in sleep. His rest was soon disturbed as a sudden, violent storm of wind whipped up the waters of Galilee and lashed the small fishing vessel. I wonder what those fishermen, who knew the lake and its tempers well enough, expected of Jesus in their precarious situation. After all, He was a carpenter, and what does a carpenter know about the sea? Yet in their unbelief they still had faith in Him—enough to believe that, if wakened to the reality of the situation, He could yet save them; not enough faith to remain calm in the midst of the storm, but enough to apply to Him in their panic. He rebukes their "little faith," yet honors it. The consternation of the disciples in the presence of His power over the elements exceeded their fear in face of the storm. Mark says that they "feared exceedingly." We are still not quite at home with divine power. Those men were just breaking through to a knowledge of the One into whose fellowship they had been called. Why should He not command the elements when He is their creator? He can surely direct the laws that He has established.

The storm on Galilee was but a prelude to what awaited Jesus on the other side in the land of the Gergessenes—turmoil and turbulence in the souls of men. Matthew says there were two demoniacs involved, although Mark and Luke speak of only one. Various harmonizations have been offered. One of them apparently was more forward than the other and probably did the speaking for the two of them, so that, while Matthew takes cognizance of the two, the second, falling into the background, was not so much as mentioned by the other evangelists.

Perhaps we should ask here, What is a demoniac? Is he simply a demented person, stripped of his reason, afflicted with some disease of the mind or of the nervous system? It is evident that our Lord did not treat them as such. Either He regarded them as really inhabited and controlled by wicked spirit beings, or He accommodated His language and actions to the popular belief.

It has been suggested that Jesus used a psychological trick, and "generally the authority of His calm, strong, gracious personality prevailed" over the delusion that tormented those poor maniacs. Such ruses may be excused on the part of doctors acquainted with our human foibles, but we shall expect something more of the King of truth. It is surely evident that our Lord believed He was dealing with demons, emissaries of the pit who had invaded human personalities and taken control. There is a difference between mental illness and demon possession. The two may indeed go together. Most mental illness has no relation to possession, whereas a possessed person may be free of the usual symptoms of mental illness, at least for a time. In such a case I should think the breakdown would appear sooner or later. Certainly the two whom the Lord delivered on that occasion were so bereft of their mental powers that their behavior was completely abnormal. Moreover, they were endued with superhuman strength to sustain their subhuman conduct.

Today the tendency is to play down the idea of demon possession, even to the point of denying its existence. But to make mental illness cover all cases of supposed demon possession is as much a mistake as to ascribe all mental illness to demon possession. There may be more demon possession today than we think, and there are Scriptures that suggest that the closing days will witness a vast increase of it. Illicit communication with the spirit world would seem to be the most inviting channel of spirit possession, and certainly that is a growing pursuit.

Another problem connected with this incident is our Lord's permission granted to the demons to enter the swine and their precipitous flight into the sea where they were drowned. Why this miracle of destruction associated with a wonderful miracle of deliverance? For one thing, it put our Lord's stamp on the value of the human soul, the human personality. The loss of a few thousand pigs is nothing compared to the salvation of one man. Did He not say on another occasion, "What is a man profited, if he shall gain the whole world, and lose his own soul?" (16:26). He meant that enough to sacrifice a herd of swine to a man's deliverance from hellish bondage. But the inhabitants of the district did not share Christ's estimate of the human soul, and, rather than risk further losses in the material realm, they asked Him to leave. They are not the last who have preferred their swine to the Savior. As for us who have professed His name, how much are we prepared to sacrifice for the deliverance of men? If my loss can help a man to God, am I willing for it?

Jesus Christ does not impose His presence where He is not wanted. Requested to leave the scene of His conquest over Legion, He recrossed the lake to "his own city" (9:1), no doubt Capernaum, which He had established as headquarters, since Nazareth had cast Him out. Here another of His notable works took place. Again Matthew omits some vivid details supplied for us by Mark and Luke. Jesus was teaching in the house, which was crowded to the door, with great numbers standing all around outside. There were delegations of Pharisees and scribes present from many parts, probably as a commission of inquiry. The paralytic was brought on a pallet by four friends, who, in their determination to get their sick friend to Jesus, took him onto the flat roof, broke it open by removing some of the tiles, and let him down into the room where Jesus was. I wonder who paid for the repairs?

"Seeing their faith," Matthew says. Whose faith? If the Lord's response had been just the healing of the body, I might have been content with the answer, "the faith of the four." But when Jesus' first response was concerning the forgiveness of sin, I must look further.

Sins are not forgiven on the strength of somebody else's faith. Certainly the faith of the four enters in, but in this case "their faith" must include the five. For what, then, were they believing? For forgiveness or for healing? No doubt it was primarily for healing. Yet I wonder if there was not in the sick man's own heart a longing for the divine pardon. We would not suggest that all sickness stems immediately from the sick person's sin. Yet in that instance our Lord does seem to connect the two, and perhaps the paralytic himself knew that there was a connection, in which case his believing for healing would be linked with a sense of spiritual need. So there would be an element in his faith that invited and secured the prime blessing of forgiveness.

Which is easier? To say, "Thy sins be forgiven," or to say, "Rise up and walk?" So far as the saying goes, the one is as easy as the other. But, then, there is no visible demonstration attached to the forgiveness of sins, so one could say, "Thy sins be forgiven," and the lack of demonstration would not prove it false. On the other hand, if nothing happened in response to "Rise up and walk," the speaker would be discredited and proved a pretender and impostor. If, however, the command to rise up and walk proves to be a word of divine power, there is a strong presumption that the word of forgiveness will also be effectual. So Jesus validated His authority to forgive by demonstrating the power of His word in healing.

That brings us to the second interlude, which also focuses on discipleship. The calling of Matthew (called Levi in Mark and Luke) was quite remarkable, as indicating that Jesus paid no heed to social distinctions, which were so rigid among the Jews. No group of men was held in such scorn as the tax gatherers, who not only were notorious for their oppressive tactics, but were also regarded as traitors to their nation in levying taxes for the Roman masters. They were classed with the "sinners," the moral reprobates. They lived in a social ghetto, from which all their wealth could not deliver them. To call one from that stratum into the intimacy of discipleship seemed to be inviting disaster, but the Lord Jesus, who had just discouraged the voluntary offer of a scribe, made room for the social outcast.

There can be no doubt that Jesus and Matthew knew each other. All Capernaum knew Jesus, at least by reputation, and those who sat in the toll booths were well enough known. There surely had been a work of the Holy Spirit wrought in the heart of Matthew to make him respond so instantly and completely to the call of Jesus, and Jesus, of whom it is said that "he knew all men," had perceived in the publican the potential of apostleship.

The banquet that followed apparently had several purposes. Primarily it was in honor of Matthew's new Master. It was also a farewell party. It was the parting of the way between Matthew and his former associates, and he wanted it to be a friendly parting, with assurances that he was not joining the ranks of their despisers and detractors. Beyond all that, it was what we might call the first evangelistic supper on record. Matthew wanted to introduce his friends to Jesus in an opportune setting. Naturally it drew the criticism of the social elites and the religious leaders. Our Lord's reply lifts the whole question above class distinction. As a physician's responsibility is to minister to sick people just because they are sick, so He as a Savior was seeking out sinners just because they were sinners. The religious performances of the Pharisees could mean nothing to God so long as they lacked the virtue of mercy. Christ was bringing God's mercy to earth, and it was extended to all who knew their need of it. But by their attitude of self-sufficiency the Pharisees were robbing themselves of that very mercy that the publicans and sinners were embracing.

Now there was a certain rivalry between the disciples of John the Baptist and the disciples of Jesus. Perhaps it was natural, although it was the last thing either Jesus or John would have wished. It is evident that the disciples of John were more rigid and ascetic in their practices than the disciples of Jesus, and that reflected the difference of the two leaders, a difference that Jesus Himself records (11:18-19). The question posed by John's disciples, then, does not seem to be out of order. Why did not the disciples of Jesus fast as they did? According to Mark's account it was a season of fasting for the Pharisees, and the disciples of John the Baptist were observing it. So the occasion raised the question.

The answer was twofold. First, it was not out of place for the disciples of John to fast, since their leader was in prison. But Jesus was still with His disciples, as a bridegroom with His chosen friends, and the marriage feast must not be clouded with mourning. John was the friend of the bridegroom, rejoicing in the bridegroom's presence (John 3:29).

Jesus had not come to patch a torn garment, nor to refill an old, empty wineskin. He was introducing a new order of things that called for new expression. "The law was given by Moses, but grace and truth came by Jesus Christ" (John 1:17). To try to fit grace and truth into the mold of the law is to destroy both.

Group 3 (9:18-34)

Matthew seems to telescope the plea of the father and the report of the friends who arrived after the healing of the sick woman. That report was probably no surprise to Jairus, as he regarded his daughter as good as dead when he came to Jesus. He exercised considerable faith; he was quite sure that a touch from Jesus would impart new life. When Jesus arrived at the house the professional mourners were already there, stirring up the emotions of gathering friends with their wild laments and piercing wails. The mourning was too suddenly turned to laughter to be real. Their response to Christ's affirmation that the child was only asleep was not one of relief and joy, but of scorn. So He put them out. Apparently they offered no resistance. Was the same overpowering presence sensed as on the occasions when he single-handedly chased the moneychangers from the Temple? Mark and Luke give some delightful details, such as Jesus' words to the dead child: "Talitha cumi." It is an infinitely tender passage. Jesus took the little cold hand in His and spoke those Aramaic words, which can best be expressed in the Scottish dialect, "My wee lammie, rise up."

But we have omitted the interruption. While Jesus was making His way through the crowds to the home of Jairus, a woman who had been suffering from hemorrhages for twelve years pressed her desperate way to Him and touched the skirt of His garment—probably the blue fringe required by the Mosaic law (Numbers 15:38) as a reminder of their covenant relation with God. She had faith that such a touch would bring healing, but she hoped that it would be accomplished without notice. Some critics have accused the Lord of embarrassing the woman by singling her out and forcing a confession, but did she not receive more as a result of her confession? His gracious words would be a cherished memory, even when the novelty of restored health wore off. More than that. We learn that Jesus knows the difference between the jostling of the crowd and the touch of need and faith. He patiently endured the thoughtless throng, but the touch that carried the prayer of a longing soul awakened a response, instantaneous and sympathetic, till a current of healing power flowed from Him into her emaciated frame. We learn also that Jesus does not bless us without cost to Himself. "I was aware that power had gone out of Me," He declared when insisting that someone had touched Him (Luke 8:46, NASB) .* There was always this self-giving for the benefit of others, and when it came to the great work of redeeming men from their sin, it cost Him His own blood.

The incident that follows must not be confused with the similar story of the healing of two blind men in chapter 20. Note the differences. This one took place in Capernaum, the other in or near Jericho. In this case the two men followed Jesus, shouting their request, while the two in chapter 20 sat still by the wayside until they were called. In the first incident no attempt was made to silence the men, but in the later incident "the multitude rebuked them, that they should hold their peace" (20:31). Here Jesus' question was, "Believe ye?" (9:28). There it was, "What will ye that I shall do?" (20:32). In the earlier instance the healing was wrought in the house into which the men followed Jesus. The later healing was wrought out on the highway. Jesus commanded the two not to report what had been done, but the other healing was a public act, and any prohibition to tell it would have had no meaning.

That all of the blind men should address Jesus as Son of David is surely significant. It was a messianic title. "What think ye of Christ? Whose son is he?" Jesus asked of the Pharisees, and they answered, "The Son of David." And they were right. Now there is a strange and difficult passage that, on one interpretation, would show David as regarding the lame and the blind with considerable scorn (2 Samuel 5:8). But a prophetic picture of the messianic kingdom promises release for the afflicted. "Then the eyes of the blind shall be opened" (Isaiah 35:5). That means that the messianic king, the Son of David, would have mercy on the handicapped among His subjects. Does that explain the wistful, "Son of David, have mercy on us?" (9:27).

New American Standard Bible.

Their very plea was expressive of their faith. Then why did Jesus question them on this matter? "Believe ye that I am able to do this?" (9:28). Notice that the question was asked in the house, away from the noise and clamor and the excitement of the following crowds. In the quietness, unsupported by the enthusiasm of the multitudes, would they still believe? They did, and the healing touch was given.

When the New Testament speaks of "a dumb man possessed with a demon," it is not affirming that all inability to speak is demonic. There are purely physical causes of dumbness in the speech organs themselves or in the hearing organs. But neither may we say that the New Testament is wrong in attributing *some* cases of dumbness to evil spirits who take hold of men and induce bondage. Jesus knew the difference. The deaf man with the tied tongue was dealt with as a purely physical case (Mark 7:32-35). But in the case before us it required only the chasing of the demon, who had subjected his victim to silence, to give him the freedom he needed. The undertones of Pharisaic criticism rose to the surface at that demonstration of authority, but Jesus made no reply on that occasion. Later He did give a shattering answer when the criticism was repeated (12:24-32).

10

THE PROMOTION OF THE KINGDOM
(9:35—11:1)

AGAIN WE HAVE AN INDICATION that the miracles described were only examples and representative of multiplied healings too many to record. Healing "all manner of disease and all manner of sickness" accompanied the teaching and preaching ministry. They must have been full and busy days, although the account does not convey a sense of rush or pressure. Nevertheless there was pressure—the pressure of a great compassion. Capernaum had its crowds, and there was little quietness for the hospitable home that was "home" to Jesus in those days. But even the quiet towns and villages and open country of Galilee, wherever He went, were overrun with multitudes—the sick, the needy, the curious, the hungry, the anxious. Shepherdless sheep they were, not knowing their way and having none to guide them; scattered, and having none to gather them; sick and wounded, and having none to heal them; rent and torn by oppressors as by wild beasts, and none to deliver them. Jesus, we read, was "moved with compassion." That is not the most elegant word in the Greek. It means literally a convulsion in the stomach. I remember G. Campbell Morgan's preaching on this very passage in Glasgow, Scotland. It made a deep impression on my young mind. Our Lord's sympathy was deep, convulsing His innermost being, and He called His disciples to share His feeling. But they were not yet ready to think in terms of sheep in need of a shepherd. The day will come when He will commission Peter to "feed my sheep," but now the figure of harvest waiting to be reaped is more appropriate to their state of mind. For the Lord talks to us in language suitable to our measure of advancement. All He asked at the moment was prayer for more reapers. Perhaps that is a hint for our own praying. If God's people would give themselves

69

to prayer for the needed personnel, the necessity for recruitment campaigns would vanish.

But God has a way of using us in the answer to our own prayers. It is really dangerous to begin praying for more workers. He may draft you! That is what He did on this occasion. He made the twelve the answer to their own prayers. After the "pray" there was the "go." But He did not send them without the needed equipment. What they had seen Him do they would now be able to do, not in any strength or power of their own, but by a delegated authority.

Matthew 10 consists of a charge to the twelve as Jesus sends them out on a mission. It is important to remember that it is not "the Great Commission." Our Lord is not here giving directions for the entire gospel age. It is a great mistake to apply the whole chapter to our present responsibility. We shall indeed find timeless principles here, but they must be distinguished from the directives that apply only to that limited mission.

First, look at the extent of the mission (verses 5-6). Definite bounds were set. Those heralds of the King were to confine themselves to "the lost sheep of the house of Israel." Our Lord used the same phrase in describing His own earthly mission ("I am not come but unto the lost sheep of the house of Israel"), while the apostle speaks of Him as "a minister of the circumcision for the truth of God" (Romans 15:8). Indeed, there were occasions when the wine of blessing spilled over from the cup of Israel, as in the cases of the Syrophoenician woman and the centurion of Capernaum. But the fact remains that Jesus Himself was "straightened" until He had accomplished the deep baptism of death. Then, and only then, could He lift the restrictions from His followers and give them a commission that embraced the whole world. So we are dealing here with a circumscribed operation, and we must not confuse it with the later, age-long mission. We shall expect the directives to differ in keeping with the distinct purposes of the two operations.

What, then, was the character of that limited mission? Two words describe it—preaching and healing. The preaching had a definite theme: "The kingdom of heaven is at hand." That was John the Baptist's text, accompanied by a call to repentance expressed in baptism. It was also the text with which our Lord commenced His own ministry. The statement can surely be used to describe any mighty break-ing in of the kingdom of heaven upon the earthly scene. How much more when the King Himself is there in bodily presence! Other facets of the gospel would be added until Paul, the apostle of the Gentiles, gave this as the gospel for the world: "That Christ died for our sins according to the scriptures; and that he was buried, and that he rose again the third day according to the scriptures" (1 Corinthians 15:3-4). Within those facts is enshrined the whole truth of the gospel. But that first evangelistic tour, of necessity, lacked what we consider the central note of evangelism—the atoning work of Christ. Thus in its message as in its scope it was a restricted mission. It is significant that the kingdom theme was reserved for the Jew, whereas the gospel of a crucified and risen Savior is for all men.

With the preaching went the healing, and notice how wide-embrac-ing is that ministry. "Heal the sick, cleanse the lepers, raise the dead, cast out devils (demons)" (10:8). It would almost seem that that in-clusive list of benefits was given to balance the restrictions already noted. Now it is generally granted that so far we have been shut up to directives for one brief mission. But there are those who insist that the list of benefactions was intended to accompany the preaching of the gospel for all time. If we accept it as our mandate we must, of course, include raising the dead, and if we cannot produce that fruit of our labors, we can only confess defeat. But if raising the dead is not part of our mandate, we cannot appeal to this verse for authorization in other areas. Any claim to a healing ministry must find its support elsewhere.

It should be noted that special authority was granted to the twelve to engage in miraculous works of healing, and that authority covered "all manner of sickness, and all manner of disease" (10:1). Suppose we grant that in modern healing movements some are truly healed. The disturbing factor is that so many are not healed. To attribute it to a lack of faith in the sick parties is an easy out. We have seen too many fully confident that the miracle would be accomplished, then sorely disappointed. It is particularly distressing when the sick are convinced that health now is their blood-bought right, and when that is denied, doubts arise as to the power of the blood to cleanse from sin. It is good to keep in mind the divine sovereignty and to remember that the will of God is always "good, and acceptable, and perfect" (Romans 12:2).

The question of demons is a large one and needs separate treatment. Let us simply say that we can go to extremes in two directions. We can deny the reality of demons and cast the whole idea of demonism into the realm of superstition, or we can become obsessed with the idea and find demonic activity everywhere. The reference to demons in our passage is a reminder that there are two great camps of supernatural beings—the angels of God and the "hosts of wicked spirits in the heavenlies." The former delight to do the will of God, and are "ministering spirits, sent forth to do service for those who shall be heirs of salvation." The latter seek to destroy the work of God and especially focus their enmity on men. What they desire is control of the human personality, to break it down and make it an instrument of evil. Demon possession is the ultimate of such control. To break that control and release the personality was part of the mission to which the twelve were sent, and they found that the name of Jesus was an instrument of power for the deliverance of enslaved men.

Our Lord deals now with the support of the mission. The late Rowland V. Bingham, founder of the Sudan Interior Mission, once met a youthful applicant for missionary service at a railway station. Pointing to his luggage, which consisted of large suitcases, the veteran said to the young man, "Do you think the apostle Paul traveled like this?" Certain it is that the twelve were not cumbered with much baggage on their mission. They carried neither cash nor traveler's checks, neither handbag nor suitcase. Those were the orders. They doubtless started out with some trepidation, wondering where their support would come from, but they obeyed and found that in the way of obedience there was ample supply, as they themselves testified later (Luke 22:35).

By that time the fame of Jesus had spread throughout the land. There would hardly be a village in all Judaea to which reports of His teaching and healing had not come. How they would accept the message of the kingdom of Heaven with its call to repentance was another question, as also how they would relate Jesus to that kingdom. There can be no doubt that wherever the twelve went they would find some with open minds and hearts, favorably inclined to the message and to the One upon whom the message focused. They were the "worthy" ones referred to in the text who would extend hospitality to the apostolic messengers during the few days of their witness in any community. So the exercise of hospitality was the divinely chosen method for sustaining the apostles on their first assignment. It was a lesson in trust for the common needs when the Lord was out of sight—a lesson that would support them when His visible presence was permanently withdrawn—a lesson that many of us fail to learn today.

Notice the place of benediction and anathema in the carrying out of the mission. There is a touch of ritual about it, but backed by the authority of the Lord Himself. The salutation of peace was effectual for the house that proved worthy, but in the event of a house failing to fulfill its early promise of responsiveness, the peace would not be lost, but would return into the bosom of those who had pronounced the benediction. Have you ever known a special surge of peace in an hour of especially severe trial? Then you know the meaning of this passage. A benediction is never lost.

The ritual of anathema consisted of a shaking of the dust of that place from the sandals of the apostles—not in resentful anger, but in prophetic judgment.

The apostle Paul used like symbolic action on at least two occasions—once at Antioch of Pisidia (Acts 13:50-51), and once at Corinth (Acts 18:5-6). It is noticeable that in each case the denunciation was aimed at unbelieving Jews who were stirring up opposition to the gospel, thus supporting their leaders in Jerusalem in their rejection of Christ. As in other situations, the antagonism of Jewry signaled the opening of the door of the gospel to the Gentiles, for Paul's order was "to the Jew first, and also to the Greek."

I wonder what day of judgment is in view here? We should remember that when our Lord was speaking those words a "day of judgment" was only one generation away, when the Roman armies would desolate Judaea, raze Jerusalem, utterly destroy the Temple, and scatter the Jewish nation. Jesus spoke of that judgment on several occasions, and specifically in what we call the Olivet discourse. Here He affirms that the judgment upon the towns that rejected the message of the twelve would exceed in intensity that poured out upon Sodom and Gomorrah. That is difficult for us to comprehend, but we accept it from the lips that never lied nor exaggerated. And there is reason. The Judaeans of our Lord's day sinned against light and opportunity that the inhabitants of the plains never knew.

It is only right to recognize another interpretation of the passage, which holds that the phrase "day of judgment" refers to the final assize, when all temporal judgments will be brought into balance and final sentence passed. That there are degrees of judgment, based upon the measure of light rejected, is a principle stated by the Lord Himself (Luke 12:47-48). If such weight was attached to the witness of the twelve, before Calvary, before the resurrection, and before Pentecost, what must be said concerning the full evangelical testimony committed to us?

To this point it is evident that the Lord was directing His instructions largely to the immediate situation, but now He is thinking in terms of a more extensive ministry that would follow, and grow out of, His death and resurrection. He speaks now of the perils of the mission, and in terms that actually preclude that brief tour of ministry. The persecution of which He forewarns the twelve did not break upon them to any extent while Jesus was with them in the flesh. Then it broke in three stages. First came the persecution from the Jews, then the added persecution from Gentile authorities as the gospel spread. With the crushing of the Jewish nation in A.D. 70, their power to persecute vanished, and now the conflict was solely with the Gentile powers. We keep that in mind as we read, "Behold, I send you forth as sheep in the midst of wolves." Elaborating on this statement, Jesus continues: "They will deliver you up to councils, and in their synagogues they will scourge you; yea, and before governors and kings shall ye be brought for my sake." How true His prediction was we learn in Acts, which records both Jewish and Gentile persecution. The Lord warned that persecution would invade even the home and assume universal proportions.

If our Lord's use of the phrase, "the day of judgment," sets us wondering, what shall we say about this statement: "Ye shall not have gone through the cities of Israel, till the Son of man be come" (10:23) ? Is the coming of the Son of man here spoken of "that blessed hope" that we hold so dear? Or has it to do simply with some plan of meeting at the end of the apostles' preaching tour? Or does it refer to "the day

of judgment" already mentioned? The destruction of Jerusalem by
the armies of Titus is certainly not *the* coming of the Lord, but surely
it is of sufficient import in the story of the kingdom of God to warrant
its being called *a* coming of the Son of man. Note that the "coming"
here referred to would find a task unfinished (10:23), which will not
be said of His final, glorious appearing, when not one of those "ordained to eternal life" will be missing. In that day the "great multitude, which no man could number" will be drawn from "all nations,
and kindreds, and people, and tongues" (Revelation 7:9).

Our Lord gave His disciples directives for the hour of persecution.
First, as sheep in the midst of wolves they must learn to be "wise as
serpents, harmless (simple) as doves" (10:16). Sheep are certainly
helpless against the ferocious attacks of wolves. Not only are they not
equipped for conflict, they will not even engage in battle. An ineffectual attempt at flight is their only answer. The epithet "silly sheep"
is well chosen. What the Lord's sheep need is what the serpent has:
wisdom. Our first introduction to the serpent is as the most "subtle"
of the animals, but in that case the wisdom was degraded to cunning.
The wisdom provided for God's people is secured from such degrada-
tion by union with the simplicity of the dove. "The wisdom which
comes from above," coupled with "the simplicity which is in Christ,"
is an excellent safeguard against the fierce assaults of the enemy.

The second directive has to do with the day of trial, when Christ's
witness is hailed before hostile courts, governors, and even kings. "Be
not anxious how or what ye shall speak; for it shall be given you in
that hour," says our Lord. Some indeed have regarded the passage as
teaching non-preparation for preaching, which is in the same category
as another fallacy that affirms that one called of God to the ministry
needs no training. Does it not say, "It is not ye that speak, but the
Spirit of your Father which speaketh in you?" (10:20)? That is an
instance of lifting a text out of its context, thus creating a pretext. It
is the occasion that makes the difference here. Our Lord would have
us without anxiety in facing trial by hostile judges, and He promises
the gracious enabling of the Holy Spirit in formulating a defense that
is really a witness. We should remember that even the most Spirit-
inspired defense will not necessarily keep us from prison or even
death. Take Stephen as an example. His defense before the Sanhedrin

was certainly a Spirit-filled utterance, yet it was the cause of his death. Paul also went to prison, and finally to the block, although his statements before rulers, both Jewish and Gentile, were of the Spirit. In such cases suffering for Christ's sake is part of the ministry, and our Lord bids us "fear not them which kill the body, but are not able to kill the soul" (10:28) .

The third directive for the messengers may seem strange to some. "When they persecute you in this city, flee into the next." It sounds a bit like the old jingle, "He who fights and runs away will live to fight another day." Certainly that was no encouragement to cowardice, a vice of which we cannot accuse either the Lord Himself or His disciples after Pentecost. There was a time when Jesus "walked no more in Judaea" because of the plots to kill Him. But that held only until His hour had come. Then we think of the apostle Paul fleeing from Damascus, where he had been converted and where he began his preaching career. Later he leaves Jerusalem on account of the persecution there and sails to Tarsus. During his evangelistic tours his progress was at times determined by persecution. Indeed that was true of the witness of the church as a whole. We recall that the persecution that Paul himself stirred up before his conversion resulted in the flight of the whole church, except the apostles, from Jerusalem. That flight launched a full-scale campaign of preaching. Fleeing is not always bad. It is often the answer to foolish recklessness and has frequently opened new doors to the gospel. When Christian missionaries were forced to evacuate mainland China, the China Inland Mission did not disband. New policies were established and new territories entered until a new name was required—Overseas Missionary Fellowship.

So there are three ways to meet persecution: first, cultivate the wisdom of the serpent coupled with the simplicity of the dove; second, trust the Holy Spirit to give the answer in the day of questioning; third, be sensible in the matter of self-preservation, being willing to die for Christ's sake yet using avenues of escape for the continuance of the witness.

Since the section dealing with the perils of the mission seem to look beyond that immediate, brief operation, we should gather that the encouragements would likewise extend to the age following Pentecost. And certainly there is nothing in this passage (10:24-33) that does not adapt itself even to our time and to ourselves individually as witnesses of Jesus Christ.

Our Lord offered a fourfold encouragement to His apostles that day. Heading the list was the encouragement of *blessed fellowship* (vv. 24-25). Suffering *for* Christ is suffering *with* Christ. That is where the fellowship comes in. There has been a strange notion abroad among us that Christians, and especially clergymen, ought to receive special treatment—clergy discounts, clergy rates, and so on. The Lord did not receive such considerations, nor did He encourage His apostles to expect them. Rather He suffered rejection and ostracism and all manner of indignities heaped upon His person and warned His servants to expect no better. We shall not seek honor where our Lord has known only dishonor; rather we shall count it honor of the highest degree to stand with Him in the place of dishonor. Beelzebub was regarded as the prince of the demons. No epithet could carry more scorn or venom. Yet the Lord's servants must be willing to endure like scorn in their identification with Him. If participation in the mission involves us in suffering, we shall "count it all joy" to be partakers of *His* suffering.

The second note of encouragement had to do with *assured results* (10:26-27). But now we are faced with a problem of interpretation. Verse 26 would seem to bid us banish fear on the ground that in due time all hidden, surreptitious, secret evil will be brought out to light for judgment. However, in verse 27 our Lord clearly indicates that the thing that is going to be made manifest is not the hidden evil, but the gospel—what He Himself calls "the mysteries of the kingdom of heaven." We recall that the apostle Paul speaks of "the mystery of his will" (Ephesians 1:9), "the mystery of Christ" (Ephesians 3:4). The mystery was hidden from the foundation of the world, but, says the apostle, "is now made manifest." Into those mysteries the Lord led His chosen band—not fully, for large areas of revelation were reserved for the Holy Spirit who should lead them into all truth. We think of those times when our Lord had private sessions with the twelve, instructing them and training them to be His witnesses. But how could that little band face the whole world? They would soon find out that sharing those secrets was costly business. The powers of darkness would summon all their devilish cunning to oppose the going forth of the glorious gospel. Both the magnitude of the task and the character of the opposition were enough to frighten the stoutest heart, yet the Lord says, "Fear not," and bases His encouragement on the accomplishment of the worldwide witness. What was a whispered secret would be a universal proclamation.

It might be interesting to note some of the occasions when Jesus said, "Don't tell." We recall Peter's great confession that climaxed a growing conviction among the disciples that Jesus was "the Christ, the Son of the living God" (16:16). One would expect the Lord's response to be a mandate to make that known. Instead He gave them strict orders to tell no man. The reason for the prohibition is clear. "From that time forth began Jesus to show unto his disciples how that he must go unto Jerusalem . . . and be killed, and be raised again the third day" (16:21). He would not have them preach His divine sonship and messiahship apart from His atoning sacrifice and His resurrection. Likewise the three who were privileged to witness the transfiguration were forcefully enjoined to keep the vision secret "until the Son of man be risen from the dead." The time would come when the secret things would be heralded abroad. What, then, do we have? In verse 26 a promise that what had been covered would be the subject of full revelation, that what had been secret would become general knowledge. No matter how vast the task confronting the little group, and no matter how the forces of hell would seek to stifle the witness, success was assured. It might not always appear so, and the cost might be great, but the message would spread to the ends of the earth. Based on this promise is the command of verse 27: "Speak," "proclaim," with the added exhortation, "be not afraid."

Further encouragement is given in the assurance of personal care. The approach to that assurance is strange. There are bounds beyond which our adversary cannot go. He can inflict death upon the body but cannot destroy the soul. If, then, the death of the body is not to be feared, those who can kill the body are not to be feared. Neither is the one who inspires the opposition to be feared, for even he has exhausted his power against us when he has compassed the destruction of the body. Only one is to be feared—God Himself, whose authority embraces the whole being and orders both time and eternity.

Now here is a remarkable proposition. We are to fear, and we are not to fear. Fear drives out fear. The fear of God is the antidote to fear. Modern medicine has developed immunity to certain diseases by means of vaccines. Can we say that the fear of God is the potent vaccine that immunizes the soul against the disease of fear? There are, of course, various "strains" of fear. One is the fear of dread and terror. That is the fear from which we seek deliverance. The fear of the Lord, on the other hand, is a reverential fear that induces obedience. That fear is fully compatible with love, and, if cultivated, saves us from the enslaving fears of the world, including the fear of man.

That jewel has still another facet. The heavenly Father's care is added reason for dismissing care. His care embraces even the sparrows that sell in the market at two for a farthing or five for two farthings (Luke 12:6). The farthing was one sixteenth of the Roman denarius, which was the usual day's wage for a laborer. But not one of those common birds, not even the one thrown in for good measure if you bought four, falls prey to the fowler without the heavenly Father. What exactly does the phrase "without your Father" mean? Dr. G. Campbell Morgan insisted that it meant the very presence of God, whereas others think in terms of the divine permission or the divine compassion. Luke's version would seem to interpret it as related to the divine remembrance: "not one of them is forgotten before God." And since we are worth more than many sparrows, we can be assured that, whether in life or in death, we shall not be forgotten. In an entirely different setting Jesus expressed the value of one human soul: "What shall it profit a man if he shall gain the whole world and lose his own soul?" More than that: Calvary spells out God's estimate of our worth, for despite our failure, the image of God is there, crying out for redemption; and so precious are the redeemed to Him that His care for them embraces our entire being, even to the last hair. "The very hairs of your head are all numbered." Note, please: not counted, but numbered. What a record system God must have!

The final encouragement offered by our Lord to His band of witnesses was that of ultimate commendation. "Whosoever . . . shall confess me before men, him will I confess also before my Father which is in heaven" (10:32). Confessing Christ is sometimes costly. A woman from Hungary recently attended a Christmas family night in one of our New York churches. The complete freedom evidenced there quite overwhelmed her as she remembered the cruel restrictions in that Communist dominated land, where a confession of Christ would mean loss of job, dismissal from school, and many other deprivations. But "our light affliction, which is but for a moment, worketh for us a far more exceeding and eternal weight of glory" (2 Corinthians 4:17). If, as we stand before the throne, the Savior says, "Father, this person was not ashamed of me in the midst of the unbelieving throng; he endured hardships for my name's sake, and honored me both in confession and in behavior"—if He can so speak of us, will not that be ample compensation for any tribulation we have known here? But let us not forget the other side of the coin. To deny Jesus now is to be denied then. What an eternity of gloom is wrapped up in the words, "I know you not"! Perhaps you are asking about Peter, who denied his Master in the hour of trial. We shall not forget the blood of atonement, the look of recall, and the tears of repentance. In the day of the great assize there will be no mention of Peter's denial—only of his sustained confession until death.

The last section in this chapter of instructions (10:34-42) has to do with response. Three groups are presented: the unbelievers who respond with hostility, the unworthy who respond with instability, and the upright who respond with loyalty.

Our Lord has already warned us that persecution would thrust its cruel fist into the family circle (10:21). Here He repeats the warning. He begins with the general statement, "I came not to send peace, but a sword" (10:34). That is very different from other words of Jesus, such as, "Peace I leave with you, my peace I give unto you" (John 14:27). His mission was certainly one of peace. He "made peace through the blood of his cross," so that rebel sinners might be reconciled to God. And the same cross is the divine instrument of peace among men. Is it not by the cross of Christ that the great barrier between Jew and Gentile is broken down, so that in Christ we are made "one new man"? That oneness, however, is secured only as men receive the reconciliation. So long as the atoning work of Jesus is rejected, the cross is a flaming sword, dividing the human race into opposing camps.

Often enough the persecution is most bitter in the home, where acceptance of Christ is interpreted as rejection of family tradition. That frequently leads to compromise on the part of the believer in an attempt to preserve the love and acceptance of the home. Spiritual instability is the result. Christ is given secondary place, and a state develops that the Lord describes here: "He that loveth father or mother more than me is not worthy of me: and he that loveth son or daughter more than me is not worthy of me" (10:37). The Lord is here claiming only what is His due—first priority in the life and affection of the believer. Anything less earns the title of "unworthy." Instability may indeed secure favor and worldly advance, but it robs one of that more abundant life the Lord Jesus died to secure for us, while on the other hand losing is gaining.

The last frame is a happy picture. Here we see one receiving Christ and being brought into right relation with God. His life takes on a new aspect. His friends are the friends of God. God's servants become his special care. He delights in the fellowship of the righteous. Humble ministries to the least of God's children are normal activities. That he does out of love, but his reward is sure. Even in the doing he will find reward. In entertaining God's servants he will find himself entertaining angels unaware, while the home will be blessed as with a sweet savor of Christ.

11

VOICES OF THE KING

(11:2-30)

IN THIS CHAPTER we hear the King speak in four voices—as Master, commending a servant (11:2-15); as Judge, condemning unbelief (11:16-24); as Son, honoring the Father (11:25-27); as Teacher, inviting disciples (11:28-30).

John the Baptist, who had come to "prepare the way of the Lord," was in jail for daring to reprove Herod's incestuous conduct. Jesus was preaching and teaching and healing, but there was little evidence of the coming of the kingdom of God. Rather, the resistance to the message was hardening. So John was puzzled and perplexed. He did the honorable and reasonable thing; he sent messengers with a straight question. "Art thou he that should come, or look we for another?" Let us remember that, as far as the record goes, John the Baptist had never seen Jesus at work nor heard any of His sermons; and now John was in prison, shut away from his own active ministry, probably receiving garbled reports of the works of Jesus. His soul cried out for certainty.

It was not a categorical answer that Jesus sent back to John, but the answer of demonstration. For the Lord would have His servant exercise an intelligent faith. The list of works performed in the presence of John's disciples, and to which Jesus drew their attention, is certainly an echo of the opening words of Isaiah 61, a passage with which John would be familiar. He would therefore reason in his heart: "The works of Jesus are clearly the works of the Anointed One spoken of by the prophet. There can be no other conclusion than that He is the Anointed One, the Christ." In that faith John finished his course, and in that faith he died.

There must have been something magnetic about John the Baptist to draw crowds from the cities and villages out to the wilderness to see and hear him. But rugged, magnificent, fearless as he was, I am sure it was more than human magnetism that accounted for his drawing power. All that strength, all that mastery, all that stirring of the conscience traced back to the fact that John was "filled with the Holy Ghost, even from his mother's womb" (Luke 1:15). We shall remember that while still unborn he leaped in recognition of Jesus in Mary's womb (Luke 1:41-44).

THE VOICE OF THE MASTER (11:2-15)

The Lord had three things to say about John. The first had to do with his place in the scheme of redemption. He was one of a great line of prophets, but he excelled them all in the unique ministry committed to him. He came as the preparer of the way for the King. The voice of prophecy had not been heard in Israel for approximately four centuries. Then suddenly a voice in the wilderness stirred the smoldering embers with the cry, "Repent, for the kingdom of heaven is at hand." Those who came before John saw things afar, but it was given to John to point to the King as present and in His redeeming capacity as the Lamb of God. Does that account for the element of violence in men's pressing into the announced kingdom? The note of urgency, of immediacy, aroused them to action.

The second thing that Jesus said about John that day concerned his place in the ranks of men. "Among them that are born of women there hath not arisen a greater than he." I wonder who else the Lord would count in the "none greater" class. What about Abraham, Moses, David? But is what follows a contradiction? "Notwithstanding he that is least in the kingdom of heaven is greater than he." The proposed explanation that John belonged to a pre-kingdom dispensation and not to the kingdom of heaven is too easy. The comparison is between natural greatness and the privilege of citizenship in the kingdom of heaven. The latter eclipses all natural gifts and powers. It is more blessed to be a member of Christ's kingdom, even if one has little natural endowment, than to possess all that makes for worldly greatness. But if greatness in the natural realm is supported by the blessings of heavenly citizenship, that man is blessed indeed.

One more statement our Lord made concerning John, posing

another problem: "If ye will receive it, this is Elijah who was to come." He is, of course, referring to Malachi 4:5, where God promises to send Elijah "before the coming of the great and dreadful day of the Lord." Now the historic Elijah appeared to Israel in a time of deep spiritual decadence and blew the trumpet of recovery from the blight of idolatry. It was idolatry of a different sort that John the Baptist challenged, but it was just as desolating. It was the idolatry of formalism, of Phariseeism. The two reformers were alike in their vehemence and their outcry against sin. Both called the nation to repentance.

After all that is said about the likenesses of Elijah and John the Baptist, we still ask what Jesus meant when He said of John, "This is Elijah." The angel Gabriel spoke of John in terms of "the spirit and power" of Elijah. But let us seek help in another direction. We know that David was the progenitor of the royal line, the line in which the Messiah was to appear. The prophets give us remarkable pictures of an age when "the earth shall be full of the knowledge of the LORD, as the waters cover the sea" (Isaiah 11:9). In that day the Lord shall be king over all the earth. And who is the Lord who shall so reign? He is God's Anointed One, the everlasting Son of the Father, but after the flesh the Son of David. Now note how the prophets refer to Him as He sits upon the restored throne of His father David. Jeremiah says, "They shall serve the LORD their God, *and David their king,* whom I will raise up unto them" (Jeremiah 30:9, italics added). Looking forward to the same messianic era, Ezekiel gives us this beautiful statement: "I will set up one shepherd over them . . . *even my servant David*" (Ezekiel 34:23, italics added). Hosea's word is, "Afterward shall the children of Israel return, and seek the LORD their God, *and David their king*" (Hosea 3:5, italics added). Now three millennia have passed since the David of history. The David of prophecy has not yet come to His kingdom. When He does, He will not be David redivivus, nor a reincarnation of the David of history. Rather, all that was promised in the son of Jesse will be fulfilled in "great David's greater Son." Likewise John the Baptist is not a reappearing of the personal, historic Elijah, but one whose ministry is both akin to, and a fulfillment of, the ministry of Elijah—a reforming ministry, calling the nation back to God in preparation for the coming of the King. That is what Jesus saw in John the Baptist. Many believe that there will be another coming of Elijah before the return of Christ in glory to prepare the King's highway. In such a case it will not be Elijah the Tishbite, but one who may rightly carry the name of the mighty prophet because of a close kinship in character and ministry. So John the Baptist is called Elijah, as our Lord is called David.

THE VOICE OF THE JUDGE (11:16-24)

The second voice with which Jesus speaks here is the voice of the judge. And indeed He has the right so to speak, since all judgment has been committed to Him (John 5:22). He passes judgment first on His own generation in general, and then particularly on the Galilean towns where He had wrought so many deeds of mercy and power.

"Children," He called the men of His generation. He called them children because they were acting like children, not like mature adults. There are both comedy and tragedy in the picture. Some are trying to direct the play. They suggest playing wedding, and strike up a merry tune. But the others are pouting, and there is no response. Then the would-be directors strike up a dirge for a game of funeral. Still no response. They will not dance to the merry tune, and they will not lament to the sad tune. They are spoiled, discontented, unresponsive children, and Jesus affirms that the men of His generation are just like that. Would He say any better of our generation? Dr. G. Campbell Morgan gets in a good side lick here. "Do not be angry with your bairns when they are discontented," he says. "They derive their nature from you."

How did that disposition show up in the men of that era? In their reactions to John and Jesus. John's ascetic ways griped them, till they accused him of being demonized. Jesus' very normal life-style offended them too, till they called Him a glutton and a tippler. Nothing could please them. Of course their criticisms were just a salve for their own consciences, but their failure to respond to a diversity of approaches only added to their condemnation.

From that general denunciation Jesus turned His attention to the Galilean cities, where He had poured Himself out in a rich ministry of preaching, teaching, and healing. Three He specifically named—

Bethsaida, Chorazin, and Capernaum—and put them in comparison with three others—Tyre, Sidon, and Sodom. But note the organization. It was two against two, followed by one against one. Let us look at them in that order. In mentioning Tyre and Sidon, our Lord was speaking about extant coastal cities. The old Tyre had been obliterated by Alexander the Great, but the new Tyre had arisen on what was an island until Alexander's causeway joined it to the mainland. The prophets had much to say about Tyre and Sidon, their pride and their attitude of enmity against Israel, so much so that the prince of Tyre was regarded as a symbol of Satan himself. That is the theme of Ezekiel's oracle in chapters 26, 27, and 28. Yet Jesus declares that Bethsaida and Chorazin, Galilean towns, were more adamant in their rebellion and unbelief than Tyre or Sidon. They are described as "the cities wherein most of his mighty works were done." Although we have no actual record of His ministry in Chorazin, we do know that Bethsaida was the home of Peter, Andrew, and Philip. So while both towns received the rich benefits of the Lord's mighty works and Jesus called some of the residents to be His disciples, the general response was thoroughly disappointing. The call to repentance went unheeded. The very works that testified that He had come from God seemed only to harden their resistance. Evidence that would have stirred the Tyreans and the Sidonians to repentance did not penetrate the conscience of those favored cities.

An even more striking picture is drawn of Sodom and Capernaum. For His comparison Jesus dips into ancient history approximately two thousand years. He recalls that luxurious city of the Jordan valley, whose name has been perpetuated in vice of the most degrading kind. Even Lot was sickened by the sights of open sin to which he was exposed. The wickedness of Sodom was as an ugly cancer, till judgment was the only answer. It was major surgery. But here was Capernaum, which Jesus had chosen as headquarters, and which therefore was both witness and beneficiary of His multiplied works of mercy, while also being hearers of His incomparable teaching. How did Capernaum react? With blind unbelief and refusal to repent. In that case it was sin against such light, such privilege, such opportunity as Sodom never knew, and Jesus declared that even the Sodomites would have been responsive to such light and so would have saved their city.

Does all that sound as if justice has gone awry and inequity in judgment has been meted out to Tyre and Sidon and Sodom? The end is not yet. In due time, God's time, judgment will be equalized, and in that day "it will be more tolerable" for those who have sinned against little light than for those who have sinned against much light, a principle that the Lord Himself has enunciated: "That servant, which knew his lord's will, and prepared not himself, neither did according to his will, shall be beaten with many stripes. But he that knew not, and did commit things worthy of stripes, shall be beaten with few stripes" (Luke 12:47-48).

"At that time," begins the new paragraph. Keep "that time" in mind. It was the time when the impenitence and the unbelief of those Galilean cities bore in upon Jesus so strongly that He was moved to utter the solemn indictment that we have just examined. But that indictment is not based upon personal resentment. He has spoken as judge.

THE VOICE OF THE SON (11:25-27)

Now He turns to the Father, and as the Son, He states His estimate of the very situation He deplores. As judge He can only condemn the evil that He has seen, but now He acknowledges the Father's right, and wisdom, and righteousness in all that has transpired. "I thank thee," He says. By all earthly measurements there was little for which to give thanks. Will a man give thanks for failure, for rejection, for disappointment? It all depends on one's focus. Here was a Man whose focus was right. His eyes were on the "Father, Lord of heaven and earth." What seemed like failure was part of a plan laid down before the world was. Rejection was in that plan as necessary to the whole scheme of redemption. And if disappointment were His Father's appointment, it also must be "good, and acceptable, and perfect," all leading to the predetermined end.

But now look more closely at that for which Jesus gave thanks. "I thank thee . . . that thou hast hid these things from the wise and prudent, and hast revealed them unto babes." It was the divine method that rejoiced the heart of Jesus. Those who gloried in their wisdom and knowledge were left to grope in their own darkness, whereas the mysteries of God were unveiled for the eyes of people of childlike faith. The apostle Paul speaks of the same divine method: "For after that in the wisdom of God the world by wisdom knew not God, it pleased God by the foolishness of preaching to save them that believe" (1 Corinthians 1:21). And again: "God hath chosen the foolish things of the world to confound the wise" (v. 27).

Who were the "babes" to whom God was revealing the mysteries of the kingdom and over whose enlightenment Jesus so rejoiced? I think Luke gives us a clue in his parallel passage (Luke 10:17-22). We noted the phrase "at that time" in Matthew's account and saw that it was a time of rejection, when even His mighty works did not effect the repentance of the Galilean cities. In the midst of that sore experience Jesus gave thanks, rejoicing in the Father's perfect ways. But there was some amelioration of the trauma. Within "that time" there was an hour that gladdened His heart. It was the hour of the return of the seventy from their preaching tour. They came with glowing reports of victories won in the name of the Lord Jesus. Now those were not the twelve who had the advantage of the Master's constant fellowship and teaching. They were beginners, "babes." It was evident that they had been taught of God, although the scribes and the Pharisees abode in their ignorance, despite their learning. So when Jesus gave thanks for the Father's method, He had a living example of it before His eyes.

There is surely something for us to learn here. For one thing, we shall be reminded of what God spoke to His servant Isaiah: "For my thoughts are not your thoughts, neither are your ways my ways, saith the LORD" (Isaiah 55:8). And shall we trust the Father's ways when they are different from our expectation? Then are we prepared, whatever our degree of learning, to become as little children that we may be taught of God?

THE VOICE OF THE TEACHER (11:28-30)

The last voice with which Jesus speaks in that chapter is the voice of the teacher. It is an invitation to rest, addressed to all who "labour and are heavy laden" (11:28). That may mean the unsaved who are laden with the burden of sin, seeking in this world for a satisfaction that they can never find; or it may refer to His own people, wearied with many afflictions and distresses. Indeed both groups are in view.

To one group He says, "Come . . . and I will give" (11:28) ; to the other He says, "Learn . . . and ye shall find" (11:29). To the one, rest comes as a gift; to the other it comes as a discovery. First comes the rest of salvation, then the rest of discipleship of which the yoke is the symbol.

That mention of the yoke reminds us of the wooden instrument that was laid on the necks of the oxen. As a carpenter our Lord had doubtless made yokes, and His care for animals would assure a good fit so that the burden would rest lightly and comfortably on the ox's neck. Now He applies that figure to the master/disciple relationship. "My yoke is easy, and my burden is light" (11:30). It does not chafe. It is in bending the neck to His yoke that we find rest, inward rest, the sabbath rest that remaineth for the people of God (Hebrews 4:9).

In this invitation to enroll in Christ's school of rest, the qualification that He claims as teacher is not what He knows, but what He is. "Learn of me, for I am." That, of course, does not lessen the measure of His knowledge, since in Him "are hid all the treasures of wisdom and knowledge" (Colossians 2:3). But it is in what He is rather than in what He knows that we find our rest. And what is it in Him that so imparts rest to weary souls? "I am meek and lowly in heart." There are some people whose very presence tires you, and others in whose company you feel relaxed and refreshed. The more we are with Jesus the more we are at rest. That meekness and lowliness of His induces a deep quietness, while reproducing itself in us. "Drop Thy still dews of quietness/Till all our strivings cease;/Take from our souls the strain and stress,/And let our ordered lives confess/The beauty of Thy peace."—John G. Whittier ("Dear Lord and Father of Mankind").

12

THE KING ENGAGED IN CONTROVERSY

(12:1-50)

ONE WOULD THINK that the Savior's gracious invitation to rest would find a ready response. It soon became evident that the religious leaders of that day preferred the heavy yoke of the law to the inward rest that Jesus offered. They were bent on bringing to God a righteousness of their own making.

THE SABBATH CONTROVERSY (12:1-21)

The law of the Sabbath was part of their concern. Only they carried it to unjustified lengths and made applications that laid heavy burdens on the people. True, the law prohibited common toil on the Sabbath, but the legalists' definition of common toil exceeded all that the law required. Their criticism of the disciples was a case in point.

The disciples were hungry. Passing through a field of ripening grain, they availed themselves of a provision of the law that allowed one to pluck and eat grain or fruit in the passing, but not to carry away (Deuteronomy 23:24-25). They plucked ears of grain, rubbed them in their hands to separate the kernels, and blew away the chaff. To the legalist that was the equivalent of cutting, threshing, and winnowing. So in the eyes of the Pharisees the disciples were guilty of a triple crime. "Behold, thy disciples do that which it is not lawful to do upon the sabbath."

The *Shorter Catechism,* upon which Scotsmen were nourished for generations, affirms that deeds of necessity and deeds of mercy may be performed on the Sabbath without creating a breach of the law. And the makers of the catechism were on firm ground, for Jesus presents that very argument in defense of His disciples. First He cites the case of David who, when fleeing from Saul, received and ate bread just removed from the table of showbread in the holy place. The law required that the two piles of six loaves each be replaced every Sabbath, and that the removed loaves be food for the priests. Yet Ahimelech the priest gave it to David, who ate it, apparently on the Sabbath. It looked like a double profanation. Its justification can be spelled in one word—necessity. David was hungry, as were those with him.

The second example is related to the first as the whole is related to the part. The ritual of the Temple required increased activities on the Sabbath. Mark tells us that one item in our Lord's purgings of the Temple was forbidding anyone to carry a vessel through the sacred precincts (Mark 11:16). If carrying a vessel through the courts was considered an act of profanity, how much more doing so on the Sabbath! Yet the priests were doing that continually, for the service of the Temple had precedence over the rule of the Sabbath. Theirs was a work of necessity, so that no guilt was attached to it. According to Dr. Edersheim, it was held as a principle that "there is no Sabbath in the sanctuary."

The Sabbath controversy continued with reference to the healing of the man with the withered hand. That handicapped person was one more call to Jesus to exercise His power in an act of mercy, whatever the day, but the situation offered the Pharisees another occasion to put Jesus on trial. For they knew very well what His answer would be to their loaded question, "Is it lawful to heal on the sabbath day?" Remarkably enough, Jesus Himself asked the same question on another Sabbath as a prelude to healing the man afflicted with dropsy (Luke 14:3).

Our Lord's reply was an appeal to the accepted practice of rescuing a distressed animal. Whether the rescue operation was based on benevolence or selfishness is not the question. It was universally regarded as the thing to do to lift the stray sheep out of the pit into which it had fallen. That argued the legitimacy and legality of an act of mercy on behalf of a human being whose worth so far exceeds that of a sheep. Whatever the day of the week, the need calls for action, and no guilt can be attached thereto. Therefore, having given verbal reply to the test question, Jesus acted in keeping with His spoken word and issued the healing command, "Stretch forth thine hand." The Pharisees had no reply, neither to the logic of the Lord's statement nor to the wonder of the healing. Exasperated with their own futility, they started to plan Jesus' destruction. They succeeded and destroyed themselves.

We are informed that after the days of Jesus the rabbis made the law, and especially the law of the Sabbath, more and more stringent. We see how Jesus used the generally accepted practice of rescuing an animal from a pit on the Sabbath day to argue the rightness of doing good on the Sabbath. Later that lenience was restricted to a situation in which the beast's life was in danger. One wonders if that new stringency were not imposed in an attempt to offset Jesus' milder attitude in matters of a ritual character. On the other hand, the strictness of the law gives us a deeper appreciation of the grace that saves apart from the works of the law, and that nevertheless builds in the believer that righteousness that the law demands but cannot give.

Our Lord's reaction to all that opposition is most instructive. For one thing, He did not allow it to impede the progress of His mission of healing. Leaving the Pharisees to their prejudiced counsel, He attracted a great crowd of sick folk, "and he healed them all," thus carrying out His own dictum that "it is lawful to do well on the Sabbath days" (12:12), and at the same time throwing down the gauntlet to His critics. That He did, however, not vauntingly, not in loud, strident speech, nor with ostentation. He sought to discourage publicity, and in that, as Matthew tells us, He fulfilled a prophetic Scripture that speaks of the gentleness and long-suffering of the Servant of Jehovah (Isaiah 42:1-4). But meekness is not weakness. The long-suffering will give place to judgment, and all nations will own the right of God's Messiah to universal rule.

Tucked away in the heart of the controversy are some basic truths that we cannot afford to miss. Those deal with the superiority of Christ. "One greater than the temple is here," said our Lord, referring, of course, to Himself. Now we shall agree that a person is of greater value than an institution. The institution is for the benefit of persons, not persons for the benefit of the institution. Indeed our Lord, according to Mark's account of this incident, applied that truth to the Sabbath (Mark 2:27). The Temple and the Sabbath, both sacred institutions by divine appointment, do indeed serve the glory of God, but do so by enabling His people to worship and commune with Him, providing a place and a time for such corporate worship. But souls are more than well set stones, however ornamented, and hearts at peace with God mean more than times and seasons. That being so, what shall be said of the Son of man, the One who instituted the ordinances, in whose person deity and humanity combine, by whom all things were made? He must be Lord of the Temple and Lord of the Sabbath. If shackling men with bonds of place and time is a perversion of the divine order, certainly we must accord complete lordship over the ordinances to Him who established them.

Perhaps a word about the consciousness of Jesus would be in order here. It was Jesus Himself who said, "In this place is one greater than the temple" (12:6), and soon we shall hear Him say, "A greater than Jonas is here" (12:41), and "a greater than Solomon is here" (12:42). Then in our present passage is this: "The Son of man is Lord even of the sabbath day" (12:8).

That sets Him above the entire levitical order with its ceaseless round of offerings that could never take away sin. As "the Lamb of God, which taketh away the sin of the world" (John 1:29) He has the right to claim supremacy over a system that was passing away. Jonas here represents the prophets. Now the prophets bore witness of the One who was to come. Jonas's witness was of an unusual kind— not in the oracles that he spoke, but in an experience that made him a sign of the coming Redeemer: "For as Jonas was three days and three nights in the whale's belly; so shall the Son of man be three days and three nights in the heart of the earth" (12:40). The One of whom the prophets testified is certainly greater than those who bore witness. Next comes Solomon, the king who reigned in splendor and whose God-given wisdom drew enquirers from afar, including the Queen of Sheba. But again the Lord said, "A greater than Solomon is here" (12:42), for "in [Him] are hid all the treasures of wisdom and knowledge" (Colossians 2:3), and He is "made unto us wisdom, and righteousness, and sanctification, and redemption" (1 Corinthians 1:31). So Jesus transcends the kingly order. Finally, He is Lord of the Sabbath, which is one way of saying that He is greater than the law. The two great law institutions were circumcision and the Sabbath. To claim sovereignty here was to claim sovereignty over the whole law.

Mind you, He honored and kept the law, though disregarding the traditions that had grown up around it. But it was in satisfying the last demands of the law that He secured emancipation for us who were vainly seeking a righteousness of the law that could never give us standing with God.

See, then, the supremacy of Christ—over the priestly order, over the prophetic order, over the kingly order, and over the legal order. Of all that He was fully aware, not in a braggart sense, but as the Son walking in the light of the Father's face, and knowing Himself for what He really was.

THE DEMON CONTROVERSY (12:22-37)

The controversy now shifts to another area. "Then was brought unto him one possessed with a devil [demon], blind, and dumb: and he healed him." Immediately the question arises, Who and what are demons? Several suggestions have been offered. Some hold that demons are the spirits of a pre-Adamic race, associated with Lucifer in his rebellion and downfall; others that they are the progeny of the illicit and unnatural cohabitation of "sons of God" (angelic beings) with "daughters of men" (see Genesis 6:2) ; yet others that they are angels who joined Satan in his revolt against the throne of God, and with him fell from their heavenly state. The last would seem to be fraught with fewer difficulties. Some things we do know: that demons are the emissaries and servants of Satan; that they are a vast host; that they manifest unremitting hatred to God and the saints; that they are bent on destroying human personality; that their aim is to "possess" man by exercising complete control; and that "possession" is frequently accompanied by psychological and physical conditions, sometimes of an extreme variety.

In the case before us the accompanying conditions were blindness and dumbness. That is not to say that blindness and dumbness or other ailments are always attributable to demon possession. There was no demonic possession attached to the blindness of the man whose healing is recorded in the ninth chapter of John's gospel. No doubt the man presented in our text manifested other symptoms of demonic control, so that he was brought to Jesus as "one possessed with a devil," and our Lord, with His perfect discernment of spirits, supported the general diagnosis and dealt with the man, not just as one blind and dumb, but as one whose physical defects were the work of an evil, indwelling spirit. When the cause was removed, the physical condition was cared for, "insomuch that the blind and dumb both spake and saw."

The reaction was mixed, as always. The people in general were aghast with wonder and even toyed with the idea that this Jesus might just be "the Son of David"—a common title for the Messiah, "great David's greater Son." The religious leaders, however, acted quickly to kill that rising thought by affirming that Jesus was in partnership with, and an agent for, Beelzebub (or Beelzebul). There is considerable doubt as to the etymological meaning of that name. The Pharisees understood the name as signifying "the prince of the demons." Jesus clearly identifies Beelzebub with Satan himself (v. 26). No matter what the name meant in heathen circles, whether lord of flies, or lord of the earth, so far as the New Testament goes, Beelzebub is the devil. Thus, in one sense, but unwittingly, the Pharisees paid Jesus quite a compliment in admitting that He was undoing the work of Satan, and actually using the power of Satan to do so.

The utter folly of their suggestion was evident, and Jesus was quick to hold it up to ridicule. Nothing will more quickly destroy an institution than division, whether that institution be a house, or a city, or a kingdom. Casting out demons is an attack on the kingdom of Satan. Will Satan, then, lend support to One who is out to destroy his kingdom? Will he lend his name to the casting out of his minions from territory that he has sorely won? Such division would be fatal to his hold on the children of men. His ultimate defeat and destruction are sure, but he is certainly not hastening that day of reckoning by allowing his kingdom to be fragmented.

Our Lord had a second reply ready to the foolish charge of casting out demons by Beelzebub. Exorcism was practiced, not only in the heathen world, but also among the Jews. There were professional exorcists, such as the seven sons of Sceva who sought to imitate the work of Paul in Ephesus (Acts 19:13-16). Those men were Jews, sons of a high priest. They regarded the name of Jesus, linked to that of the apostle, as a new, magic formula for their trade. Would those Pharisees suggest that their sons who made profession of exorcism were in league with the devil? And if not, how could they accuse Jesus of such partnership in face of the real effectiveness of His works of deliverance? "Therefore they shall be your judges."

Now comes argument number three. In so many of the robberies that plague our society the common technique is: bind the owner, take the goods. It seems strange to have the Lord Jesus applying to the world of crime for an illustration, but it is certainly *a propos*. In criminal circles, however, it is often the weak, the aged, the infirm, who are bound and robbed. In our Lord's case there are two differences. Here we are dealing with a "strong man" who will guard his property to the last ditch; and here the purpose is not robbery, but emancipation. The emancipation of the demon-possessed man was evidence that the strong man, the devil himself, had been bound. Christ binds the devil in order to unbind the prisoner.

One option is thus disposed of, and that effectually. It could not be "by Beelzebub the prince of the demons" that Jesus cast out demons. There is only one other option—the Spirit of God. No middle ground can be granted here, and no third alternative exists. The implications are tremendous. Casting out demons "by the Spirit of God" means that God is operating in power, that the kingdom of God is challenging the kingdom of Satan. The battle lines are drawn, and every man must choose under what banner he will fight.

> To every man there openeth
> A Way, and Ways, and a Way,
> And the High Soul climbs the High Way,
> And the Low Soul gropes the Low,
> And in between, on the misty flats,
> The rest drift to and fro.
> But to every man there openeth
> A High Way, and a Low.
> And every man decideth
> The way his soul shall go.
>
> JOHN OXENHAM
> ("The Ways") [1]

"The kingdom of God is come unto you," and it is the kingdom of life and light and liberty.

"Wherefore." That opening word in 12:31 tells me that what follows is linked with what goes before. What follows is a most solemn affirmation concerning sin that can never be forgiven—sin against the Holy Spirit. Now the only reference to the Holy Spirit in the preceding passage is in verse 28 where the Lord says, "If I cast out devils by the Spirit of God, then the kingdom of God is come unto you." In Mark's record the reason for that solemn admonition is given: "Because they said, He hath an unclean spirit" (Mark 3:30). Some have concluded that the Pharisees who charged Jesus with an unholy alliance had committed the unpardonable sin by attributing the work of the Holy Spirit to the devil. I think that is going a little too far. When Jesus said, "The kingdom of God is come unto you," He was actually inviting their entrance—not, of course, without repentance. Invitation was also implicit in the statement that "whosoever speaketh a word against the Son of man, it shall be forgiven him." But why the stern caution attached to an implied invitation? Because those men before Him were perilously close to the unpardonable sin. They were speaking against the Son of man, a sin for which there is pardon, but it was a very fine line between their blasphemous criticism of Christ and the blasphemy against the Holy Spirit, in whose power and by whose anointing our Lord wrought His mighty works. To continue in their present rejection of Christ and refusal of the witness of the Holy Spirit would inevitably lead to the sin that knows no forgiveness. To be blasphemed was part of the humiliation that the Son of God must endure in securing our redemption. No such humiliation is appointed for the Holy Spirit. To turn His testimony into a lie, to speak of Him in terms of abuse, to say an ultimate no to His call, is to put oneself outside the pale of the divine pardon. It would be presumption on our part to say that any particular individual had committed the unpardonable sin. We may warn, but we cannot convict. Even Jesus, on this occasion, refrained from anything beyond warning.

But another lesson must be given. The Phariees had spoken, and what they had said was a revelation of their inmost state. What is in comes out, and what comes out is what is in. "Thy speech betrayeth thee" applies to more than local dialect or accent. It is an echo of the heart. "Out of the abundance of the heart the mouth speaketh." You cannot have a heart full of evil and lips full of grace. Neither can you have a heart full of grace and lips full of iniquity. As is the tree, so is the fruit. We can surely see, then, how our words become a criterion of judgment. They spell out what we are. The "idle word" bespeaks the idle heart, or, if we may combine two connotations of the Greek term (*argos*), the unprofitable word betrays the pernicious heart. If we would effectively discipline our lips, we had better go deeper and have our heart renewed.

THE SIGN CONTROVERSY (12:38-50)

The solemnity of the warning issued by our Lord seems to have had little effect upon the scribes and Pharisees. There was no evidence of repentance. Instead they answered with a haughty demand for a sign. One who set himself up as a rabbi and expressed himself in such burning terms had better produce acceptable credentials! True, they addressed Jesus as Teacher (*didaskalos*), but I wonder was there not a tinge of sarcasm and bitterness in their bold request? For the open mind signs had been multiplied, but for those adamant unbelievers no sign would have been convincing. We remember that the answer of the same group to the raising of Lazarus was a plot to kill Lazarus as well as Jesus (John 12:10-11). By all means, get rid of the evidence! Such was the spirit of those who heckled Jesus on that day of controversy.

The Lord's answer was positive and firm. No sign such as they desired would be given, but another kind of sign would be granted that would effectually separate believers from unbelievers, namely, His death and resurrection, so clearly and prophetically dramatized in the experience of Jonah.

See how Jesus lifts the entire Jonah incident to a new plane of significance. It is now more than a story. It is a sign, an action prophecy, a foreview of what would be the pulsating heart of the gospel. We may be sure that the Lord Jesus would not take up a tale that was half fiction and affirm, "That depicts my death and burial and resurrection." The objection that a whale's gullet is too small to swallow a man is not only outmoded by greater knowledge of sea mammals, but is a slight on the intelligence of Jesus, who certainly would not jeopardize His cause by building it on a fable.

We must not ignore the supernatural element in the event. God was in it, ordering the course of things. He prepared the storm; He prepared the sea monster; He prepared the gourd; He prepared the east wind—not just to have Jonah's commission with respect to Nineveh carried out, but to plant in the course of history, and in the holy Scriptures, a picture of the Son of God in His redemptive activity. To secure that end, a miracle was quite in order.

Here Jesus affirms that He would be "three days and three nights in the heart of the earth" (12:40). Literalists require, therefore, that we count three full days of twenty-four hours each for the period from our Lord's burial to His rising from the dead. To secure that count they date the crucifixion on the Wednesday of Passion Week, and the resurrection on our Saturday evening, which would be the Jewish Sunday morning, since their day began at sundown. It is an academic matter that I really do not care to discuss, except to say that in ancient reckoning a part of a day (or day and night) was frequently counted as a whole. I think we can safely apply that idiom to our Lord's statement regarding Jonah and Himself. If we understand the idiom it should not present a problem, much less a challenge to faith.

From the experience of Jonah on his way to Nineveh Jesus passes to the response of the Ninevites to the preaching of Jonah. Nineveh was an ancient city, built by Nimrod, that "mighty hunter against God" (Genesis 10:8-11). Although not the official capital of Assyria at the time of Jonah's visit, it had been a part-time royal residence, adorned with palaces and temples. Its mounting sins called loudly for judgment, and Jonah was the chosen herald of judgment. It was surely unusual for a Hebrew prophet to be sent to a Gentile city as a messenger from God. Still more surprising is the message that Jonah brought—no listing of the sins of Nineveh, no call to repentance, no promise of amnesty, only a bald statement, "Yet forty days, and Nineveh shall be overthrown." Most remarkable of all was the response of the entire city. We recall that Noah's preaching brought none to repentance outside his own family. Sodom gave no heed to the testimony of Lot. The witness of the prophets for the most part fell on deaf ears in Jerusalem. But the Ninevites, from the king (perhaps governor) on his throne to the lowliest cotter, humbled themselves in repentance before God, and the city was spared. In this case it was the response of the prophet himself that left something to be desired (Jonah 4:1, 11). Nevertheless it looks as if Jonah continued as a minister to the Ninevites, since his reputed tomb is there in the mound named Nebi-Yunus.

"A greater than Jonas is here." That is no empty boast. Jesus, "the Christ, the Son of the living God," is incomparably greater than all the prophets. One might expect, then, that His own people would give at least as much heed to His word as the Ninevites, a heathen people, gave to the dark sentence of a foreign prophet. But it was not so. In the presence of those who repented on receiving little light, how great will be the condemnation of those who receive the greater light and repent not!

The lesson is emphasized by recalling another Old Testament incident. The fame of Solomon had reached the distant places. The wisdom with which God had endowed him drew many from afar, seeking counsel. Notable among the visitors was the Queen of Sheba, whose realm was doubtless in the southern part of Arabia, about twelve hundred miles from Jerusalem. She made that journey by camel "to hear the wisdom of Solomon." She is even more noteworthy than the Ninevites. To them the message was brought, but she sought it out at the cost of a long, hazardous journey. By that the Queen of Sheba becomes a judge of those who reject the "greater than Solomon," refusing the wisdom from above brought to us in the person of our Lord Jesus Christ. We condemn the complacency and the unbelief of that generation to whom Jesus spoke in the days of His flesh, but does not the same judgment apply to our generation, perhaps to ourselves?

The passage that follows (12:43-45) calls for careful attention. Let us keep in mind that it is part of the controversy in which the King has been engaged with His opponents. He wishes to present a picture of "this generation," represented by the religious leaders of His day. But who are "this generation"? Are they His contemporaries, or is He using the term in a racial sense? There can be little doubt about the meaning of the word in verses 41-42 where the contemporary generation stands condemned by the people of Nineveh and the Queen of Sheba. We should assume, then, that the same connotation would attach to the word in verse 45. But when we come to apply the passage, we strike difficulties. The application seems to demand a wider range of history, and that has given support to the dispensational views so well expressed by such Bible teachers as A. E. Gabelein and Merrill Unger.

I am persuaded that the description of the unclean spirit's movements should be regarded as a parable rather than as a rule of demonic activity. The parabolic character is supported by our Lord's closing statement, "Even so shall it be also unto this wicked generation" (12:45). Let us see, therefore, whether the parable fits the history of the Jewish people. The unclean spirit may be regarded as the sin of idolatry, which plagued Israel from the time of the Exodus to the captivity in Babylon, and which indeed brought about the captivity. The return from Babylon found a people freed from the scourge of idolatry. There was a resurgence of the Mosaic ritual, with many embellishments. The national life could be described as "swept and garnished," but alas! the word *empty* would have to be added, with special reference to the religious leaders of our Lord's day. When religion becomes an empty shell, the door is open for the entrance of all kinds of "unclean spirits." Our Lord's portrait of the scribes and Pharisees in chapter 23 is certainly suggestive of the "seven other spirits more wicked." Happily that is not the last word in Israel's history. Zechariah tells us of the day when a spirit of repentance will come upon that favored people, and "there shall be a fountain opened . . . for sin and for uncleanness" (Zechariah 12:10—13:1). Then shall Ezekiel's word from the Lord be fulfilled: "A new heart also will I give you, and a new spirit will I put within you" (Ezekiel 36:26). That waits the coming again of the Messiah, when they "see Him whom they have pierced," and give their allegiance to "great David's greater son."

But there is surely a personal application of this strange parable. There is such a thing as self-reformation, assisted often by rehabilitation centers, Alcoholics Anonymous, and the like. There can be the turning over of a new leaf, and one may be proud of his attainments in the field of moral conduct. If, however, we have reformed on our own, we have no guardian to keep the way to the heart, and the vacated house becomes an open invitation to intruders. The only security against the invading powers of darkness is the presence of Jesus as Lord of the life.

The chapter of controversy closes on a deeply emotional note, having to do with family relationships. But first we ask, Why did Jesus' mother and brothers come at all? What was their errand? In Mark's gospel we read of His friends coming "to lay hold on him, for they said, he is beside himself." Notice, they were friends, not enemies. They were concerned about Him, but they just did not know Him, who He was, and what was His mission. In their eyes such zeal and self-abandon as Jesus manifested were marks of insanity. One wonders if His own family shared those sentiments when they came to see Him that day. We remember John's statement that "neither did his brethren believe in him" (John 7:5), so it would be easy for them to put such a restriction on His activities, and they may even have persuaded Mary that He needed some home care.

At any rate, Jesus used this occasion to help along a difficult, delicate task—to terminate the relationship after the flesh in favor of the new, spiritual relationship. That was surely part of the sword that must pierce Mary's own soul (Luke 2:35). "Who is my mother?" He asks. And with a sweep of His hand, He acclaims His disciples as "my mother and my brethren"—as much as to say to Mary, "Resign your office of mother on any natural ground, and share your motherhood with these women who believe in Me;" and to His half brothers, "You are not my brethren until you join the ranks of my disciples." The qualification for relationship with Jesus is doing the will of God.

That terminating of the natural relationship was brought to its climax at the cross, when Jesus turned over the care of His mother to John with the words, "Woman, behold thy son." There He did not even use the term *mother*. The apostle Paul states doctrinally: "Though we have known Christ after the flesh, yet now henceforth know we him no more" (2 Corinthians 5:16). Does that mean anything to us personally? Let the Lord Himself speak. "Every one that hath forsaken houses, or brethren, or sisters, or father, or mother, or wife, or children, or lands, for my name's sake, shall receive an hundredfold, and shall inherit everlasting life" (19:29).

NOTES

1. James Dalton Morrison, ed., *Masterpieces of Religious Verse* (New York: Harper, 1948), p. 300.

13

THE PARABLES OF THE KINGDOM

(13:1-53)

IT WAS IN GRADE SCHOOL IN SCOTLAND that I learned the old, brief definition of a parable—"an earthly story with a heavenly meaning." Some indeed will see little or none of the heavenly meaning. To those to whom is given a knowledge of the mysteries of the kingdom of heaven the parable is luminous and full of meaning, but it is darkness to those who are not so initiated. To the "little children" of God's family the apostle John writes: "Ye have an unction from the Holy One, and ye know all things" (1 John 2:20). As for the others, "they seeing see not; and hearing they hear not, neither do they understand" (13:13). That is the penalty of unbelief, in keeping with the ancient prophetic Scripture that says, "And he said, Go, and tell this people, Hear ye indeed, but understand not; and see ye indeed, but perceive not. Make the heart of this people fat, and make their ears heavy, and shut their eyes; lest they see with their eyes, and hear with their ears, and understand with their heart, and convert, and be healed" (Isaiah 6:9-10).

If some fail to see the heavenly meaning in the earthly story, others see more than is there. The parables have suffered from over-interpretation, and in some quarters one's spirituality is measured by the superabundance of meaning that he attaches to the details. For example, in the parable of the rich man and Lazarus in Luke 16:19-31 (some regard it as more than a parable), the rich man and Lazarus are observed carrying on a conversation over the impassable gulf between heaven and hell. Shall we conclude that the parable is intended to teach that such intercourse is a feature of the life to come? We shall, then, look for the thrust of each of the parables in that cluster, and not force the trimmings to do more than make the main truth or truths more vivid.

There are altogether eight parables in this chapter. Six of them are in pairs, dealing respectively with sowing and reaping, mustard and yeast, seeking and finding. The seventh, the parable of the dragnet, is a kind of summing up of the foregoing, while the eighth is a special word for those who are entrusted with the mysteries of the kingdom. The first two the Lord Himself explained to the disciples, so we should have little difficulty understanding them. But as soon as we get away from His own expositions we find ourselves bombarded with divers schools of interpretation. Where our Lord indicates the meaning we can afford to be positive and dogmatic, but the more interpretation is required, the more is caution called for—and the more charity toward those who differ from us.

THE PARABLE OF THE SOWER (13:1-23)

Although the first of the series carries the title, "The Parable of the Sower," so given it by the Lord Himself (13:18), nevertheless the focus is on the soil as the determining factor. Whether the Sower be the Lord Himself or one of His servants, the same good seed, the word of the kingdom, is what is being sown, and it has to contend with some very unpromising soil—compacted soil, rocky soil, and thorn-infested soil. The seed on the pathway, trampled hard by many feet, has no chance to take root. Lying on the hard surface it makes easy provision for the birds. The stony soil offers no depth to the roots, so that the supply of sap is soon exhausted in the scorching sun. The thorny shrubs present unequal competition to the tender wheat and strangle it. Fortunately those three do not make up the whole field. A careful farmer would see to that.

Our Lord attributes the first loss to a lack of understanding. And indeed truth that does not penetrate the understanding is easily lost, especially when the archenemy of truth stands by, ready to snatch it away. Even in nonreligious matters what we do not understand is soon forgotten. But what is the connection between the wayside and the want of understanding? Could it be that the mind has been so buffeted by the philosophies of this world that it is incapable of thinking clearly and intelligently about the things of God? We remember the words of our Lord: "I thank thee, O Father, Lord of heaven and earth, because thou hast hid these things from the wise and prudent, and hast revealed them unto babes" (11:25).

The second group described are surface people, highly emotional, responding quickly and emotionally to any new situation, but just as quickly turning to another experience that offers a thrill. Their first response to the gospel may be speedy and enthusiastic, but they are not equal to the inevitable tests of temptation and persecution and affliction. They resemble Pliable in John Bunyan's *The Pilgrim's Progress,* who was easily persuaded to accompany Christian on the pilgrim journey, but his first taste of hardship, the Slough of Despond, withered his enthusiasm. Hear him in his first zeal: "The hearing of this is enough to ravish one's heart!" But a little later he says to Christian, "Is this the happiness you have told me all this while about? May I get out again with my life, you shall possess the brave country alone for me." A question that is frequently asked concerning great evangelistic campaigns is, Do the converts stand? Here we have our Lord's own expectation that some will not stand. That being so, our evangelists have no need to blame themselves for the dropouts. We accuse the evangelist of being too emotional and criticize the churches for poor follow-up, and in some cases we may be correct in our judgment; but Jesus turns the failure upon the would-be convert, saying, "Yet hath he not root in himself" (13:21).

Many there are who become unfruitful by permitting rival interests to crowd out the growing exercises of the Christian life. They are caught in the rat races of commerce, career, competition; or success lures them to indulge carnal appetites at the expense of spiritual progress; or lack of success fills them with anxiety for their families, so that their time and energy are absorbed in making a living, to the neglect of higher things. Jesus says that they *become* unfruitful, suggesting that there was a time when they were fruitful, but had allowed those carnal interests to obscure "those things which are above." We shall have to confess that that is an all-too-common experience and can come upon us at any stage of life. To change the figure, in this war we need to be on guard continually.

The good soil, in which the seed grows to maturity, is described by Luke as "they, which in an honest and good heart, having heard the word, keep it, and bring forth fruit with patience" (Luke 8:15). Note should be taken of that word *patience*. It differentiates the good from the stony ground. Jonah's gourd came up in a night but perished in a night. I am not saying that conversion is always a long process, but the preparations may be long, and the process of growing is certainly long. The "honest and good heart" calls for attention, indicating as it does a preparation of the heart by the Holy Spirit.

It has been suggested, on the ground of this parable, that the sowing of the seed of the Word is three quarters ineffective and one quarter effective. I do not think that we can reduce the kingdom of heaven to such mathematical terms. Even in the agricultural scene presented, the farmer does not lose a quarter of his seed to the beaten path, another quarter in the stony ground, another quarter among the thorns, with only a quarter reaching the well-tilled area. We may have four situations here, but they are not equal situations. One would expect that the prepared area would be much larger than the other three combined. But that does not tell us that the saved are three times as many as the unsaved. The fact is that arithmetic does not enter the scene at all.

The question is often asked, how many of the four soils represent saved people and how many depict unsaved people? There can be no dispute about the first and the last, the first clearly indicating a complete lack of response and the last a full response. The seed among the thorns at least shows life, although that life is interfered with by the intruding lower interests—let us hope only temporarily. That leaves only the stony soil; there the Lord indicates a lack of rootage and only a superficial show of spiritual interest. But rather than disputing which are saved and which are not, let us see that our own hearts are good soil, well prepared for the entrance of the Word, whether it be for salvation or for "grow[ing] in grace, and in the knowledge of our Lord and Saviour Jesus Christ" (2 Peter 3:18).

That parable has an importance all its own. It is in a sense the keynote parable. In Mark's record, when the disciples, and those with them, asked the Lord to interpret it, He answered, "Know ye not this parable? and how then will ye know all parables?" (Mark 4:13). Implicit in that negative question is the positive suggestion that this parable, if properly understood, will provide the key for opening the others. Then, to help His disciples, and us, to use the key, He propounded and interpreted another major parable, generally referred to as the parable of the tares.

THE PARABLE OF THE TARES (13:24-30, 36-43)

Two basic truths emerge from the parable of the tares—the great admixture and the great separation. There are two competing sowers, the Son of man and the devil, who sow contrary crops, each in keeping with his own character. Notice that, although Satan is called "the prince of this world" (John 12:31), Christ regards "the world" as His legitimate territory for sowing, while the devil does his sowing surreptitiously, well knowing that his princedom is forfeited by his rebellion, and that Christ, the Son of God and Son of man, is the rightful heir and supreme owner. The writer of the letter to the Hebrews reminds us that "not unto angels did he subject the world to come . . . but we see Jesus . . . crowned with glory and honor." He is in the business of populating His kingdom, and the present intermingling of the seeds will not hinder a pure harvest at the end. The separation is not entrusted to human hands or to lesser servants who might prove inexpert in the task and damage the wheat while uprooting the darnel. How often we have heard Christians say of other believers who held different views on secondary matters, "I just don't believe that he is saved!" It is not without reason that Jesus said to us, "Judge not, that ye be not judged," or that the apostle exhorted, "Let us not therefore judge one another any more" (Romans 14:13). We just are not equipped to pass final judgment. What secret criterion will enable the angels to make the great separation infallibly? Perhaps they are more discerning of the presence of the Holy Spirit, who is the seal of the true believer.

The separation is determinative of destiny. There is no escaping the furnace for the children of the devil, while the children of the kingdom shall "shine forth as the sun in the kingdom of their Father" (13:43). Notice the identity of the kingdom of the Son of man (13:41) and the kingdom of the Father (13:43).

It would be a mistake to use the parable to determine the chronological order of eschatological events. The ultimate separation of the wicked and the righteous, with the appropriate destinies, is here in

view, not the detailed sequence. The same is true of the parable of
the dragnet (13:47-50), and that of the sheep and the goats (25:31-
46). The apostle Paul, however, puts last things in sequence, as in
1 Thessalonians 4 and 2 Thessalonians 2, but the time for such revelation had not yet come while Christ was still with us in the flesh. Here
we are informed of two opposite destinies—the everlasting burning or
the everlasting shining. And we have the responsibility of deciding
which will be ours. What we do with Jesus will determine.

THE MUSTARD SEED AND THE LEAVEN (13:31-33)

The next brace of parables is left open. It is not surprising, then,
that students of Scripture differ widely as to their meaning. Admittedly we are prone to make them conform to our general prophetic
outlook rather than give them a voice of their own. The postmillen-
nialist of former days naturally saw in the parables of the mustard
seed and the leaven pictures of the invincible advance of the kingdom
till the consummation. The premillennialist, who looks for a cataclysmic coming of the kingdom at the end of this age by the return of
Christ Himself, cannot allow such a gradual and total expansion, so
he must find in the parables that element of evil that he expects will
be operative till the King comes back.

Let us have a closer look at these two parables, briefly stated, but
full of significance. First we shall discuss the mustard seed, grown into
a tree, large enough to offer nesting space to a flock of birds and to give
shelter to the beasts. The "gradual influence school" makes three
points: the small beginning—a tiny mustard seed; the amazing growth
—to the dimensions of a great tree; and its beneficent ministries to
God's creatures—giving nesting to the birds and shade to animals.
That all is applied to the gospel, and on first view seems to fit well.
The apostolic band, at one point a group of runaways (Mark 14:50),
can be likened to the mustard seed. But see to what it grows! It is a
giant tree with great branches spreading out over the world—the Roman branch, the Eastern branch, the Anglican branch, the Methodist
branch, the Presbyterian branch, the Baptist branch, with many more,
including the new branches of the Third World. And who can deny
the beneficent influence of those ecclesiastical shelters? Despite weak-
nesses and failures and divisions, that tree of the kingdom has sus-

tained the witness of Christ and has lifted up its voice for righteousness while ministering to the physical, social, and spiritual needs of multitudes.

But is that what the parable is intended to teach? There are those who believe otherwise, and their contrary position finds strong support in Scripture. We recall the giant tree of Nebuchadnezzar described in Daniel 4:10-27. It certainly was no symbol of the onward advance of the kingdom of God. Rather it depicted the Babylonian monarch, in all his pomp and pride, brought down to the dust until he acknowledged the sovereignty of God. No doubt the birds and beasts of that dream could be regarded as those who basked in the royal patronage, of which they were now bereft.

With that Old Testament example before us, we can see other meaning in the parable of the mustard seed. As Nebuchadnezzar's tree grew to unnatural proportions, so the tree that sprang from a tiny seed. Mustard is not by nature a tree. We might even call the mustard tree a freak. Spreading out its branches to nest the birds of the air, it has harbored many dark creatures. We think of the crusades of the Middle Ages, the oppression of the Jews, the persecution of nonconformists, the "conversion" of the American Indians at sword point, all tagged with the Christian name. Add to those the many cults that have claimed to be Christian while undermining the faith at every point of doctrine. One might say that the body ecclesiastic is overgrown and bloated. That is not the whole story. We shall not forget "the true vine," which is Christ Himself, whose branches are true believers. Even there there are unfruitful branches that must be cut off. But there is a striking difference between the two trees.

The mate of the parable of the mustard seed is the parable of the leaven. Once again there are divers schools of thought regarding its meaning and application. Let us suppose for a moment that the parable stands all by itself, and that there are no other references to leaven in all the Bible. Then several interpretations might suggest themselves very naturally. "The kingdom of heaven is like unto leaven" (13:33). Now in another place the Lord speaks of the kingdom being within us (Luke 17:21). Put these two together, and what do we find? We have the kingdom of heaven (or "of God," for we are not pressing any distinctions here) implanted within us, as leaven in the meal, working silently, steadily, affecting every part of our inward being, to bring all—mind, heart, will—into the control of the Holy Spirit, forming in us the likeness of Christ. In such case, leaven is a picture of good. It depicts the operation of the kingdom within, the work of the Holy Spirit. And that is exactly how many regard this parable.

It is not difficult to expand the operation of the kingdom of heaven from the individual to the universal. It could go like this: the woman is the church, the meal is the world, and the leaven is the gospel. The church interjects the leaven of the gospel into the life of the world, resulting in a gradual transformation until the kingdom of heaven is established on earth. Admittedly the process has its setbacks, but the overall trend is to moral and spiritual improvement till at last "the kingdoms of this world are become the kingdoms of our Lord and of his Christ." That teaching fitted well the optimistic philosophy of the early part of our century. Back in 1920 I had evangelistic meetings with a very dear pastor who held that view. We had blessed times of prayer together. We tramped the village streets together in pursuit of souls. And we had hot discussions on that very question. To him it was axiomatic that the regeneration of the world would be accomplished through the leavening influence of the gospel. "The kingdom of heaven is like unto leaven" could have but one meaning. In his thinking it stood alone.

But exactly here is where we have to retrace our steps. We shall strip away our suppositions and see whether we must qualify our position. This brief, one verse parable does not stand alone. Leaven appears in the Mosaic ritual, almost entirely as a forbidden element in the offerings of God's people. The Passover was linked with the feast of unleavened bread. No meal offering might contain leaven. (For exceptions to this prohibition see Leviticus 7:13 and 23:17). Turning to the New Testament, we observe the place of leaven in our Lord's teaching. He used the term to describe the doctrine of the Pharisees, the Sadducees, and the Herodians. The Pharisees were the legalists, and the Lord did not hesitate to categorize their teaching as hypocrisy. The Sadducees were the skeptics, denying the supernatural, such as angels, the resurrection, and the like. The Herodians were the Quislings, who sought their own ends by supporting the cause of Herod, which in turn depended on the good graces of the Roman power. Against those three forms of "leaven" Jesus warned His disciples.

The apostle Paul is equally consistent in his use of leaven as something to be avoided. Sin in the church is a leaven that must be purged out as a corrupting element (1 Corinthians 5:6-8). Sin in the life of a Christian is incompatible with our partaking of Christ as our Passover. Leaven speaks of "malice and wickedness," whereas the bread of the Passover is "the unleavened bread of sincerity and truth."

Surely we have sufficient ground on which to base a categorical statement that in the Holy Scriptures leaven is treated as a symbol of sin and corruption. Or do those two passages in Leviticus to which reference has been made prevent such a statement? I think not. A careful reading of Leviticus 7:13 will show us a worshiper at peace with God, yet acknowledging his shortcomings. Here we see David as in Psalms 51 and 32. As for Leviticus 23:17, the typology points to Pentecost and the first fruits of the New Testament church, in which, despite its true relationship with Christ the Head, yet are found elements of corruption, as witness the sin of Ananias and Sapphira. I dare to affirm, then, that if the leaven of the parable is a symbol of good, then that is the only exception to an otherwise unbroken rule. I prefer to go by the rule and see here the kingdom of God on earth invaded by corrupting forces that will continue their nefarious activity until that cataclysmic day when "the Son of man shall send forth His angels, and they shall gather out of His kingdom all things that offend."

But some will say, "Is not the statement clear, that 'the kingdom of heaven is like unto leaven'? If the kingdom of heaven is good, then that to which it is likened must also be good." That raises a question of semantics. Is the likeness simply to leaven as such, the rest of the verse being only the trimmings? Or is the likeness referred to the whole situation? Surely the latter is the case. Wherever this language is used, as in verse 47, it refers to the whole situation. It must be so here, as elsewhere.

Then the context must be brought into account. These parables, strikingly different as they are, have some common notes. One is the element of struggle, of encounter. In the first of the group there is the struggle with unresponsive soils; in the second with alien seed; in the third with spurious growth; and now here with corrupting influences. It would seem that the Lord is enforcing a truth concerning the kingdom of heaven to which His disciples were blind, namely, the age-long conflict with the powers of darkness, a conflict taking many forms, but ending at last in glorious conquest. Sometimes we are taken with panic when we are thrust into the thick of the battle, or when we sense the subtle power of satanic influences, but we know the King who leads us to battle, and "we are more than conquerors through him that loved us" (Romans 8:37).

Ever since sin entered our race, the trend has been downward, and God has consistently borne with the mounting evil until sin had come to full expression. When defining His covenant with Abraham, God gave as the reason for delaying the transfer of the land, "the iniquity of the Amorites is not yet full" (Genesis 15:16). The judgment of the flood came when God saw that "every imagination of the thoughts of his [man's] heart was only evil continually" (Genesis 6:5). Such was the deterioration of Sodom that ten righteous persons could not be found there (Genesis 18:33). Speaking prophetically of the last days, the apostle Paul does not foresee moral improvement, but rather "evil men and seducers shall wax worse and worse" (2 Timothy 3:13). And certainly the trend of our age has not been upward. We have advanced technologically, we have vastly increased our store of knowledge, we have attained new standards of living, but they have not diminished the sordid tales of vice and crime and violence and corruption that meet our eyes and ears with painful regularity. What once was sin is now a way of life clamoring for acceptance. Our Lord's phrase, "till the whole was leavened," would seem to have come true in our time.

THE TREASURE AND THE PEARL (13:44-46)

The third pair of related parables has to do with finding, selling, and buying. In the first, the parable of the hidden treasure, we are not told whether the man involved was seeking treasure, or whether he just ran across it in the course of some other occupation. We understand that many in those days used the ground as their bank, thinking it safer than the financial institutions, with the result that many died without divulging the secret of their hidden treasure. No doubt there were those who made a business of hunting for such unclaimed, unknown, loot. In other cases it would be an accidental find, if a man, say, were digging to plant a garden. The parable does not indicate to which class the finder of the treasure belonged. The law apparently allowed that what was found in a field belonged to the buyer of the field. Having discovered the treasure, then, the finder thought no more in terms of the value of the field itself, but in terms of what lay buried there. He was willing, therefore, to cash in on everything he had, knowing that he would more than recover his investment. Now, says our Lord, the kingdom of heaven is like that. The question is, In what respect is the kingdom of heaven like that?

One of our greatest hymns, translated from the German of Johann Franck by Catherine Winkworth, begins, "Jesus, priceless Treasure," and I have no doubt that the parable engaging our attention was the inspiration of that ascription. Surely we shall not find fault with such an expression of devotion to the Savior. If, however, we regard Christ, or salvation in Christ, as the treasure, then we see the man of the parable as the sinner, seeking and finding the treasure.

We agree that salvation is all of grace, provided for the bankrupt sinner who has nothing wherewith to purchase eternal life. Nevertheless we shall not forget the Lord's demand upon the rich young ruler who desired an inheritance in the kingdom of God: "Sell whatsoever thou hast, and give to the poor, and thou shalt have treasure in heaven; and come, take up the cross, and follow me" (Mark 10:21). Or what shall we make of this?—"If any man come to me, and hate not his father, and mother, and wife, and children, and brethren, and sisters, yea, and his own life also, he cannot be my disciple" (Luke 14:26). To put it simply, while "the gift of God is eternal life," entering the kingdom of heaven is costly business, for which reason Christ Himself warns us to count the cost, and adds, "whosoever he be of you that forsaketh not all that he hath, he cannot be my disciple" (Luke 14:28-33). Whatever else the parable of the hidden treasure has to teach us, it certainly reminds us that it costs to enter the kingdom of God, but that it is more than worth the cost.

Having said all that in defense of those who interpret the parables in terms of the sinner finding the Savior, I must affirm my preference for an entirely different meaning. In three of the four preceding parables we see a man sowing. We have identified the Man as Christ, and, in keeping with His own statement, the field as the world. The world is the sphere of Christ's saving operation. But in what kind of world is He operating? It is a world far from uniformly responsive to His sowing. Some of its soil is wayside soil, some of it is stony, and some overrun with thorny shrubs. It is a world plagued by adversaries who seek to destroy the good seed by sowing darnel. It is a world inimical to the work of God, but amicable to evil spirits that find shelter in the overgrown branches of a spurious Christendom.

But Christ is the master optimist. In that so unpromising field He finds a treasure. Through the mists of corruption, violence, and vice He sees the kingdom of heaven. He sees "the kingdoms of this world . . . become the kingdoms of our Lord, and of his Christ." He anticipates the answer to the prayer which He taught His disciples: "Thy will be done in earth, as it is in heaven." He looks down the corridors of time and beholds the rebel province of the kingdom of God restored, renewed, and reconciled. He looks out upon a world "filled with the knowledge of the glory of the Lord as the waters cover the sea" (Habakkuk 2:14). He foresees as fact what poets and philosophers have dreamed, well-expressed by the Scottish poet, Robert Burns:

> Then let us pray that come it may
>   (As come it will for a' that)
> That sense and worth o'er a' the earth
>   Shall bear the gree an' a' that!
> For a' that, an' a' that,
>   It's comin' yet for a' that,
> That man to man the world o'er
>   Shall brithers be for a' that.
>
> ROBERT BURNS
> ("A Man's a Man for a' That") [1]

Yes, Jesus saw that, not as a dream, but as a certain goal. But well He knew that it would cost. There could be no renewed world, no restored world, no reconciled world, except it be a redeemed world. The prince of this world must be cast out, his claims must be canceled once and for all, the powers of darkness must be robbed of their stranglehold. So the Man who has seen the treasure of the kingdom of heaven hidden in the field of this world lays all that He has on the line in order to secure undisputed right to that treasure. And here is the price: "Existing in the form of God, [He] counted not the being on an equality with God a thing to be grasped, but emptied himself, taking the form of a servant, being made in the likeness of men; and being found in fashion as a man, he humbled himself, becoming obedient even unto death, yea, the death of the cross" (Philippians 2:6-8, ASV).* He bought His kingdom with His blood.

Although only one treasure is here spoken of, and its reference is to the kingdom of heaven, our Lord had, from all eternity, foreseen another treasure, variously described for us in the New Testament. "Christ loved the church, and gave himself for it . . . that he might present it to himself a glorious church" (Ephesians 5:25, 27). Gathered from every tongue and tribe and people and nation, this "great multitude that no man could number" constitutes that "people of possession," which Peter describes as "a chosen generation, a royal priesthood, a holy nation" (1 Peter 2:9). Jesus Himself refers to this company as "them which thou hast given me" (John 17:9). They were chosen in Christ from the foundation of the world. They are not a second thought. The church is Christ's peculiar treasure, standing in a unique relationship to Him as His body and His bride. So while we draw a distinction between the kingdom of heaven and the church, the one the ultimate political establishment and the other the ultimate ecclesiastical establishment, we cannot think of Christ being oblivious to the treasure of the church while speaking in terms of the treasure of the kingdom.

If we understand the parable of the hidden treasure, we shall have little difficulty with its mate, the parable of the priceless pearl. Of course the division among interpreters of the parable of the treasure persists among those who seek the meaning of the parable of the pearls. Here we have one of the favorite texts of the evangelist. Who can read Spurgeon's powerful sermon entitled "A Great Bargain" and not be deeply stirred? According to the evangelistic view, the merchant-man of the parable is a seeking sinner. He is not interested in cheap

*American Standard Version.

merchandise. He is in the market for goodly pearls, perhaps knowledge, perhaps culture, perhaps success in business, perhaps power,
perhaps money. But none of those satisfies him. Then he discovers
Jesus and sees in Him the answer to his every need. But he cannot
put this "pearl of great price" in the same category as the goodly pearls
with which he had traded. In comparison they now appear tawdry.
He now says with the apostle Paul, "What things were gain to me,
those I counted loss for Christ . . . for whom I have suffered the loss
of all things, and do count them but dung, that I may win Christ"
(Philippians 3:7-8). The idea of bartering is foreign to the spiritual
truth presented and must be considered a part of the earthly trimmings. I am sure many a soul has been saved through an exposition
of the parable after this order.

But if we are bent on theological and exegetical consistency, we
shall want to see in the man of the parable the same as we saw in the
parable of the treasure—our Lord Jesus Christ. In like manner the
"pearl of great price" will be what He purchased, not with lesser
pearls, but with His own blood. And what may that be? Again we
cannot fail to see a twofold return for the sacrifice—the kingdom of
God come to earth, and the church with Him in glory.

THE PARABLE OF THE DRAGNET (13:47-50)

Although a different figure is used, the parable of the dragnet has
much in common with that of the two seeds. The two main truths
in both are the present admixture and the final separation. The lesson from the dragnet would have a special appeal to the fishermen
among our Lord's disciples. Incidentally, here is a timely hint for the
soul winner: there is great value in speaking to a man in his own
language and illuminating our presentation of the gospel by means
of personal interests. Too often our witness is couched in theological
language that simply goes over the head of the one we would win.
But present the gospel in terms of the farmer, the accountant, the
baker, the lawyer, and interest is more easily aroused.

It is evident that not all caught in the gospel net are truly born
again and exercise faith unto salvation. Once again, the task of sep-
arating the spurious from the real is not committed to us, but to more
able hands and higher wisdom. The end of the pretender, as of all
unbelievers, is "the furnace of fire." The Lord calls it "fire," and

we gain nothing by discussing what kind of fire it is. We are given this solemn word—"there shall be wailing and gnashing of teeth" (13:42). The wailing speaks of perpetual sorrow. The "gnashing of teeth" suggests unrelenting hate and unmitigated resentment, which is the fixed attitude of the lost toward God. We remember that the same term is used of the members of the Sanhedrin as their anger boiled against Stephen (Acts 7:54). Our Lord's use of it would tell us that there is no repentance in hell.

THE HOUSEHOLDER (13:51-53)

The disciples affirmed their understanding of "all these things," a statement that presumably covered all seven parables. If we could have a record of their understanding, I wonder if we would find a diversity of interpretations such as we have noted in today's teachers, or would they be of one mind? One thing is sure. When the day comes that we no longer know in part, but fully, even as we are fully known, we shall then have so much grace that we shall not say one to another, "I told you so!"

In the meantime, we are called upon to be faithful stewards of the truth as we know it, always digging deeper into the divine revelation. What our Lord states here in picture language is defined for us theologically in the Hebrews letter: "Therefore leaving the principles of the doctrine of Christ, let us go on unto perfection; not laying again a foundation of repentance from dead works, and of faith toward God, of the doctrine of baptisms, and of laying on of hands, and of resurrection of the dead, and of eternal judgment" (Hebrews 6:1-2).

With this affirmation elicited from the disciples, Jesus in this final parable compared them as scribes (interpreters of God's law) to the head of a household who has at his disposal great resources with which to perform his duties. "Things old and new" no doubt refers not only to the great truths of the Old Testament but also to truth as represented in these parables—all of which the disciples now possessed as a wealth of divine resources that they would draw on continually in their ministries. We as His ministers today should always be prepared to do as much, since we now have the fullness of the divine revelation, both old and new.

NOTES

1. James Dalton Morrison, ed., *Masterpieces of Religious Verse* (New York: Harper, 1948), p. 286.

14

THE KING IN ACTION

(13:54—16:21)

HAVING SHOWN, IN A SERIES OF PARABLES, the nature of the progress
of the kingdom, the King continued the type of ministry that at once
amazed and confused even His own disciples. He was not raising a
standard and rallying forces for a military thrust against the Roman
overlords, but He was calling men to repentance while ministering
to the needy as the prophets had foretold (Isaiah 61:1-2). That
period of ministry, extending roughly from the death of John the
Baptist to Peter's great confession, would seem to be in three movements, recorded for us respectively in 13:54—14:36, 15:1-39, and
16:1-21.

At this time a double grief came to our Lord. First He experienced
scornful rejection by His own townsfolk; then He heard of the death
of John the Baptist.

A PROPHET WITHOUT HONOR (13:54-58)

It was not our Lord's first visit to Nazareth since the beginning of
His ministry. Luke gives us the account of that earlier visit when
amazement at His gracious words turned to wrath at His faithful
words. That was the occasion of the Nazarenes' abortive attempt to
hurl Jesus over the cliff to His death. Now near the close of His
public ministry He returns to His hometown. By that time He is a
public figure, whose name has spread abroad throughout the land.
How would they receive Him now? As a hero? As a superstar? As
an ornament to their little town? They were too provincial for that.
They could not endure the thought of one of their own rising higher
than themselves. It is related that when Sir William MacDonald, the
first Labor Prime Minister of Great Britain, returned to his home-

town on the northeast coast of Scotland after his appointment to that high office, he decided to pay a visit to a former schoolmate who was confined in a mental institution. He had difficulty stirring recognition from his feeble-minded friend.

"Jock," he said, "this is Willie MacDonald. Ye ken, the Prime Minister!"

"Och aye," was the reply, "ye'll get over it. When I came in here, I was Napoleon."

But they are not always mentally deficient people who refuse to recognize those who have gone beyond the provincial bounds. The story is told of a writer who visited the home territory of Thomas Carlyle to gather material for an article. He interviewed the farmer who was neighbor to the Carlyles. Replying to the visitor's questions, he said, "Aye, there was a Tammas in that family. He went to London to write books and things. But the real man o' that family was Dave. He drave mair pigs to the Ecclefechan market than ony ither man."

Well, here we have the men of Nazareth, men of sound mind and normal intelligence. But Jesus was more than they could accept. As one of themselves He could not possibly be so much above them. They could raise carpenters, but not prophets. That is exactly what Nathanael said when Philip invited him to meet Jesus of Nazareth (John 1:46). So "they were offended in him" (13:56). That is what a prophet is to expect from his peers who do not wish to have their tranquil way of life disturbed. "And he did not many mighty works there, because of their unbelief" (13:58). Notice it does not say, "not any." There were some cases when the compassion of Jesus surmounted the general unbelief (Mark 6:5). But we learn the extent to which mighty works depend on faith, not faith on mighty works.

In Matthew's account, Jesus is referred to by the inhabitants as "the carpenter's son," quite a normal nomenclature. We do not expect a witness to the virgin birth of our Lord to arise from those quarters. Some of the old timers may still have harbored suspicions from those days when Mary was found with child "before they [she and Joseph] came together" (1:18). More to the point at the moment is the fact that in Mark's record of this incident, the question asked is, "Is not this the carpenter?" (Mark 6:3). There is no contradiction there. Some would express their query one way, while others asked it another way. The point of interest is that Jesus was not only the carpenter's son (in the legal sense), but He too was *the carpenter*. Till the age of thirty He labored with His hands, and we can believe that His productions set a standard for all the workers of Nazareth.

The Death of John the Baptist (14:1-12)

Now we come to a slight chronological problem. Chapter 14 opens with the statement that "at that time Herod the tetrarch heard of the fame of Jesus." Herod Antipas, son of Herod the Great and tetrarch of Galilee and Peraea, appears in the narrative here as a man whose conscience was tormenting him. There was a time when he listened to John the Baptist, so there seemed some hope of his moral recovery. Instead, he chose the path of indulgence, which led to the beheading of the prophet to satisfy the cruel and bloodthirsty whim of a woman. Soon after, Herod heard of the mighty works being wrought by Jesus, and his guilty conscience linked those with the works of John, whom he had killed. "This is John the Baptist," he says, with trembling voice and blanched face; "he is risen from the dead; and therefore mighty works do shew forth themselves in him" (14:2).

That statement concerning Herod's associating the works of Jesus with the death of John the Baptist called for an account of that death. Matthew, therefore, must retrace his steps to give us such a record. To explain the present he must go to the past. He is still in that past when he says concerning the disciples of John that they "went and told Jesus." Now it is quite generally thought that the phrase, "when Jesus heard of it, in 14:13 follows chronologically the statement "went and told Jesus" in verse 12. But when we see that the account of John's death is inserted to explain Herod's reaction to the miracles of Jesus and is therefore out of chronological order, we must find another link for "when Jesus heard of it." That link would seem to be verses 1 and 2. In verse 13 we get back on the track which we left in verse 3. The order of sequence now is, first, the death of John the Baptist (vv. 3-12); second, Herod's fear on hearing of the miraculous ministry of Jesus (vv. 1-2); and third, our Lord's departure to a desert place on hearing of Herod's attempt to link Him with John. We shall follow that order.

Harmonizing the three accounts of the death of John the Baptist reveals a progressive deterioration in his relations with Herod. At first that part-Jewish puppet of Rome rather favored the rugged preacher of the wilderness. He heard him gladly, we are told, a practice that apparently continued when John was made a prisoner. Again we are informed that Herod "did many things" in response to the fearless preaching. But one thing he did not do: he did not repent, and failing that, all the "many things" went for nothing. A contrary force was working in this man's life—an illicit union with his sister-in-law Herodias. John could not let such corruption go unrebuked. His bold witness against the unlawful union aroused the ire of Herodias so that she set her mind on John's death. That created a dilemma for Herod. He had to placate Herodias, yet he stood in awe of John, recognizing him as a prophet, and knowing that he was so regarded by the populace. So, sharing the wrath of his wife, yet at the same time sharing the sentiment of the people, what course could he follow? The answer was prison. That would be punishment for speaking out against the royal delinquents. Herod added to all his evil when he cast John into prison. But that served another purpose. As long as John was at liberty, the murderous passion of Herodias could catch up with him. In prison he would at least be safe. So we read that Herod "kept him safely," and no doubt soothed his conscience with the thought.

But the revenge of Herodias reached the dungeon. The tetrarch's birthday was a fine occasion to spring the trap. A drunk monarch and an alluring dancing daughter, Salome, set the stage. The king's extravagant oath to give the young dancer anything she asked left him not only vulnerable, but a helpless prey. Whatever moral fortitude he ever had collapsed, and the doubtful approval of the sycophants who basked in his favor was more to him than righteousness. The request for the head of John the Baptist momentarily shocked him as he saw how he had trapped himself, but soon he was making the gory presentation a feature of the night's revelry.

The bloody head of John the Baptist haunted Herod. The Baptist dead terrified him more than the Baptist alive. So, when reports were multiplied of a Rabbi accompanying His teaching with mighty works, going as far as raising the dead, the terrified king could draw only one conclusion: it was John the Baptist risen from the dead. Others might think otherwise, but Herod's fear brooked no alternative. There would seem to be truth in the old adage, "Conscience doth make cowards of us all."

THE FEEDING OF THE FIVE THOUSAND (14:13-21)

"Now when Jesus heard it." Heard what? Not the death of John. That was in the past. It was Herod's interpretation of His ministry, making Him out to be John redivivus, that decided Him to retire for a season to a quiet spot across the lake. An additional reason for going apart was the return of the twelve from a tour of ministry (Luke 9:10-11). There was need for rest, evaluation, and instruction. The chosen spot was in the vicinity of Bethsaida, which was situated on the north shore of the Sea of Galilee. Going by boat was an escape from the hubbub of the pressing throngs, but the quietness was not to last long. The distance by foot was little more than the crossing by boat, so by the time Jesus and His few disciples reached land the crowd was already assembling.

Our Lord knew how necessary it was, both for Himself and for His apostolic band, to withdraw from the crowds. We can take so much of the pressure; then we need replenishing. "Come ye yourselves apart and rest awhile," He said on one occasion, and that was indeed part of the pattern of His life.

That withdrawal did not indicate any feeling of revulsion on the part of Jesus. He did not share the attitude of the Roman poet Ovid, who wrote, "*Odi profanum vulgus,*" which might be rendered, "I hate the vulgar throng." One word spells our Lord's reaction in the presence of the multitude—compassion. We have already come across the word as indicative of our Lord's emotional response to the needy crowds whom He saw as sheep scattered, having no shepherd (9:36). To the disciples the throngs were an embarrassment and a burden. To Jesus they were a call and an opportunity. Wth Him compassion was not a passive pity. It translated itself into action. In this instance it was the activity of healing.

The disciples became uncomfortably aware of the passing of time. It was already past supper time, and soon they would have on their hands not just a crowd, but a weary, hungry crowd. Doubtless they were feeling like that themselves, and the Master must have been exhausted. So they undertook to counsel, if not to command, the Master. It was time to terminate the meeting and let the people secure food before closing time. It seemed like a reasonable proposition, except for one consideration. It was not a called meeting, but a spontaneous gathering of which the village merchants had had no warning. Their normal stock would soon be exhausted if thousands rushed in on them. Not many had brought lunch with them, as did the lad with the five loaves and two fish (John 6:9). If others did, they certainly did not offer to supplement the lad's gift.

This is one of the few incidents related in all four gospels. There must be some special significance attached to it. For one thing, the young lad giving up his lunch is a delightful touch. Although he is mentioned only in John's account, we cannot read the synoptic versions without thinking of him. The very fact that he was in the crowd that day and carrying a lunch indicates his desire to know Jesus and to be as long in His company as possible. The handing over of the loaves and fish was surely an act of faith. He even may have had more faith than the disciples. We recall Andrew's qualifying question, "What are they among so many?" (John 6:9). The boy really worked with Jesus that day. If there is a museum in heaven, the lad's five barley loaves and two small fish will take their place beside Mary's cruse of precious ointment.

Notice the hands that came into play that day. First the giving hands, an act of consecration on the part of a young boy; the multiplying hands, where the miracle was wrought; the distributing hands, for the disciples were pressed into service; and the receiving hands that eagerly grasped the portion provided for every one. Are we permitted to say that without the giving hands there would have been no receiving hands? Perhaps it is better to side with Mordecai when he said to Esther, "If thou altogether holdest thy peace at this time, then shall there enlargement and deliverance arise to the Jews from another place" (Esther 4:14). In other words, God's purposes will not fail of realization, even if some of His servants fail of their responsibility. But rather than argue the point, let us see how God uses human instrumentalities and welds them into the total pattern. Here only the Lord's hands were the miracle-working hands, but He associated other hands with His own in the performance of that great miracle of provision. Nor were those instrumentalities drawn from the nobility of the earth. On one side an unnamed boy with a boy's lunch; on the other side a group of ordinary men who were only beginners in the life of faith. Yet it was no insignificant part that they played in the drama of that hour.

Matthew 14:20 presents two seemingly contrary facets of God's character. "They did all eat, and were filled: and they took up of the fragments that remained twelve baskets full." First, see the lavishness of God. Nobody was policing the ranks, crying, "Go easy, eat light, just a little for each!" Instead, "they did all eat, and were filled." Not only so. Jesus provided twelve baskets full more than was needed to fill all five thousand men, plus women and children. God is a lavish God. See Him in creation. That little phrase, "the stars also" (Genesis 1:16), embraces billions of heavenly objects, beyond the count of the strongest telescopes. See how such words as *abundantly* and *multiply* are applied to creatures of the deep, the birds of the air, and man. Then the provision for those creatures was just as generous. The same lavish trait is visible in the realm of grace. The apostle Paul speaks of *abundant* grace and *sufficient* grace. Likewise in the sphere of prayer: He is "able to do exceeding abundantly above all that we ask or think, according to the power that worketh in us" (Ephesians 3:20).

But alongside lavishness is economy. Our Lord, as we have seen, produced much more than was needed to give all five thousand more than they could eat, but the excess was not for waste. John's record includes the command of Jesus, "Gather up the fragments that remain, *that nothing be lost*" (John 6:12, italics added). What was done with the twelve baskets full we are not told. On one occasion our Lord said, "The poor always ye have with you" (John 12:8). Doubtless there were poor among the five thousand, and in the region around Bethsaida. Economy is as much a part of God's character as abundance. He has written it into nature itself. So often what we regard as waste is just part of nature's process of recycling. No doubt man is the most guilty of all creatures in the crime of waste. If we would be godly (Godlike), we must learn to give more and waste less.

WALKING ON WATER (14:22-36)

Why did Jesus *constrain* His disciples to go without Him across the lake to Capernaum? The word used suggests a degree of pressure. The same word is translated *compel* in Luke 14:23. For one thing, there was a delicate task to perform—the dismissing of the crowd—and the presence of the disciples might have made it more difficult. The situation needed a masterful personality, free from such bungling as the disciples manifested before the miracle. John tells us that Jesus "perceived that they would come and take him by force, to make him a king" (John 6:15). At least some of the twelve, as, for instance, Simon the Zealot, would heartily have joined such a movement. It was better that they be out of the picture and let Jesus Himself handle the situation. Above all, He desired to be alone with His Father in the quietness of the mountain. Surely that has something to say to us concerning the necessity of secret communion with the Lord. Let Harriet Beecher Stowe express our heart's need:

> Alone with Thee, amid the mystic shadows,
>   The solemn hush of nature newly born;
> Alone with Thee in breathless adoration,
>   In the calm dew and freshness of the morn.
>
>   HARRIET BEECHER STOWE
>   ("Still, Still with Thee") [1]

The emotional pressure was heavy on the disciples. They had been witnesses to, and participants in, an amazing miracle; they had fought a stubborn storm throughout the night; and now, in the fourth watch, which merges into early dawn when morning mists rest upon the lake, they see approaching them through the mist the form of a man walking on the water. Perhaps it seems strange to us that they did not immediately think in terms of their absent Master. In their emotional confusion they thought only of an apparition and cried out in fear. I suppose people differ in their responses to fear. My own experiences of fear have been mostly in nightmares when I became voiceless. Whether the fright be in sleep or awake, crying out will tend to relieve the pent-up feeling. But a better than psychological relief came. It was the voice of the Beloved, speaking peace to their hearts.

Peter could not let such an incident pass without getting into the

act. Impetuous Peter, indeed! At first view he is just like a child who
wants to do what he sees his elders do. But there is more to it than
that. He believes what Paul later wrote, "I can do all things through
Christ which strengtheneth me" (Philippians 4:13). He is beginning
to learn to dare at Christ's command, and although there will be
failures, he will become one of the chief pillars of the church. True,
he bungled it by letting the boisterous wind scare him, but the fact
remains that "he walked on the water," which none of the others did,
and he knew where to apply for help when he felt himself sinking.
The lesson is simple and clear. With our eyes upon Jesus we can ride
the stormy waves, but if our eyes are upon the stormy waves, they will
engulf us. David did lots of sinking, but, like Peter, he knew the
source of deliverance. "I cried unto the LORD with my voice, and he
heard me out of his holy hill" (Psalm 3:4).

I think I detect a touch of humor in the Lord's gentle rebuke of
Peter. At least there was a smile on His face when He said, "O thou
of little faith, wherefore didst thou doubt?" (14:31). And Peter will
tread many a stormy sea with Jesus before the day of assembly on the
crystal sea. In John's record we are given this detail, that "immediately the ship was at the land whither they went." But not before
they had turned the little ship into a temple, for "they that were in
the ship came and worshipped him, saying, Of a truth thou art the
Son of God" (14:33).

We can hardly leave the passage without reminding ourselves of the
typical and dispensational value of that sequence of events. First, the
breaking of the bread is a picture of Calvary. Do we not read that on
another occasion "Jesus took bread, and blessed it, and brake it, and
gave it to the disciples, and said, Take, eat; this is my body"? (26:26).
Second, sending His disciples across the rough lake suggests the
launching of the church upon the stormy seas of this age of witness.
Third, our Lord's ascent of the hill for prayer speaks of His ascension
to the right hand of God to exercise a ministry of intercession on behalf of His church in the midst of her "toil and tribulation, and
tumult of her war" ("The Church's One Foundation," Samuel J.
Stone). Fourth, His coming to the toiling disciples and their immediate arrival at their destination remind us of His coming for His
church, when "in a moment, in the twinkling of an eye" (1 Corin-

thians 15:52) we shall be gathered to Him, "and so shall we ever be with the Lord" (1 Thessalonians 4:17).

"They besought him that he would depart out of their coasts" (8:34). They "besought him that they might only touch the hem of his garment" (14:36). That was the difference between the Gadarenes and the men of Gennesaret. In the one case we see men of this world who preferred their swine to the Savior, having no care for the deliverance of devil-tormented men. Here we see "the milk of human kindness" coupled with a remarkable surge of faith, as they welcomed the Savior to their borders and rounded up the sick of the community for their one chance of healing.

What we have in that incident is a multiplication of an earlier action on the part of one woman, who said to herself, "If I may but touch his garment, I shall be whole" (9:21). She touched, and immediately her ailment was gone. No doubt the story of the woman who touched and was healed had been told all over Galilee, so that, when Jesus came to Gennesaret, He was confronted, not with a wall of unbelief, but with a clamor to touch and be whole. If the touch of faith could save one woman, it could save a multitude. So they believed, and so it came to pass. Jesus does not disappoint faith.

In Luke's account of the woman who touched, there is a significant note introduced. Jesus said, "Somebody hath touched me; for I perceive that virtue [strength] is gone out of me" (Luke 8:46). Healing was costly business to Jesus. The touch of faith took a toll of His strength. If there was a perceptible drain upon Him from that one touch, what would be the demand of a multitude of such touches? Yet He put no limit on the number who might touch Him. "As many as touched were made whole," but He paid for it in weariness. If we, then, are willing to share His weariness in ministering to others, we shall also know Him as the source of renewal, for He suffered His last great weariness on the cross.

Can there be some special reason for the emphasis on the *hem*, or *border* of our Lord's garment, both in the action of the woman and in the request of the men of Gennesaret? We must tread lightly here and not allow our imaginations to run away with us. At the same time, one is justified in asking whether the Old Testament references to the hem of the garment cast light upon the emphasis here. We think of the blue border (or fringe) commanded by God through Moses, intended to remind the Israelites that they were a holy people, set apart for God. Now the only one who has ever completely fulfilled the meaning of that border and lived out the life of holiness of which it spoke is the Lord Jesus. It is as that wholly separated One that Jesus was the completely open channel through which the power of God could operate in unlimited measure for the alleviation of human need.

Again we think of the robe of the ephod in the high priest's vestments. All around the skirt of the robe were alternating bells and pomegranates. We cannot go into detail on that subject. In general, those seventy-two bells and alternating pomegranates were surely symbolic of the ministry of the high priest as the bearer of the testimony of God and of the divine benediction. Once more, the only perfect High Priest, the ultimate bearer of God's saving grace, is the Lord Jesus. To touch the border of His robe, as an act of faith if not of understanding, was to lay claim to all the benefits of His ministry as God's appointed High Priest.

Tradition Versus Commandment (15:1-20)

The second movement (15:1-39) begins with an encounter. Nothing so angered the Lord as hypocrisy, and here He is faced with a prime example of it. His encounter was evidently with an official delegation from Jerusalem come to Galilee for the set purpose of finding some way of incriminating Jesus. It was no open-minded enquiry, but a determined prosecution. The issue on which they laid hold revealed the weakness of their case. Jesus' disciples did not observe all the rules that tradition required regarding ablutions. One evident omission was a failure to wash their hands before eating. With us the washing of hands before meals is a hygienic matter, but with the Jews it was a religious observance. True, the law of Moses laid down certain rules for the priests in relation to their handling of the holy things, but tradition had expanded the rules to include all the people in a multitude of occasions. In the eyes of the Pharisees neglect on the part of the disciples of Jesus was a serious religious error.

It is rather interesting to note that the Pharisees did not include Jesus Himself in their accusation. That raises the question whether

Jesus did actually practice washing before meals. What the incident makes clear is that He did not bind Himself to observances that had no higher authority than tradition. At the same time He would not disregard a practice simply on the ground that it was tradition. A tradition must be evaluated in the light of the law of God and must stand on its own merit. It could not be given authority that belonged only to the Word of God. That is how Jesus dealt with the situation before Him. Over against "the tradition of the elders" He places "the commandments of God." If the Pharisees are out to champion the traditions of the elders in a nonmoral and rather insignificant matter, Jesus will champion the law of the Lord in matters of high moral import.

He goes directly to the heart of the law, the Ten Commandments, where we are shown the sum of man's duty to God and man. He chooses the one that most nearly touches both Godward and manward obligation, since the parent stands in God's stead until the child is of age to discern right from wrong. "Honor thy father and thy mother" is, therefore, a command of the first importance, and whatever contravenes that law brings upon the doer a heavy load of guilt. In such a setting, honoring father and mother is more than saying nice things about them and treating them with outward courtesy. It embraces the obligation to care for one's parents and to see that the needs of their advanced years are met. But a tradition had grown up in Israel that voided that law in its more practical application. One who desired to be released from the obligation to support his aging parents need only go to the priest and have his possessions declared *corban* (Mark 7:11)—dedicated to God. Thereafter not only was he not required to support his parents; the law of corban forbade his giving to them of the consecrated goods. The perversity of that system was that money so dedicated was not necessarily given to the treasury of the Temple. It was only declared given. So the man who claimed the benefit of the law of corban kept on enjoying his wealth while his parents suffered their penury, shut off from filial support by a wicked tradition. And *that* was an act of worship! Jesus called it hypocrisy. It is a good example of the moral tangle in which we find ourselves when we forsake the pure Word of God and give divine authority to human gurus.

So far our Lord had not answered the Pharisees' criticism of the disciples concerning the washing of hands before eating. Now He replies to that by means of a great general principle: "Not that which goeth into the mouth defileth a man" (15:11). The error of those religious leaders was that they confused the physical and the moral. They made a moral issue out of something purely physical and failed to see the moral values in the fundamental laws of God.

It is interesting to note that although our Lord addressed the religious leaders on the matter of corban, He called the multitude together to hear His statement about defilement. The common people would be less involved in the legal niceties of tradition than the Pharisees and scribes, whereas defilement was a matter of common interest to all who took part in the ritual worship of the synagogue or Temple. Even Peter, doubtless among those criticized for failure to wash his hands, was punctilious in the matter of unclean meats (Acts 10:13-14). We may be sure that if Peter and Andrew and James and John were criticized for failure to wash before eating, that negligence was shared by the people in general. Our Lord's dictum, then, was of immense value to the multitude. It was one more section of the manifesto of freedom that Christ came to inaugurate. So, while we shall continue to wash our hands before meals and teach our children to do so, it will be for hygienic reasons, not as a religious observance.

It is not surprising that the Pharisees took offense at their esteemed tradition being so set down. They expressed their displeasure to the disciples, who conveyed it to the Master. His reply was rather startling, considering His unusual care for men. "Let them alone," He said (15:14). It reminds us of another seemingly harsh injunction: "Give not that which is holy unto the dogs, neither cast ye your pearls before swine" (7:6). Men who exhibit the propensities of dogs and swine in their reaction to the holy things are put in that category. So there are those who are no longer amenable to the truth, and regarding them Jesus said, "Let them alone." Those men represented a system of religion that the Father had not planted and was therefore foredoomed to failure. They claimed Abrahamic ancestry, but they were far from Abrahamic faith. Many are the systems today that are not of God's planting. We are apt to panic when we see some of those taking root and flourishing, and we launch our crusades against

those "blind leaders of the blind." We are indeed exhorted to in-
struct those who have been deceived, in the hope that they may escape
from the snare (2 Timothy 2:24-26). But if one has turned his back
upon known truth and has committed himself to the way of error,
the apostle Paul says, "From such turn away," and that is in keeping
with the word of the Lord, "Let them alone." It sounds harsh to us,
but when we remember that the One who spoke that word cared
enough for men to die for them, we shall know that it is the harshness
of perfect righteousness and wisdom. Like John and James we should
like to be given permission to call down fire from heaven, but judgment is not in our hands. There may even be an element of mercy
in that "Let them alone." It means that judgment is held in abey-
ance and time given for repentance.

Our Lord gave further clearance of that question to His disciples
in answer to the request of Peter, who regarded the dictum as a parable. Several lessons may be adduced. First, defilement is a moral condition for which we must look for a moral cause. Second, what we
consume orally is not such a moral cause. Third, the cause of moral
defilement lies within ourselves. Fourth, when we give expression to
the evil within, we are adding defilement to corruption.

THE CANAANITISH WOMAN (15:21-28)

After that round with the Pharisees, Jesus withdrew, along with
His disciples, to the coastal area of Tyre and Sidon. He sought quiet-
ness for a season. Mark tells us that He "would have no man know"
(Mark 7:24) of His presence. But need sought Him out. Even in
Gentile country He could not be hid. The woman who broke in on
His rest period is called elsewhere a Syrophoenician. The Romans
had united the two regions, Syria and Phoenicia, hence the compound
name.

The incident is in three movements: the woman's plea is presented,
the woman's faith is tested, and the woman's petition is granted. Several questions present themselves. How did this Gentile woman learn
that Jesus had come to her vicinity? How did she know of His power
over demons? Where and how did she learn to call Jesus "Son of
David" (15:22)? Was there some Jewish influence in her background? We shall remember that "Son of David" was a messianic

title. So here is a Gentile woman pressing a Jewish claim! Perhaps that partly explains the manner in which Jesus dealt with her. But whether or not she had a right to seek blessing on messianic ground, she was exercising a faith which, after it was tried, rejoiced the heart of the Lord Jesus. Then too she addressed Him with all reverence. We shall not say that in using the term *Lord* she was acclaiming the deity of Christ. She hardly knew enough for that as yet. But she used the highest term that she knew for One whom she believed capable of performing the deliverance from Satanic bondage of which her daughter stood in need. Faith, reverence, and then the passion of motherly love. "My daughter," she cries, "is grievously vexed with a devil" (15:22). And she believes that Jesus, the Son of David, will share her grief and longing.

Peter speaks of the trial of our faith as "being much more precious than of gold that perisheth" (1 Peter 1:7). That woman's faith was subjected to a threefold trial. First there was the trial of silence. The silence of God is more awful than His speech. David the psalmist realized that and cried out, "Be not silent to me: lest, if thou be silent to me, I become like them that go down into the pit" (Psalm 28:1). There is something terrifying about silence, and that Greek mother must have felt terror gripping her heart. *Let me know the worst, if worst it must be, but save me from the awful suspense!* That thought must have been in her mind. Even the disciples felt the tenseness of the situation and urged the Master to act negatively if He were not going to act positively. Then came the second test of the woman's faith. We may call it the test of limitation. The ministry of Jesus had specific bounds. "I am not sent but unto the lost sheep of the house of Israel." We recall that when out Lord sent His disciples out on their first preaching mission He laid this limitation upon them: "Go not into the way of the Gentiles, and into any city of the Samaritans enter ye not: But go rather to the lost sheep of the house of Israel" (10:5-6). In the light of such a clear directive it would surely seem inconsistent in the eyes of the disciples if the Master broke through that limitation. Here, then, He is using the order as a test of the woman's faith. How will she respond? Will she consider the matter closed and give herself and her daughter over to hopelessness? Or will she summon up arguments against such discrimination and claim equal rights? Or will she in desperation cast herself at Jesus' feet and plead mercy? That she does. And I think she might have poured a little more content into that word *Lord*. It is a word (*kurios*) that carries meaning all the way from a respectful "sir" to an address to deity. Perhaps the very struggle in which she was engaged pressed her to a recognition of deity in the Man whose word commanded the forces of hell. At any rate she offered no argument, save that of desperate need. "Lord, help me!" (15:25).

Surely Jesus cannot resist such a plea. But one more test must be applied that we may describe as the test of humiliation. The woman has addressed Jesus as Son of David and sought His blessing on messianic ground, so claiming equal privilege with the sons of Abraham. That could not be allowed to pass. The order of privilege must be recognized and sustained, and Jesus depicts that order in vivid language—we might almost say cruel language. "It is not meet to take the children's bread, and to cast it to dogs" (15:26). We cannot believe that Jesus spoke those words in the spirit of scorn in which the Jews were wont to speak of "the Gentile dogs." There was actually an invitation tucked away in them. It is found in the word for dog that Jesus used, different from the term applied to the dogs that licked the sores of Lazarus, but referring rather to puppies—pet dogs that had access to the dining area and fed on what dropped from the table. In other words, any benefit that Jesus might bestow upon a Gentile suppliant would be a spillover from Israel's cup of blessing. Will that Gentile woman accept such a place of humility? She does, laying hold of the hope in that word *puppy*. One can sense a burst of delight in Jesus' response: "O woman, great is thy faith: be it unto thee even as thou wilt." Great faith is humble faith; humble faith is great faith.

The day of discrimination would soon end. Calvary embraced the whole world. Jesus Himself sensed the limitation placed upon Him in the days of His flesh and on more than one occasion expressed it. "I have a baptism to be baptized with; and how am I straitened till it be accomplished!" (Luke 12:50). Or again: "And I, if I be lifted up from the earth, will draw all men unto me. This he said, signifying what death he should die" (John 12:32-33); aye, and signifying how that death should give Him access to all men, and give all men access to God through Him. The few benefits bestowed on Gentiles, as in the case of that Syrophoenician woman, were foregleams of the "whosoever" gospel that it is our privilege to proclaim without restraint.

On many occasions our Lord demonstrated His authority over demons, but here is an added dimension. Distance did not diminish His power. Jesus did not go to the home, nor require that the demonized girl be brought to Him, as in the case of the boy at the base of the Mount of Transfiguration. Just as He could command healing by "remote control" (as witness the healing of the centurion's servant), so His command of the demons was as effective at a distance as in a face-to-face encounter.

THE FEEDING OF THE FOUR THOUSAND (15:29-39)

From the area of Tyre and Sidon Jesus and His disciples returned to familiar Galilean territory. Mark says that they went "through the midst of the coasts of Decapolis" (Mark 7:31), a region that stretched north, east, and south of the Sea of Galilee. There Jesus sought rest on a mountain slope overlooking the waters of Galilee. But the quiet was soon broken by the hurrying crowds bringing their sick and infirm, their blind and deaf, their lame and dumb, to the feet of the Great Physician. Mark tells us of one of those healing incidents that fired the wonder of the crowds, who exclaimed, "He hath done all things well; he maketh both the deaf to hear, and the dumb to speak" (Mark 7:37).

For three days the crowd kept pressing in upon Jesus, seeking and obtaining healing for their sick and infirm. Considering that healing was a drain on Jesus' strength (see Luke 8:46), we might have expected Him to say to His disciples, "We have had enough of this; let us get away." But His thought was not for His own weariness, but for the needy, eager, and now hungry multitude. To dismiss them would mean for many hardship to the point of fainting. It is interesting to note that on the occasion of the feeding of the five thousand, the disciples took the initiative by suggesting that the people be sent away to buy provision before closing time of the merchants, but now the initiative is with Jesus Himself, calling attention to a condition that demanded action.

If one is happily surprised (or should we be?) at Jesus' reaction to the situation, we are sadly surprised at the response of the disciples.

They seem to have forgotten the miracle of the feeding of the five thousand, or else they doubted if it could be repeated. Their vision went no farther than "a desert place" and "so great a multitude." Oblivious to the multiplying hands, they could see only an impossible situation. I have no doubt, however, that when Jesus began to organize for a "repeat performance," their memory was awakened, their faith revived, and they became glad participants in the miracle of feeding four thousand with seven loaves and several small fish—not in scanty measure, but until all were filled, with seven hampersful of remnants. Once again the bounty and the economy of God are brought into bold relief. How the remnants were distributed we do not know, but that they were put to good use we can be assured.

Where the King James version reads, "He . . . took ship," the literal rendering of the Greek would be "He . . . entered into the boat." It is that definite article that intrigues me. It suggests that Jesus had a boat at His call for His frequent crossings of the lake. Whose boat was it, Peter's? Or John's? It appears that Peter had not disposed of his boat at the time of his call to follow Jesus. Indeed he still had it after the resurrection of Christ, when he said to his fellow disciples, "I go a-fishing" (John 21:3). As far as our record goes, that was his last fishing trip. But it is interesting to think that Peter's boat was the Lord's ferry. No, it is not an article of faith, but it suggests that we may have in possession something that the Lord would put to regular use if it were at His disposal. So the crossing was made to Magdala, otherwise known as Magadan, on the west shore of the lake.

A WARNING ABOUT LEAVEN (16:1-12)

Like movements 1 (13:54—14:36) and 2 (15:1-39), movement 3 (16:1-21) had a stormy beginning. The old question of a sign was revived by the joint delegation of Pharisees and Sadducees. A sign can be a directive, as in athletics; or it can be an omen, heralding coming events; or it can be an indication of some condition of strength or weakness of character; or it can be a token of authority, in confirmation of a claim or a message. It was a sign in the latter sense that the critics of Jesus demanded, and of course they were thinking in terms of some miraculous manifestation such as calling down fire from heaven. Actually the whole life of Jesus was a sign from heaven, with

His beauty of holiness, His multiplied works of mercy, His manifest power over the devil and his legions, and His incomparable teaching. But His enemies were blind to all that and were bent on pushing Him into a corner where He would have to give the kind of sign they asked for or stand exposed as a pretender.

Now Jesus had replied to that demand before (see 12:38-42). On that occasion He turned the question back upon His detractors. They were smart enough, He indicated, to read the weather signs, but they were evidently poor interpreters of current events. As news commentators they were miserable failures, unable even to appraise such a phenomenal character as was walking in and out among them, distributing the beneficences of heaven. Jesus knew right well that if they did not believe His gracious works of mercy, neither would they be convinced by some dramatic display. We recall that in the parable of the rich man and Lazarus (Luke 16:19-31), the rich man in Hades asks Abraham to send Lazarus to his brothers on the plea that they would repent if someone came to them from the dead. The reply was, "If they hear not Moses and the prophets, neither will they be persuaded, though one rose from the dead" (Luke 16:31). So Jesus left them to ponder the sign that He had given them before—the sign of the prophet Jonah. Jonah, having come from three days in a living tomb, was a sign to the people of Nineveh. But Jonah's living death and resurrection were but a foreview of our Lord's death and resurrection, which therefore was the ultimate sign to that and all succeeding generations, calling men everywhere to repentance and salvation.

It is remarkable to find the Pharisees and the Sadducees united in their attack on Christ, for they were at opposite poles theologically and politically. The Pharisees were the traditionalists, the ultraconservatives, while the Sadducees were the liberals, rejecting such supernatural doctrines as angels and resurrection (see Acts 23:8). The two factions were usually at loggerheads, but their common opposition to Christ brought them together.

That alliance did not escape Christ's notice. He turned it into an occasion to warn His disciples of the peril of both Pharisaic and Sadducean teaching—hypocrisy on the one hand and unbelief on the other. The language that He used reminded the disciples of a negligence on their part. In all the excitement of the feeding of the four thousand and the encounter with the Pharisees and Sadducees they had failed to replenish their own supply of loaves. Now they thought that Jesus' mention of leaven had reference to failure on their part, and they began to worry about their next meal. The lessons of the feeding of the five thousand and the four thousand had not yet penetrated, and Jesus was compelled to recall those events and apply the lesson. It is noticeable that our Lord laid emphasis on what was left over in each case, twelve basketsful after the feeding of the five thousand, and seven basketsful after the feeding of the four thousand.

According to the Greek text, our Lord spoke of two kinds of baskets—the *kophinos,* which He linked with the five thousand, and the *sphuris,* which He connected with the four thousand. It has been affirmed by some that the *kophinos* was smaller than the *sphuris* and was used widely by the Jews as a lunch basket, whereas the *sphuris* was more in Gentile use as a traveling bag. From that it has been suggested that the five thousand were Jews, while the four thousand were Gentiles who thronged after Jesus for the healing that He gave them. I think that is reading something into the text that is not intended, especially since both types of baskets were of various sizes and were put to divers uses.

The lesson of the hour was twofold. First was the warning to avoid the hypocritical legalism of the Pharisees and the gross liberalism of the Sadducees. Their teaching was a corrupting leaven in the national life and must by all means be kept from polluting the life of the infant church. The Lord's figurative use of the term *leaven* was at first misunderstood by the disciples, who thought of leaven in the literal sense and panicked over their lack of bread. So the second lesson was a rebuke for their poor memory and a reminder that He who could so multiply the loaves and the fish that the fragments left over far exceeded the original supply could care for the physical need of twelve men.

Caesarea Philippi was roughly thirty miles north of the Sea of Galilee. Formerly called Paneas (after the god Pan), it was renamed Caesarea by Herod Philip in honor of Tiberius Caesar. The designation "Philippi" not only commemorated the Herod who so named it, but distinguished that city from the Caesarea on the Mediterranean coast that played so large a part in the ministries of both Peter and

Paul. Caesarea Philippi was probably the most northerly point of our Lord's journeys. Little did the disciples know that they were walking into a situation of crisis. Two vital truths were about to be brought into sharp focus—one bearing on the person of Christ, and the other on His mission.

It is evident that the twelve, although walking with Jesus, were not cut off from communication with others. Otherwise there would have been no point in His inquiring of them concerning the popular view of His identity. Nor was it idle curiosity or pride that prompted the question. The whole scheme of redemption required a recognition of the Christhood of Jesus. And where would that recognition first appear, if not among those who were closest to Him? Later, in the upper room, the Lord was grieved at the incompleteness of the disciples' understanding of His person so that, in reply to Philip's request, "Show us the Father," He said, "Have I been so long time with you, and yet hast thou not known me, Philip? he that hath seen me hath seen the Father" (John 14:9). Why, then, did not Jesus immediately address His question to the disciples on this occasion but enquired about the guesses and conclusions of the generality of people? I can only believe that it was in preparation for the personal question. Perhaps the disciples, some of them at least, had hardly formulated their thoughts concerning Jesus, but the question, "What are people saying about Me?", with the diversity of answers, would challenge them to come to some decisive conviction and so prepare them to answer the follow-up question, "What do *you* think of Me?"

I wonder what brought the people to those varied opinions. John the Baptist, Elijah, and Jeremiah were all great men. Our Lord Himself ranked John the Baptist foremost among those born of women. Elijah had a chariot of fire to glory instead of a funeral coach to the grave. Jeremiah was the prophet of the captivity, whose love for his people opened the fountain of tears. We must say that in a sense they were very complimentary opinions, but they fell far short of the truth. If Jesus is only a man, those sects that give Him a place with Confucius and Buddha and Moses in their "hall of fame" do Him great honor. But if He is the true, eternal Son of God, then He stands in a category all by Himself. Not even *primus inter pares* is a sufficient designation for Him who, "existing in the form of God, counted not the being on an equality with God a thing to be grasped, but emptied himself, taking the form of a servant, being made in the likeness of men" (Philippians 2:6-7, ASV). Those who associated Him with John the Baptist, Elijah, and Jeremiah had a long way to go. The question now was, How far along the road of understanding and recognition had the disciples come?

PETER'S GREAT CONFESSION (16:13-20)

In the few sentences following we shall observe a confession, a commendation, a pronouncement, an appointment, and a prohibition.

We have come to expect Simon Peter to act as speaker of the house. While the others were mentally formulating their answer to Christ's so personal question, Peter spoke out with an air of finality: "Thou art the Christ, the Son of the living God" (16:16). He is Jesus of Nazareth, but Peter sees in Him the Christ, the Messiah, God's Anointed One, the One "of whom Moses in the law, and the prophets, did write" (John 1:45). At that point, if you had asked Peter to write out his image of the Messiah, I wonder how his statement would read! Of course his concept of Christ would be based on the Old Testament picture. Or would it? Shortly we are going to hear Peter repudiate a very important part of the Old Testament revelation of the Christ. No doubt his thought was colored by the popular expectation of Messiah's mission—to deliver Israel from Gentile domination and establish the throne of David to perpetuity. How much more was in Peter's mind we cannot say. But we can say that by the time he wrote his two epistles his understanding of the messiahship of Jesus was vastly richer than when he first said, "Thou art the Christ." The cross, the resurrection, the ascension, and Pentecost made the difference.

But if Peter's concept of messiahship was inadequate and immature, another fact concerning the person of Christ had taken hold of his mind: "Thou art . . . the Son of the living God." Jesus had just applied to Himself, as on many occasions, the designation "Son of man." That was an assumed title, the title of incarnation, of self-abasement, signifying His being made in all things like unto His brethren. Our Lord's very question, however, pointed to something more than could be wrapped up in the name "Son of man." Peter saw that something more, that something that spelled out eternity, even deity. "Son of the living God" was his answer. Once again, we cannot know how much of the mystery of Christ was conveyed to Peter's mind by this title. At any rate, he sensed that the divine title applied to the Man Christ Jesus as well as to the Godhood within Him, a fact made clear to Mary by the angel Gabriel when he said, "That holy thing which shall be born of thee shall be called the Son of God" (Luke 1:35). Whether we think in terms of the incarnation begetting, or the resurrection begetting, or the eternal begetting, we affirm with Peter, "Thou art . . . the Son of the living God."

Here, then, was revelation, incomplete no doubt, but basic. The Messiahship and Sonship of Jesus had surfaced, and Simon Peter was the chosen vessel to hurl the credo into the stream of Christian witness. The Lord was quick to take up Peter's declaration and to make clear its origin. It was no second-hand faith that Peter expressed, no repetition of some rabbi's affirmation, no conclusion arrived at by human reason. Miracles had been wrought before in Israel, validating the ministry of Moses, of Elijah, of Elisha, and of others. The multiplied miracles of Jesus were certainly sufficient to demonstrate that He was come from God (see John 3:2), but it took more than the miracles themselves to establish, not only that God was with Him, but also that He was very God, God the Son. The mighty works were the outward manifestation, accompanied by divine illumination. "Flesh and blood hath not revealed it unto thee, but my Father which is in heaven" (16:17). Here again is the mystery that has puzzled and disturbed many minds. Jesus offered His works as a call to faith and held men responsible for their response to those works; yet He accounts every confession of faith a work of God. So it was with Peter. So it is with us.

We must not fail to see what is implicit in the commendation. Jesus is affirming the truth of Peter's statement, and the form of His affirmation makes it stronger than if He had simply said, "You're right, Peter!" That benediction, that pointing to the source of the revelation, indicates Jesus' acceptance of the double title. He did not suggest that Peter was carrying his great admiration for his Master a little too far. The acceptance of titles of joint humanity and deity is one of the most notable features of our Lord's self-consciousness.

After commendation comes pronouncement. "Thou art Peter, and upon this rock I will build my church" (16:18). Simon Johnson was his name. On first meeting him, Jesus indicated a new name for him—in the future (John 1:42). The future tense has now given way to the present tense. That bold, confident confession has revealed the new man, and the new man must carry the new name. "Thou art Peter," a rock of a man. Now of course we can point to a number of subsequent occasions when Simon did not act like a rock of a man, especially those three unhappy denials that so saddened the Lord. Here is a case of the faith of Jesus. He knew that Peter would fail, and fail badly, but He knew what He would make of this impulsive, unstable man, and how this weakling would become the strengthener of His brethren (Luke 22:32).

"Upon this rock I will build my church." First let us look at the institution that the Lord calls "My church." The best definition is from the Lord Himself, given in the seventeenth chapter of John's gospel, in the words "those whom thou hast given me" (John 17:11; compare also verses 2, 6, 9, 12, 24). That company of "given" ones is made up of "these," namely, those who were with Christ as His disciples, and "them also which shall believe on me through their word" (John 17:20). The body of believers, then, constitutes the church, and the church is the Father's gift to the Son. Since believing is a condition inwrought by the Holy Spirit, we perceive a mystic union of the church with the blessed Trinity.

The Greek word translated "church" (*ekklesia*) is one of a cluster of terms that the Spirit of inspiration has lifted from their old uses and made part of the vocabulary of revelation. Such a word is *charis* (grace), which has advanced from describing anything sensually pleasant to declaring God's gracious attitude to sinners, then God's basic *modus operandi* in salvation ("by grace are ye saved," Ephesians 2:8), then God's reservoir of help for His believing people ("My grace is sufficient for thee," 2 Corinthians 12:9), then the Godlike virtues, such as generosity, inwrought by the Holy Spirit in the character of the Christian. *Ekklesia* has been likewise ennobled. The word is found in Acts 19 in its secular sense, once of a mob assembly and once of a legal, official assembly. Two thoughts seem to combine in the word—a calling out, and a gathering together. Combine the two, and you have an assembly of called out, and therefore of favored,

people. Such is the church. We are called out from the world, not
to be so many isolated units, but to be "bound together in the great
bundle of life in the Lord our God." We are a company, an assembly,
and while perforce we must operate as many assemblies now, the
"general assembly" will include all who have "washed their robes and
made them white in the blood of the Lamb." So we have the churches
and the church.

Although the church is God's gift to His Son, it is also the purchase
of blood. "Christ . . . loved the church, and gave himself for it"
(Ephesians 5:25). Every called-out soul is Christ's by right of purchase. After the purchase, then, comes the building. "I will build my
church." He is the Master Builder, and in the day of presentation not
one living stone will be missing. We have seen Edinburgh's disgrace,
that unfinished erection on Calton Hill, and McLeod's folly in Oban,
a dream that never came true, but when Jesus says, "I will build my
church," we are assured that the work decreed from the foundation
of the world, and the contract sealed in the blood of His cross, will be
brought to completion, despite the incessant opposition of the prin-
cipalities and powers of darkness. "The gates of Hades shall not prevail against it" (16:18, ASV).

Admittedly that is a strange statement. Gates suggest a city, and
here Hades, the place of death, the realm of darkness, is regarded as
having gates—gates that are in defiance of the church of Christ. I think
we can find a little help in the incident of Samson in Gaza. When the
Gazites learned of the presence of Samson, they closed the gates
against him, with intent to slay him when morning broke. But the
gates of Gaza could not prevail against him to deny him exit. So the
powers of hell may seek to barricade and bar the ongoings of the
church, but always the church is empowered to break through the
barriers, to defy the gates of Hades, and march on to the goal. There
are times when it would seem that the gates of hell were prevailing,
when great areas are closed to the missionary, when inimical govern-
ments seek to crush the Christian testimony, when martyrdom becomes a way of life; but it is at such times that the church grows
stronger, and the absence of the foreign missionary finds compensation in renewed and miraculous workings of the Holy Spirit. The
twentieth century has been called the century of the martyrs, but

where the pressure has been the most severe, there the church has been most triumphant. "The gates of hell shall not prevail against it."

"Upon this rock I will build my church." What rock? Controversy has raged around this question for many centuries. The whole concept of the papacy rests on the belief that "this rock" is Peter, a dogma rejected by all who follow the reformed faith. It is both exegetically and linguistically unacceptable. The Old Testament, by its repeated uses of the term *rock,* establishes it as one of the chief symbols of God in His saving activity. Take this from David: "The LORD is my rock, and my fortress, and my deliverer; the God of my rock; in him will I trust" (2 Samuel 22:2-3). Or this: "Thou art my father, my God, and the rock of my salvation" (Psalm 89:26). That could be multiplied. Then Paul has something to say about the rock that gave its water to the thirsting people of God in the wilderness: "They drank of that spiritual Rock that followed them: and that Rock was Christ" (1 Corinthians 10:4). To take a figure that has consistently been used to present God in His saving activity and apply it to a fallible man is not good exegesis. Besides, we cannot ignore the different terms in the Greek: "Thou art Peter (*petros*), and upon this rock (*petra*) I will build my church." The first refers to the rocklike character of the man, as Christ would train and fashion him. The second speaks of the living rock, not just a piece of stone, however it may have something of the character of rock. Not upon the first (*petros*), but on the second (*petra*), is the church built. And who may the *petra* be? It must be One who answers to the Rock so frequently mentioned throughout Scripture as the God of our salvation. To take up Paul's words again, "that Rock was Christ." Jesus, confessed by Peter as "the Christ, the Son of the living God," is the church's one Foundation, the chief corner stone.

Appointments are expected to be made on the basis of qualification. Peter, by his great confession, had qualified for promotion in the kingdom of heaven. The appointment was announced in picturesque terms: "I will give unto thee the keys of the kingdom of heaven" (16:19). Keys are a symbol of authority, as several references make clear. Isaiah predicted the fall of Shebna from his high post as treasurer of the realm under King Hezekiah, and his replacement by Eliakim, whose elevation to office is stated in the words, "The key of the house of David will I lay upon his shoulder." We shall remember that King Hezekiah was the current representative of the house of David, and the house of David represented the kingdom of God on earth. The degree of authority granted to Eliakim is indicated in the statement, "He shall open, and none shall shut; and he shall shut, and none shall open" (Isaiah 22:15-22). Now we turn to Revelation and we see Jesus in His exalted office as Head of the church. To the church at Philadelphia He writes, "These things saith he that is holy, he that is true, he that hath the key of David, he that openeth, and no man shutteth; and shutteth, and no man openeth" (Revelation 3:7). Eliakim was then, with respect to his office, a type of Christ, and now our Lord uses the same figure in defining Peter's place in the kingdom of heaven.

Notice the progression. First the key represents the authority of Eliakim in the house of David; then the keys speak of authority granted to Peter in the launching days of a new aspect of the kingdom of heaven; finally the key indicates Christ's own enduring authority in His church. In every case the authority is exercised on behalf of another. Eliakim serves Hezekiah; Peter serves Christ; and Christ, to whom all things are subjected, exerts His universal authority in service to Him who sitteth upon the throne (1 Corinthians 15:24-28).

How were the keys of the kingdom to be used? That is quite generally associated with two critical points in the advancement of the gospel. It was Peter who preached the first post-resurrection sermon of the Christian era on the great day of Pentecost when the principle "to the Jew first," was put into operation, and three thousand men of the house of Israel were brought into the kingdom of God through faith in the Lord Jesus Christ. Later, when God would open the door of the kingdom to the Gentiles, it was Peter who was summoned to Caesarea to lead Cornelius and his household into the light of the gospel. If that is what is meant by the keys of the kingdom of heaven, then we can say that all of us who believe have been entrusted with the keys. It is our privilege, by witness of lip and life, to open the door to others.

What about the authority of binding and loosing? We cannot dogmatize too much here. But to me it speaks of apostolic authority in the area of Christian conduct. Speaking as a Spirit-filled, Spirit-taught man, the apostle declares such and such modes of conduct unworthy of the name of Christ and is assured in his spirit that heaven stands with him in his condemnation of such conduct. Again, there are areas of behavior in which the liberty of individual judgment should be preserved. The apostolic voice calls for such liberty, and the witness of the Spirit indicates the support of heaven in such loosing. One cannot read the New Testament without discerning that this power of binding and loosing was granted also to the apostle Paul—perhaps to all of the apostles; but it would be presumptuous on the part of any man-appointed or self-appointed teacher to assume such a prerogative.

Some scholars have suggested, on the basis of the form of the verbs here, that the passage should read, "Whatsoever thou shalt bind on earth shall have been bound in heaven: and whatsoever thou shalt loose on earth shall have been loosed in heaven." We shall agree that the initiative of all this binding and loosing is in heaven, and the human agent of those powers receives his instructions from the Holy Spirit.

The next statement shocks us. The Lord had sent out His disciples to preach the message of the kingdom of heaven, with a call to repentance. Their preaching was very much like that of John the Baptist, and like the Lord's own early message. Now His disciples, with Peter leading, have come to recognize Him as "the Christ, the Son of the living God." Surely that would be the theme of their message from now on. First, the kingdom; now, the King. But instead of organizing another preaching tour with emphasis on the new theme, Jesus said, "Tell nobody." What a strange prohibition in face of such a glorious revelation! There must have been a reason. That we shall try to explore in the next division of our study, the King in His Passion.

NOTES

1. James Dalton Morrison, ed., *Masterpieces of Religious Verse* (New York: Harper, 1948), p. 75.

PART THREE

The King in His Passion

(16:21—27:66)

15

DWELLING IN HIS PASSION

(16:21–20:16)

JESUS MUST HAVE HAD GOOD REASON for commanding silence concerning His identity as "the Christ, the Son of the Living God." It might be suggested that publishing that abroad would bring Him prematurely into conflict with the Jewish hierarchy and hasten His death. He was indeed on a time schedule, to which reference is made a number of times, sometimes by Himself, as in John 7:6, where He answers His brothers' taunts with the statement, "My time is not yet come." But I think the reason goes deeper. He has been recognized by His disciples for whom He really is. It would have seemed logical to organize a preaching tour for the proclamation of that wonderful revelation. In that case the message, however true, would be incomplete. We shall remember that Jesus came, not simply to be acclaimed "the Christ, the Son of the Living God," but to accomplish the great sacrifice for the redemption of men. Whatever was preached concerning His person, then, must be accompanied by a proclamation of His mission.

THE LAW OF THE CROSS (16:21-27)

So "from that time"—that is, when Peter made his great confession—"began Jesus to shew unto his disciples, how that he must . . . suffer many things . . . and be killed, and be raised again the third day." He would not allow His followers to go out with a message that lacked the note of the cross. It is surely significant that in this portion of Matthew's gospel that we have entitled "Dwelling in His Passion" we find four intimations of His approaching death (16:21; 17:9, 12; 17:22-23; 20:17-19). The apostle Paul set the cross at the heart of his preaching. We remember his resolve on the way to Corinth: "I determined not to know any thing among you, save Jesus Christ, and him crucified" (1 Corinthians 2:2). That was in spite of the fact that the preaching of the cross was "unto the Jews a stumblingblock, and unto the Greeks foolishness" (1 Corinthians 1:23).

Is it not strange that the first opposition to the message of the cross should come from the apostolic band, and of all places, from Peter? "Be it far from thee, Lord: this shall not be unto thee" (16:22). It was but a little while before that Peter had acclaimed Jesus as the Christ, not from human reasoning, but by revelation. Now he repudiates the very work that Jesus came to perform in compliance with His messianic mission. Peter will have his Christ, but not a Christ crucified—not yet, at any rate. Later he will write to the scattered tribes, "Ye were . . . redeemed . . . with the precious blood of Christ" (1 Peter 1:18-19), and "who his own self bare our sins in his own body on the tree" (1 Peter 2:24). But he is not ready for that yet. In the exuberance of his recent blessing he will stand squarely in the path of the cross and say with even more vehemence, "Not this way!"

Peter was not the best logician in the world. He had a strange habit that took him some time to overcome. "Lord," he would say, and then, "No." Those two words are incompatible. Here he says no to the course that the Lord has set before Himself. Later, in Joppa, we shall find him saying no to the Lord's command to kill and eat. It is not an uncommon habit among the Lord's people. Calling Jesus Lord demands that we learn to say yes to all His will as "good, and acceptable, and perfect."

Peter loved Jesus. Indeed it was his love for Jesus that moved him to chide Him. He would spare His dear Master all the humiliation and suffering of which He had just spoken. One may love and still be a stumbling block. For love needs enlightenment, and in that hour Peter's love was unenlightened. Even that luminous word *Must* failed to penetrate the mist of Peter's affection. That is the great imperative that stretches from eternity to eternity in the heart of which our Lord lived all His earthly life and all the way to the cross. "I *must* work the works of Him that sent me while it is day." And that leads to this other: "As Moses lifted up the serpent in the wilderness, even so *must* the Son of man be lifted up" (John 3:14, italics added). Had Peter known the power of that "must," he would never have attempted to stand in the way of our Savior's progress to the cross.

But was it altogether love for Christ that drew from Peter that word, "This shall not be unto thee"? (16:22). Was there not a tinge of self-love in it? For if Jesus went forth to death, what would become of Peter and the others? Would they fare any better? Peter certainly had no appetite for the cross at this point, so he tried to block the Master's road to it.

If Peter's behavior was contradictory, so the responses of the Savior were in striking contrast. Those ranged from "Blessed art thou" (16:17) to "Get thee behind me, Satan!" (16:23). In the first event Peter is in close enough rapport with God to receive revelation concerning the beloved Son; here, and not long after, he is in unwitting cooperation with the devil in an attempt to hold Jesus back from the cross. For remember that our Lord's life work was His death work. To interfere with that was to be a satan, an adversary. Avoiding the way of the cross is man's way. Marching right on when the cross looms before us is the divine way.

The cross is the central law of the kingdom of heaven. "It is the way the Master went; Should not the servant tread it still?" Notice how the Lord lays down the same law for us as He does for Himself: "If any man will come after me, let him deny himself, and take up his cross, and follow me" (16:24). Need we remind ourselves that "taking up the cross" is not humbly and patiently enduring the trials that come our way, however noble and virtuous that may be? It is a deliberate act of committal in which we hand ourselves over to the fellowship of the cross, to be joined to Christ in His death in order to be joined to Him in His resurrection life. It means "not I, but Christ."

Jesus has a wonderful way of leading us from particular situations to great general principles. Here is such a two-edged thrust: we save by losing, and we lose by saving. Quite apart from the ultimate application to the kingdom of God, this is really a law of life. Those who spend themselves in the promotion of a good cause enrich their lives, while those who seek only their own advancement, whether in money or power, develop an impoverished personality. That law comes to its fullest application in association with the kingdom of God. One cannot seek to fill his life with the baubles of this world and inherit the kingdom of God. By the same token one cannot devote his life to the kingdom of God, just to find himself a pauper at last. That leads to two questions. The first concerns profit. What profit is there in obtaining the wealth of the world at the cost of the soul? The second has to do with recovery. How can you recover that lost soul? You lost it for money, but money cannot buy it back.

All that is enforced by the expectation of Christ's return in the role of judge. His coming again will be "in the glory of his Father, with his angels." No dispensational distinctions are made here. But whether it be the judgment of the saints at the *bema* or the final judgment at the great white throne, perfect equity will prevail. "According to his works" applies to all, whether the issue be service rendered or degree of rebellion. The only thing which is not according to works is salvation. "By grace are ye saved, through faith . . . not of works, lest any man should boast" (Ephesians 2:8-9). See, then, how our Lord looked beyond the gloom to the glory.

THE TRANSFIGURATION (16:28–17:23)

The kingdom of God is not simply "one far off, divine event to which the whole creation moves." It is nearer than we think, and certainly the presence of the King made the kingdom very near—so near, in fact, that Jesus could affirm that some of those present would live to see it in power, or, as Matthew states it, "Some of them that stand here . . . shall in no wise taste of death, till they see the Son of man coming in his kingdom." They did not have to live long to know the fulfillment of that promise. Only six days, and Peter, James, and John climbed Mount Tabor with Jesus and witnessed the transfiguration. But can we be sure that what they saw there was what Jesus had promised—the Son of man coming in His kingdom, the kingdom of God coming with power? According to Peter's testimony it was exactly that. Here is his own recollection of the event: "We did not follow cunningly devised fables, when we made known unto you the power and coming of our Lord Jesus Christ, but we were eyewitnesses of his majesty. For he received from God the Father honor and glory, when there was borne such a voice to him by the Majestic Glory, This is my beloved Son, in whom I am well pleased: and this voice we ourselves heard borne out of heaven, when we were with him in the holy mount" (2 Peter 1:16-18, ASV). There can be no doubting Peter's reference to the transfiguration and to the promise given six days before the event. It is another case of "this is that." At the same time, while the three privileged disciples saw the glory of the kingdom in the glory of the King, that scene was but prophetic and representative of what is yet to come, when He shall appear to exercise His full rights as King of kings and Lord of lords.

The transfiguration was truly a foreview of glory to come, but it had its dark side too. For two visitants from heaven, Moses and Elijah, engaged our Lord in conversation, the theme of which was not the glory beyond the gloom, but the gloom before the glory. They "spake of his decease which he was about to accomplish at Jerusalem" (Luke 9:31, ASV). Just what they said about that coming "exodus" we do not know. This we can believe, that His "dwelling in His passion" took on new depths, not indeed depths of despair, for they were accompanied by a constant assurance of resurrection. "Tell nobody," He again says to His disciples, "until the Son of man be risen from the dead."

How did Peter, James, and John recognize Moses and Elijah? There is no suggestion that Jesus introduced them. That may help to answer the question, Shall we know one another in heaven? It may be that the better we get acquainted with Moses and Elijah in their works, the more easily shall we recognize them in heaven. But we must not go off on speculative tangents. It is interesting to note that Peter proposed a camp meeting with three preachers and an audience of three. Or was it a seminary with three instructors and three students? No wonder he said, "It is good for us to be here," with such individual attention from three such notable teachers, one of whom was doctor of the law; one doctor of prophecy; and the third, "the Christ, the Son of the living God." The third? That will not do. The cloud came down upon them. The voice from heaven focused attention on Jesus, saying, "This is my beloved Son, in whom I am well pleased; hear Him! . . . And lifting up their eyes they saw no one, save Jesus only." He is the fulfillment of both law and prophets. In His presence Moses and Elijah must step aside. Having borne witness to Him, they resign the place of preeminence to Him. They all must join John the Baptist in saying, "He must increase, but I must decrease" (John 3:30).

The transfiguration is variously described, but the main features seem to be the radiance of our Lord's countenance and the dazzling white of His garments. From whence came this glory? We read of Moses that "the skin of his face shone as he talked with him (God)," but the radiance gradually faded, a parable of the fading glory of the law in yielding place to the more glorious economy of grace (2 Corinthians 3:7-13). The point for us at present is that the brightness of Moses' countenance was not native, but induced. Our sun worshipers expose themselves to the sun till their skin takes on a darkened hue. Sun tan they call it. But when the season for sunbathing is over, the tan fades and the lighter shade returns. So the glory of God beat upon Moses until his very countenance glowed with a heavenly light, so bright that the children of Israel could not endure the sight. For the comfort of the people, Moses wore a veil when he spoke to them until the glow wore off. My purpose in saying all that is to make a negative comparison. The transfiguration of Jesus was not like that. With Him it was native glory shining through the veil of flesh till even His garments shone with an unearthly whiteness. Then the glory was withdrawn, and Jesus completed His humiliation at Calvary, from whence He returned to former glory by way of resurrection, ascension, and exaltation. Then, and forever, the Son of man wears all the glory of the Son of God. Moses and Elijah returned to the abode of the blessed, but Jesus to the valley of human woes.

As they descended the three disciples were puzzled. Jesus had indicated that some of His followers would live to see Him "coming in His kingdom." Quite evidently what had occurred on Mount Tabor was a fulfillment of that promise. At least those three understood it so. But an old prophecy seemed to cast doubt upon their understanding. The Bible students of the day clung to the last prophecy of their ancient Scriptures in which God promised the coming of Elijah "before the great and terrible day of Jehovah come." So far as the disciples knew, that harbinger of the great and terrible day had not come. How, then, would the transfiguration event be regarded in any sense as Christ's "coming in his kingdom"? Our Lord's answer to their puzzlement was twofold: first, a confirmation of Malachi's prophecy as still waiting fulfillment; second, an affirmation that the ancient prediction had already had fulfillment in the person and work of John the Baptist. Although He did not mention the Baptist's name, Jesus left no doubt as to the one of whom He spoke.

The theological discussion was quickly interrupted. An episode was transpiring at the base of the mountain that deeply grieved the Lord. The story can be told by considering the needy child, the pleading father, the helpless disciples, the mighty Savior, the faithful Teacher, and the faithless age.

The distraught father described the boy's affliction as lunacy (KJV), or epilepsy (ASV), but Jesus treated it as demon possession. His keener discernment recognized the root of the trouble. In times past, lunacy and epilepsy have been associated with demon possession in the popular mind. It is a totally wrong view. Those are physical and mental ailments that may be linked with demon possession, as in this case, but have no necessary relation. Demon possession may have many expressions. In chapter 9 Matthew tells us of a demoniac whose physical affliction was inability to speak. When Jesus cast out the demon, the dumb man spoke normally. We do not conclude that all cases of dumbness are the work of demons.

The case before us was indeed a grievous one. The father told Jesus how the boy often fell into the fire and into the water. Doubtless he was driven to acts of self-destruction by the demon. How he had survived such experiences we are not told. We can imagine the constant fear and anxiety of the parents, as they kept unending watch over their afflicted boy. The father's language is indicative of the deep sorrow that tore at their hearts continually.

The inability of the nine disciples who had not accompanied Jesus up the mountain is really surprising, considering that Jesus "gave them power against unclean spirits, to cast them out" when He sent them on the preaching mission described in chapter 10. There is no indication of the withdrawal of that power. Indeed they were themselves taken aback when they found themselves helpless in the face of this situation, which is doubtless the reason for their asking, "Why could not we cast him out?" The Lord's answer was, "Because of your unbelief." It would appear, then, that the gift of exorcism is operative only by an exercise of faith. So the gift may be effective in one situation and ineffective on another occasion, depending on the measure of faith brought into play at the moment. In that instance the lack of faith was more in evidence than faith, which afforded Jesus an opportunity to give a brief, but tremendously telling lesson. We think that moving mountains would be beyond the reach of faith altogether, but according to Jesus mustard seed faith is sufficient for such an accomplishment. And we shall remember that Jesus referred to the mustard seed as "the least of all seeds" (13:32). In other words, such is the power of faith that just a modicum of it is enough to effect any action that could properly be categorized as moving mountains. In the situation before us the disciples had run out of faith, like a car run out of gasoline, so that the power that had been given them was inoperative. This lack of faith on the part of His disciples was one of our Lord's chief griefs (16:8), while the presence of faith rejoiced His heart (15:28). I have wondered how Peter and James and John would have fared if they had been with the nine instead of with the Lord on the mountain.

Matthew 17:21 is omitted by many ancient authorities, but in the parallel record (Mark 9:29) the same statement regarding "this kind" is found, in some manuscripts with the reference to fasting and in others without. Despite the textual difference we can draw some valuable truths from the passage. For one thing, there are different "kinds" of demons, requiring the application of differing techniques. Second, possessing a "gift" of power does not eliminate the need for prayer. And third, we should discern when a situation calls for fasting in addition to prayer.

Our Lord's Galilean ministry was drawing to a close. The shadow of the cross lay across His path, and now for the third time He rehearsed to His disciples the sufferings awaiting Him in Jerusalem, adding, as always, the note of triumph, His resurrection on the third day. "And they were exceeding sorry," for their faith could not penetrate the darkness. As yet they did not know the meaning of His approaching death, nor could they anticipate the victory of the rising again.

The Payment of a Tax (17:24-27)

The little interlude that follows took place on our Lord's final visit to Capernaum. It had reference to the Temple tax that every male

Jew was expected to pay. Unlike other taxes, it was the same for all, rich or poor. The collectors of that non-Roman tax apparently thought that Jesus was delinquent in His payment. So the form of their question to Peter would suggest: "Doth not your teacher pay the half shekel?" Peter's answer was a simple yes; but it turned out to be not so simple a matter as he thought. It was indeed a theological question, distinguishing between the subjects of the kingdom who were liable to the taxation and the children of the king who were exempt. The application was not difficult to make. Our Lord's claim to official exemption was equivalent to an affirmation of His unique Sonship. But while recognizing His special privilege, He did not use it, lest He should cast a stumbling block before others. The apostle Paul was of the same mind. Having an apostolic right to monetary support from the young churches, he did not exercise his right, so as to avoid any hindrance to his ministry. He paid expenses by plying his trade of tent making. There are times when our highest right is to forego our rights for the gospel's sake.

Jesus went one better and took care of Peter's tax also. True, He made Peter work for it, which reminds us that what we can do He expects us to do. There is no doubt that the Lord, the Master of all skills, brought that fish to Peter's hook. And it was not a Roman coin that was in its mouth, but one acceptable to the Temple agents—the shekel.

A SERIES OF LESSONS (18:1—20:16)

All that time the disciples were having their dreams regarding the kingdom of heaven and their respective places in it. But Jesus' conversation led out in other directions. While they were dreaming about position and rank and greatness, He was speaking about suffering and a cross. Perhaps the incident of the Temple tax aggravated the situation. It surely was out of reason for "the Christ, the Son of the living God," the Lord of the Temple, to identify Himself with Peter in the payment of the tax. So in their confusion the disciples brought their question to Jesus: "Who then is greater in the kingdom of heaven?" What they are saying amounts to this: "In view of all you are saying about suffering and death, what comes of our expectations of cabinet appointments in your kingdom?" That such ambitions were present was clearly in evidence when the mother of James and John lobbied for her two sons (20:20-21).

The question about greatness was the prelude to some very practical and searching lessons, not only on the subject of greatness but, growing out of that, offenses, discipline, and forgiveness.

Before discussing greatness *in* the kingdom of heaven, our Lord took up the previous question, entrance *into* the kingdom. Now if Jesus had been a mediocre teacher, He would have philosophized on the relation of childhood to the kingdom of heaven. Being the Master Teacher, He called upon a little child to help Him—much more effective than just talking about a child. Here was a living text. Here were the simplicity, the submissiveness, and the trustfulness that qualify for entrance into the kingdom of heaven. But only too soon those qualities fade, and in their place come complexity, stubbornness, suspicion, pride, hypocrisy, with other symptoms of the disease of sin. Exactly here lies the need for that conversion of which Jesus speaks—a return to childhood's simplicity, trust, and sincerity, a turning from self to God.

As for greatness within the kingdom of heaven, the answer is still "a little child." Jesus Himself defines what it is in the little child that makes for greatness—his humility. "Whosoever therefore shall humble himself as this little child, the same is greatest in the kingdom of heaven" (18:4). That "therefore" is important. It indicates a relation between the childlikeness that opens the kingdom to us and the childlikeness that gives one a place among the greats of the kingdom. The former being so, it follows that the latter must be true also. Said one of our Puritan divines: "Stoop, stoop! It is a low, low door by which we enter the kingdom of God." The same applies to admission to heaven's "hall of fame."

Having made a little child the answer to His disciples' question about greatness Jesus, with the child still present, expatiates on our responsibility to young believers. Stated negatively, we are to refuse not, offend not, and despise not. "Whoso shall receive one such little child in my name receiveth me" (18:5). We are reminded of the King's commendation of those who had ministered to His people in the days of their need: "Inasmuch as ye have done it unto one of the least of these my brethren, ye have done it unto me" (25:40). But what does the receiving mean? Without dogmatizing I offer my thought that the Lord was referring to the fellowship of the church, from which believing children should not be barred. It is indeed a sensitive question at what age children should be received. I am persuaded that they think more deeply than we give them credit for, and being refused on account of age can be discouraging, whether in matters secular or matters religious. I have had experience of both. At one point I was barred from a departmental examination that qualified for university, because of my age, although others with lower grades, but older than I, were permitted to take it. As a small child I asked for baptism. Our minister somewhat glibly indicated that I was too young. Both experiences were disheartening. It took some time to get over the hurt. Certainly such delicate matters as voting rights have to be dealt with, but the believing child must know and feel that he belongs.

Refuse not. Then offend not. The word *offend* here means causing to stumble, putting a stumbling block before the feet of the young believer. In the mind of the Lord that is such a serious offense that tragic death would be preferable to committing it. The millstone here referred to was the great upper stone which required a pack animal to turn. The Lord further emphasizes the tragedy by speaking of "the depth of the sea." It is evident that the care of the young takes high ranking in the kingdom of God.

We live in a world that is inimical to the kingdom of heaven, whose prince will use every means at his command to trip up the children of God, causing them to fall and thus rendering their testimony ineffectual. That should not surprise us. But the fact that occasions of stumbling are to be expected does not lessen the guilt of the one who lends himself to Satan as his agent in thus seeking the Christian's downfall. Upon such a person Christ pronounces a woe of judgment.

From offenses against the young, Jesus passes to stumbling blocks of our own making. Here is a man who is a perfect physical specimen. That can be a cause of pride, and the body becomes his god. He acts as if he had no soul. "God is not in all his thoughts." The end of that man is "everlasting fire." A wheelchair and heaven at the end would surely be a better bargain. Now what we have said concerning the whole body is applicable to any part of the body. If your eyes prove to be instruments of lust, dragging you to the eternal fire, it would be more profitable to be blind. Or if the skill of your hand robs you of your sense of need of God and so marks you for the gehenna of fire, you would be better off without hands. So we are warned against casting stumbling blocks in our own way as well as being hindrances to others.

Refuse not. Offend not. And now, coming back to the child in the midst, He says, "Despise not." Jesus hurled that dictum into a society in which childhood was despised. In the Augustan age of Rome, a father had the right to sell, abandon, or kill his children if he did not care to rear them. A deserted child could be retained as a slave by anyone who found him. The great Roman orator, Cicero, affirmed that the death of a child was no cause for grief. Weak children were cast out to be a prey of wild beasts, particularly in Hibernia and Sparta. Children were frequently whipped to death before the altars of Diana. There was the Savior's challenge to the world with respect to childhood. And He gives right good reason for His command. The honor afforded children in heaven argues our obligation to honor them here. "In heaven their angels do always behold the face of my Father which is in heaven." We acknowledge that we are all born sinners and that sin separates us from God, but here we see God commissioning His angels to engage their mighty energies to bring in the children, and they have full access to the throne in the pursuit of their high endeavor, for "it is not the will of your Father which is in heaven that one of these little ones should perish" (18:14). It is doubtless "one of these little ones" who is the subject of the parable, whose coming to the fold makes the bells of heaven ring. One for whom so much angelic and divine energy is expended, whose being found stirs so much joy in heaven, is not to be despised. So the triple exhortation comes from the Savior's lips: Do not refuse. Do not offend. Do not despise.

Now suppose I am the object of another's offensive behavior, calculated to make me stumble; and suppose the one who so offends me is my brother. What shall I do? Our Lord lays down a three-step procedure. The first step is the private interview, in which the attempt is made to bring the offender to an acknowledgement of his wrongdoing, in which case you have won your brother (18:15).

That immediately tells us what is the objective in the entire procedure—not to humiliate the brother, nor to require compensation of him, but to win him. The Lord is here calling us to a ministry of healing, and our approaches are much more likely to succeed if we go in that spirit. Of course we have no guarantee that the brother will respond to our first gesture. In the event of his turning a deaf ear, we take the second step and seek the support of one or two others who know the situation—men (or women) of Christian maturity and good judgment. Once again, the purpose is not to browbeat the offender into submission, but to "gain [win] thy brother." If he remains adamant in face of the two- or threefold testimony, the third step is in order—"Tell it unto the church." Keep the purpose in mind. We are not out for self vindication, but for restoration. That is one big reason for bringing our cause to the church rather than to the courts, a practice that the apostle Paul strongly denounced (1 Corinthians 6:1-8). We may win a case in the courts, but we shall never gain our brother there.

What if the brother is still recalcitrant, despite the action of the church? Then "Let him be unto thee as an heathen man and a publican" (18:17). But how do we treat the Gentile and the tax-gatherer? Do we not treat him as one for whom Christ died, but who has not known the blessedness of a full salvation? Does he not become an object of our pity, our love, and our prayers? In other words, the sanction of the church does not end our effort to win our brother. The church may impose discipline on the offender, but we continue to "pour in oil and wine," the healing balm of true Christian love.

Such action carries heavy sanctions. It is recorded and sealed in heaven. A church that is being regulated by the Holy Spirit in obedience to the holy Scriptures has an authority from the great Head of the church to act in His name, and He promises His own presence to direct the binding and loosing that will have their confirmation in heaven. So when a church, large or small, imposes discipline on an unrepentant offender in conformity with the teaching of the Lord, that action is given the sanction of divine confirmation; and when that church lifts the discipline from a penitent brother, that loosing carries heavenly approval.

I shall not suggest that the application exhausts the meaning of that almost frightening verse (18), but, gathered from the context, it would seem to set the direction.

"Then came Peter" (18:21). That does not surprise us. Peter generally had a question ready, and not infrequently in the area of application. The teaching just given by Jesus would seem to call for some directives concerning forgiveness, and Peter was the one to see that it was not overlooked! Now the rabbis taught that one might forgive a first and a second offense, but not a third. The third called for retribution. Peter was prepared to stretch pardoning grace to cover seven offenses, and I am sure he sensed a quiver of self-righteousness as he emphasized that *seven.* Perhaps he expected hearty commendation from the Master for having gone so far ahead of the rabbinic teaching! The Master's reply, to the contrary, was a stunning blow—that is, to Peter's sense of superior virtue: "I do not say to you, up to seven times, but up to seventy times seven" (NASB). What that actually says is, "Quit counting. Just keep on forgiving!" That is the law of forgiveness in the kingdom of heaven, to go on forgiving as long as God keeps on forgiving. For, as a matter of fact, we shall never have occasion to forgive others as often or as much as God has forgiven and still forgives us.

That is the theme of the parable that follows. Here is a servant who owes his lord, the king, ten thousand talents. How much is that? In these days of changing values it is difficult even to make a guess. A talent, we are told, was 750 ounces of silver.

That servant must have been a high ranking official to have access to so much. It amounted to a national scandal. But the king was willing to sustain that loss out of pity for the disgraced and bankrupt servant. Forgiven so much, the servant showed no pity to his fellowservant who owed him a pittance. Such ingratitude, such ruthlessness deeply grieved the king, who now required "all that was due unto him" (18:34). But what was due? Surely not the debt that was canceled, but that the forgiven man should learn to forgive. That is the lesson of the parable.

Thus ends the Galilean ministry. There is a gap in Matthew's record at that point, taken care of in John 7:11—10:39 and Luke 13:22—17:10. Since we are not attempting a harmony of the gospels, we shall stay with Matthew as he follows Jesus to Perea, east of the Jordan, and finally to Judaea and Jerusalem.

It is worthy of note that much of our Lord's teaching grows out of questions posed to Him, and those not always friendly questions. The Pharisees were continually bombarding Him with matters of controversy in attempts to embarrass Him or to find some cause of accusation. So it was on that occasion. Their trick question concerned divorce, always a touchy subject, and at that time a live issue, since two influential rabbis, Hillel and Shammai, had championed contrary views, Hillel holding a liberal view and Shammai taking the stricter position. It all revolved around the interpretation of Deuteronomy 24:1—"When a man taketh a wife, and marrieth her, then it shall be, if she find no favor in his eyes, because he hath found some unseemly thing in her, that he shall write her a bill of divorcement, and give it in her hand, and send her out of his house" (ASV). Crucial to the question was the phrase, "some unseemly thing." Does that embrace any physical, mental, social, or moral blemish that would be revolting to the man, or is it confined to a lack of moral integrity? Opinion was divided, and the legalistic Pharisees made it a test question for Jesus, who met it head on but approached it in a manner that must have shaken the inquisitors. He took them right back to the beginnings and from those beginnings showed how incompatible was divorce with the divine intention. Look briefly at this divine intention:

First, marriage calls for the establishing of a new household. "For this cause shall a man leave father and mother, and shall cleave to his wife" (19:5).

Second, the union is of such a character as to make of the two "one flesh." That goes right back to the creation of man and woman. Eve was actually a part of Adam, "bone of my bones, and flesh of my flesh" (Genesis 2:23). The marriage bond perpetuates that oneness.

Third, in the divine intention the marriage bond is inviolate. "What therefore God hath joined together, let not man put asunder" (19:6).

In such an arrangement there is no place for divorce. Yet Moses, the great lawgiver, allowed it. Why? Surely it was not ignorance of the divine intention; nor was it a deliberate thwarting of the will of God. Jesus gives the answer: "Because of the hardness of your hearts" (19:8). Moses was dealing, not with people newly created in the image of God, but with a generation of sinners to whom the divine intention was beyond reach. It was a permission, not an abrogation of the original ordinance. The command element had to do with the certificate of divorce that was a measure of protection for the woman. The man could not impulsively tell his wife to go. The preparation of the article of divorce gave time for a cooling of tempers and some weighing of the situation.

At that point our Lord issues an authoritative dictum regarding the implications of divorce and remarriage. If a man divorces his wife for any reason other than fornication and marries another woman, he is guilty of adultery. That is an adulterous union, and we have no right to call it by any other name than sin. The same applies to the one who marries the divorced woman. The multiplication of divorces in our day does not make it any less sinful.

The phrase, "except for fornication," is variously interpreted. For one thing, the word *fornication,* as here used, cannot be limited to irregular conduct before marriage. It refers rather to moral perversion, whether before or after marriage. Then again, it is a matter of dispute whether that "exception" clause applies only to the act of divorce, or whether it allows remarriage to the innocent party. The answer for the Christian is surely to do what our Lord did, go back to the beginnings; there see God's noble intention, and walk therein.

The reaction of the disciples to the teaching is evidence of the discipline involved in marriage. They reckoned that if marriage were so binding, the single state would be preferable. Jesus did not give a definitive answer to that statement, but indicated three groups who practice celibacy, rightly or wrongly. The first group are those born with a physical or mental deficiency that rules out the marital state. Of the second group Jesus says that "they were made eunuchs by men." That is enforced celibacy. As for the third group, they have dedicated themselves to the service of Christ and, seeing that marriage would restrict them in the kind of work to which they are called, forego the comforts of marital union. The apostle Paul belonged to this company, whether as a widower or as a bachelor we cannot be sure. He commended the unmarried state as freer from distractions in the service of the Lord. But neither he nor the Lord suggested that celibacy was a higher order than the marital state. Jesus does make it clear that since celibacy cuts across the normal course of nature, it should be entered into only as a special calling, requiring and obtaining special grace.

Look at the mothers who desired to have Jesus lay His hand in blessing upon their children. Was that desire based on faith in Him as "the Christ, the Son of the living God"? Some may have arrived at that belief, like Peter, but I rather think that the mothers represented various shades of belief. Certainly all held Jesus in high esteem as a rabbi, as a prophet, as one come from God, and sensed that His touch would confer a benediction on their little ones. We cannot read the minds of all the mothers beyond this—they desired a blessing for their little ones.

Children respond readily to kindly contacts. When I was a child in Alloa, Scotland, the parish (Presbyterian) minister was Lachlan Maclean Watt, who later became senior minister of Glasgow Cathedral. One day I was standing at a street corner when Mr. Watt came along. Smiling, he put his hand on my head and said some kind word that I have forgotten. But that "laying on of hands," if you care to call it so, was never forgotten, and I have no doubt that it was part of God's dealing with me to bring me, still a child, to faith in the Lord Jesus. Now there is power in the hand of Jesus far more than in the hand of Lachlan Maclean Watt, and we can believe that those Perean children would never lose the impact of that touch.

But now look at the disciples. They are appalled at the temerity of those women in trying to present their children to Jesus. In the Roman world children were little accounted of, and it is just possible that, in spite of the teaching of the Hebrew Scriptures, something of that low esteem had crept into the Jewish thinking and attitude. Then, too, the disciples could not as yet link greatness and children, although Jesus had insisted that greatness in the kingdom of heaven was measured by conformity to the childlike spirit. To their thinking, greatness called for remoteness, and a group of children breaking in upon that remoteness amounted to desecration.

Another consideration was the fact that in bringing their children to Jesus, those mothers—*women,* if you please!—were pressing in upon Him, which was contrary to rabbinic protocol. We recall that when the disciples returned to Jacob's well from their shopping in Sychar, they found Jesus talking to a woman and were amazed. It is true that a few women accompanied Him from Galilee to Jerusalem, who "ministered unto him of their substance" (Luke 8:3). In other words, these devoted women cared for His (and His disciples') physical needs (Luke 8:1-3). That was allowable, but for women who were not of their company to break in upon Jesus was carrying "women's rights" too far! So "the disciples rebuked them."

Now look at Jesus in that situation. According to Mark's record He was "moved with indignation." We are so accustomed to think of Jesus as "moved with compassion" that that is almost a foreign concept. The apostle Paul exhorts us to "be angry and sin not." We can be sure that our Lord's anger was indeed of the sinless sort. Always it had good reason, as when the Pharisees held Him guilty of Sabbath breaking when He restored a withered hand (Mark 3:5). But on that occasion it was with His own disciples that He was deeply grieved. Their treatment of the mothers and their children was evidence that they still had an imperfect knowledge of Him and of His mission. They were slow to learn, and that disturbed Him. But for all that, He did not dismiss them as unqualified for the apostolic task. He knew what He would yet make of them. Our Lord never gives up, although He must often be grieved at our lack of comprehension.

Bringing the three records together, we see Jesus calling the children to Him, taking them in His arms, laying His hands upon them, and blessing them. There was no hurry as if to get through with an unwelcome task, but deliberate action that manifested His deep and loving care for the children. Notice that He was acting out His own teaching. We remember how He had called a little child to be His text when He answered His disciples' question about greatness in the kingdom of heaven, and the three points of His sermon were: Do not refuse. Do not offend. Do not despise. So here again: stop blocking their way, allow them to come; for the kingdom of heaven is made up of people who have the child heart, and it rightly belongs to them.

Then, as if to confirm it all, and as a parting blessing, He "laid his hands on them, and departed thence" (19:15).

In this rich chapter we have seen our Lord in a variety of situations. First we see Him ministering to the multitude as healer of their diseases (19:1-2); then in encounter with the Pharisees, presenting the divine intention for the marital relationship (19:3-9); then in more intimate conversation with His disciples, expounding the sensitive doctrine of celibacy (19:10-12); then relating to the little children, emphasizing their place in the kingdom of heaven (19:13-15). Now we come to His meeting with one generally referred to as "the rich young ruler." Three fundamental questions surface from that incident: one asked by the young man himself; one posed by the disciples; and one urged by Peter. The first had to do with the way of salvation (19:16); the second had the subjects of salvation in mind (19:28); the third dealt with the nature of future reward (19:27). Let us look at them in order.

"Good Teacher, what shall I do to inherit eternal life?" Such was the question of the young man who came running and knelt before Jesus in manifest urgency and humility (Mark 10:17). The enquirer's question revealed two facts: first, that he regarded eternal life as something to be earned; and second, that he sensed a deficiency in his own efforts to attain. Now there is some variation in the text of our Lord's answer, but Mark's record is in accord with the King James version of Matthew's text: "Why callest thou me good? there is none good but one, that is, God." When Jesus said that, was He disclaiming goodness, or was He claiming Godhood? At least He gave the young man opportunity to go further than "Good Teacher."

Jesus started with the youthful seeker where He found him, namely in the realm of law. The question was, "What good thing shall I do?" The law tells us. Was not the law ordained for eternal life (Romans 7:10)? Well, let the law speak. Let it tell us what is that "good thing" that will earn the life that we strive after. But somehow we are not satisfied. Having diligently practiced the tenets of the law to the best of our ability we remain unassured, till we cry out, "What lack I yet?"

I think we have maligned that young man. I remember hearing a dashing young preacher expatiating on the rich young ruler. He began: "My first point is, he was a liar." That is hardly fair. When the young fellow said to Jesus concerning the commandments, "All these things have I kept from my youth up" (19:20), he was not engaging in bombast. He was in a state of utter frustration. The keeping of the law to the utmost of his power had not given him the peace and assurance that he sought. That is what inspired the cry, "What lack I yet?" But there was one commandment to which "the utmost of his power" was not equal. It concerned, not outward behavior, but inward disposition. "Thou shalt have no other gods before me." That interview with Jesus was about to bring to light an idolatry that barred the way to eternal life. "Sell that thou hast, and give to the poor, and thou shalt have treasure in heaven: and come and follow me" (19:21). But "he went away sorrowful: for he had great possessions" (19:22). His great possessions meant more to him than eternal life; they meant more to him than treasure in heaven; they meant more to him than God. He was an idolater. His wealth was his god. The law upon which he had leaned condemned him. And never again did he enjoy his possessions. "He went away sorrowful."

I wonder did he ever return to lay his treasures at Jesus' feet. We read that "Jesus beholding him, loved him," and if the Master's love for him calls for special mention, it would not be surprising if the power of that love finally drew him. But it remains an unresolved mystery.

We come to the second question: "Who then can be saved?" And here is how it came about. The rich young ruler had given evidence that his love of riches was greater than his love for God. He had turned away from the course that Jesus had invited him to follow. He had "gone away, sorrowful." But his sorrow was nothing so deep or so pure as the sorrow of Jesus. With Jesus it was wounded love. Analyzing the case, our Lord saw the peril of riches as illustrated in the one, but so common a disease. Calling His disciples, He conveyed to them the meaning of what they had just seen. Riches are a strong deterrent to entering the kingdom of heaven. They tend to give one a sense of security apart from God, and a feeling of superiority over one's fellows. "Stoop, stoop," wrote the godly Samuel Rutherford, "it is a low, low door by which we enter into the kingdom of God." And because it is hard for a rich man to stoop, it makes entering into the kingdom of heaven harder than for a camel to go through the eye of a needle. Now some commentators hold that "the needle's eye" is a figurative phrase for the wicket gate of a city, utilized for entrance and exit when the large gates were closed. To get a camel and its load through was difficult and tedious work. But whether we regard the needle's eye in that figurative connotation or in a completely literal sense, it is clear that our Lord was bearing down hard on the peril of riches as an obstacle in the way of life.

Such emphasis surprised the disciples, as did many of our Lord's teachings. Wealth being regarded as a sign of the divine favor and approval, they could not see how it would be a stumbling block. Holding the view of riches that they did, their question was entirely logical: "Who then can be saved?" We have heard the Lord say, "Except ye be converted, and become as little children, ye shall not enter into the kingdom of heaven" (18:3). Will the wise man of the world, the mighty man, the aristocrat, bow to the humility of a little child and take his place with fools, weaklings, plebeians—all penitent sinners—for the sake of his soul's salvation? Left to his own resources of moral courage—no! "With man this is impossible; but with God all things are possible." A member of the British aristocracy used to say, "I was saved on the letter *m,* and in explanation would refer to 1 Corinthians 1:26, where it is written, "Not many noble are called." There is no case beyond the practice of the Great Physician, whether he be a man on Skid Row or a king on his throne.

Now while the Lord was answering the question, "Who then can be saved?", Peter was occupied with another matter. He had heard the Lord tell the rich young ruler that if he disposed of his earthly treasure to follow Him, he should have "treasure in heaven." That rang a bell with Peter. He and his fellow apostles had divested themselves of their worldly interests to accept the Master's call. In the light of Jesus' statement to the young aristocrat it would be normal and logical for them to expect some compensation, and now seemed the moment to enquire as to the nature of that recompense. So here is Peter's blunt question: "What shall we have?"

If you or I had been in Jesus' place that day, I suppose we would have answered something like this: "Peter, this reward-seeking is very carnal. You must learn to follow Me out of pure love for Me, without regard to reward." In other words, we would have been more "spiritual" than the Lord Himself! For not only did He answer Peter's question, but He laid it down as a principle and practice of the kingdom of heaven that all sacrifices for Him would have recompense beyond all expectation.

See what rises out of Peter's question. First, there was something special for the twelve, introduced by the pronoun *ye*. It looks forward to the establishing of the kingdom under the universal scepter of Messiah Jesus, seated on the throne of David. In that context the twelve apostles will have governing powers over the twelve tribes of Israel. That, of course, presumes that the resurrection of the just will have taken place. I do not see how that passage can be successfully spiritualized. The only difficulty I have is the matter of a replacement for Judas. If the "election" of Acts 1 was valid, then it would be Matthias. But the apostle Paul might be regarded as a strong contender for that vacated place. It is not our business, however, to make appointments in the kingdom of heaven.

After the "ye" comes the "every one." Here is where the principle of recompense is stated, and I should think that, if the Lord took pains to enunciate that principle, we cannot despise it as an unworthy thing. It would appear that the Lord, knowing the weakness of our hearts and the pressures under which we serve Him, has given us that for our encouragement. Every sacrifice made for Christ and for the gospel's sake will be amply rewarded, both now and in the life to come. The recompense may not always be evident in the eyes of the world, but our Lord will not fall down on His "hundredfold" promise.

The Guthries are a notable family in the history of the Scottish kirk. William was one of those who held high the torch in the seventeenth century. As eldest son of the family, he was heir to the lairdships of Pitforthy and Easter Ogle. Under the tutelage of the godly Samuel Rutherford he sensed the call of God to the work of the ministry; he made over all his estates to a younger brother, lest the care of them should in any wise hinder his service to God and the kirk. It might be difficult to recognize the hundredfold recompense in that devoted minister's death in his middle forties, but although he died in great pain, he died adoring the kindness of God through all the strenuous years of ministry. The eternal reward will be witnessed by all the heavenly host.

"Ye," a special provision; "every one," a general principle; and now "many," marking a division—"Many that are first shall be last, and the last first." Criteria of judgment are different in the kingdom of heaven. The time factor plays no part. It is not length of service that counts. Moreover, acclaim here is no assurance of commendation there. We may do well in all outward appearances, but that is no guarantee of receiving the Master's "Well done!" "Many that are first shall be last, and the last first." To enforce that law of the kingdom our Lord gave us the parable of the workers in the vineyard, in which three attributes of God are vividly presented.

First is the justice of God. The long-time workers in the parable complain bitterly that they received no more than those who joined the forces at the eleventh hour. That certainly would not sit well with the unions. But the lord of the vineyard defended the justice of his action by reminding the complainers that they had made their wages a matter of contract, and he had kept his contract. Justice required no more.

Second is the sovereignty of God. "It is my will," says the ASV, "to give unto this last, even as unto thee. Is it not lawful for me to do what I will with mine own?" (20:14-15). Now it is the mere fact of sovereignty that is here pressed, but we learn elsewhere that the will of God is "good, and acceptable, and perfect" (Rom. 12:2), so there is no reason to dispute it. Moreover, there is no higher court of appeal. God is the supreme Judge, not only of the actions of His creatures, but of His own actions. If His ways are past finding out, we know that they are in keeping with His character. Here is a sovereignty calling for both submission and trust.

Third is the goodness of God. The evil eye cannot perceive the goodness of God. Eyes that are filled with lewd, vile, unclean pictures are blind to the truly lovely and pure. So the covetous eye distorts even the holy things, seeing in the goodness of God only injustice. "The LORD is good to all; and his tender mercies are over all his works" (Psalm 145:9). So says the man who truly knows God, but the stranger is full of resentment and dissatisfaction, like those in the parable who, instead of admiring the generosity of the lord, accused him of unfair dealing.

That elaborate parable is designed to establish a law of the kingdom, that "there are first that shall be last, and the last first."

16

APPROACHING HIS PASSION

(20:17—25:46)

ON TO JERUSALEM (20:17-34)

WE HAVE SEEN OUR LORD dwelling in His passion. We now accompany Him as He is approaching His passion. That movement is introduced by the words, "As Jesus was going up to Jerusalem," for now it meant the cross. Deeply conscious of the cross, Jesus took His disciples aside, and for the fourth time told them what awaited Him in Jerusalem. Note how positive and detailed is His statement, ending, as always, with the note of victory—"the third day He shall be raised up."

Then is an important word in that setting. It is incredible that the mother of James and John should choose that hour, when Jesus has been expatiating on His passion, to lobby on behalf of her sons, seeking for them the two highest offices in the kingdom. Can we probe her thoughts? On the positive side it is evident that she, and her sons with her, had unshakeable faith in Jesus as the one who would "restore the kingdom to Israel." But were they so obsessed with the idea of the kingdom, after the pattern of their thinking, that they were impervious to the thought of suffering and crucifixion? Or was it a form of protest against the path that Jesus was laying out for Himself? We recall Peter's protest when the Lord first intimated that a cross, not a throne, awaited Him. It would not be surprising if the others harbored the same protest in their hearts.

The Lord sought to bring them back to the reality of suffering and death with a question regarding their ability to suffer with Him, for if we suffer with Him, we shall be also glorified together (see Romans 8:17). The King James version gives a double description of the suffering, as a cup, and also as a baptism. The cup reminds us of the upper room and Gethsemane, while in Luke 12:50 He speaks of His

175

passion in terms of a baptism: "I have a baptism to be baptized with; and how am I straitened till it be accomplished!" The two brothers replied, "We are able." That was a boast that neither the two nor the ten could make good. Do we not read a little later, "Then all the disciples forsook him, and fled"? Some of them did worse than that. Peter denied Him and Judas betrayed Him. However, Jesus took the two at their word, knowing that the coming of the Holy Spirit would endue them with power from above, in the strength of which they would drink of His cup and share His baptism of suffering and death.

In the economic order of the holy Trinity, some things are reserved to the care of the Father. One example of this is "the times or the seasons" (Acts 1:7). Here is another special prerogative of the Father: to appoint the chief ministers of the kingdom of heaven.

So much for the ambition of the two. Now we see the resentment of the ten—a resentment that demonstrated that they were just as ambitious as the sons of Zebedee. The only difference was that James and John had a good lobbyist in their mother. Out of that bit of friction came another law of the kingdom. We have already learned that greatness in the kingdom of God is spelled H-U-M-I-L-I-T-Y. Now we are given another spelling lesson. Greatness spells S-E-R-V-I-C-E. And if we are aiming for top position, we must know that it is reserved for bond servants.

Jesus has now crossed to the west side of the Jordan and has come to Jericho where He gives sight to two blind men. But now we face a problem in harmony. Matthew places the miracle at the exit from Jericho, with two blind beggars involved. Mark speaks of just one man, and names him—Bartimaeus. Luke also indicates one man, but has the miracle take place "as they were going out from Jericho." The number problem is slight. Two of the three recorders focus on one of two men, whereas Matthew includes both in his report. As to location, several attempts at harmony have been made. One suggestion is that there were two Jerichos, the old and the new; that they were contiguous; that departing from the one meant entering the other, so that either statement was correct. We can wait for further light and in the meantime draw all possible spiritual benefit from that remarkable incident. Here we have three portraits: two men in dire need, crying for help; a crowd disturbed by the cry of need but unresponsive to it, though doubtless many among them had had their own ailments healed by that "Son of David"; and the majestic figure of Jesus as He halts the crowd, calls the blind men, and grants them their request for full sight. Jesus knows what awaits Him in Jerusalem, but He is not succumbing to self-pity, nor allowing His approaching grief to diminish His compassion for men in need.

THE RECEPTION OF THE KING (21:1-22)

As we proceed through that section of the gospel, we see the entry of the King, first into the city and then into the Temple; the controversies of the King with various groups of religious leaders; and the predictions of the King as He replies to the questions of His disciples.

Former entries into the city of Jerusalem had been quiet, unobtrusive, but not this one. Not that there was anything dazzling about it. There were no bands, no chariots, no banners, nothing that would match a Roman triumph. The crowds gathered to Jesus spontaneously, both those from Galilee and those who heard of His arrival and came out of the city to meet Him. The point is that He not only allowed it, but encouraged it by securing a beast of burden on which to ride. Nor did He try to dissuade His followers from spreading their garments and palm branches on the road before Him. Neither did He command them to cease their chanting: "Hosanna to the Son of David: Blessed is he that cometh in the name of the Lord; Hosanna in the highest" (21:9).

The word *Hosanna* is used in the New Testament only in the records of the triumphal entry, but it is found in Psalm 118:25, where it is translated *"Save now, I beseech thee, O LORD"* (italics added). It is a term that was used in welcoming kings and other royal visitors. Its use by the joyous multitude that day would seem to suggest their belief that Jesus was their promised and expected King. That would be confirmed by their adding, "To the Son of David," for Messiah comes of the Davidic line.

Some instructive points lie beneath the surface, such as our Lord's knowledge of the whereabouts of the ass and her colt, seeing He had not been in that area for quite some time; the readiness of the owner to give Jesus the use of his beasts, and Jesus' confidence that such readiness would be found; the fact that it was an unbroken colt (see

Mark 11:2) that nevertheless was completely tranquil under its un-
wonted burden, with the crowds shouting all around.

Our curiosity might ask some petty questions, such as, "How did
the ass and the colt get back home?" But there is one important question: Why? The reason for that change of behavior pattern is, happily, given us. "All this was done, that it might be fulfilled which
was spoken by the prophet, saying, Tell ye the daughter of Sion,
Behold thy King cometh unto thee, meek, and riding upon an ass,
and a colt the foal of an ass" (21:4-5). It was an official act, studied
and deliberate, fulfilling the prophecy of Zechariah 9:9. It was a rare
combination of meekness and regality—a Servant and a King. Now
how will Jerusalem receive Him?

We have noted the change in our Lord's behavior. What follows
reveals a maintaining of this sterner pattern. It is seen in the cleansing of the Temple, in the cursing of the fig tree, in the parables of
rejection, and in the pronouncement of woes upon the scribes and
Pharisees.

The traffic that so stirred the wrath of Jesus was in itself legitimate,
even necessary. Worshipers coming from distances could not bring
their sacrificial animals. They were permitted to turn them into
money, with which they purchased acceptable beasts for religious
purposes in Jerusalem. That allowance was based on Deuteronomy
14:24-25. In addition, Roman money was not accepted for the Temple tax, or any gift to the Temple for that matter. Therefore there
had to be money changers to change denarii into shekels. So it was
not the traffic itself that Jesus rebuked, but its location and its fraudulent practices. The Temple court was not the place to transact business. Moreover, it had become a priestly monopoly, with all the
abuses that generally attend a monopoly.

That was not the first cleansing of the Temple. Early in His ministry, as recorded by the apostle John, Jesus used stern measures with
the traffickers in the Temple, but they were soon reinstated in their
usual place. Evil is hard to curb. On a television program dealing
with prostitution in Times Square, New York, one woman, when interviewed, affirmed that she had been arrested for prostitution over
forty times but had never spent a night in jail. So the fraudulent

business in the Temple was as active as ever when our Lord came to Jerusalem to complete His earthly task.

But there was a difference in the rebukes on the two occasions. The first cleansing was accompanied by the words, "Make not my Father's house an house of merchandise" (John 2:16). The second time His words were much sterner: "It is written, My house shall be called the house of prayer; but ye have made it a den of thieves" (21:13). Evil does not improve. It waxes worse and worse. Notice the "It is written," and read Isaiah 56:7 and Jeremiah 7:11, passages that Jesus brought together in His condemnation of the iniquitous traffic.

The cleansing prepared the way for the healing. Immediately "the blind and the lame came to him in the temple; and he healed them" (21:14). So the stern judge is still the Man of compassion. If our churches submitted to a work of purging, the needy would be beating a trail to our doors.

Look, then, at those three pictures in the court of the Temple: a scene of activity, the hubbub of merchandising; then a scene of confusion and panic as tables are overturned, money is strewn everywhere, animals and men in flight; then, despite the scattered debris, a scene of subdued excitement and joy as the blind receive their sight, the lame walk, and ailments vanish at the touch of Jesus. If some understanding and skilled artist were to paint those three scenes in a series, we should have one of the most significant works of art ever produced. But let not the artist forget the singing children in picture number three!

How will the ministers of the Temple respond to that transformation? One should expect them to join the song of the children. Instead, they are thoroughly incensed. They shut their eyes to the fraudulent practices, but regard the singing of the children as a profanation of the sacred place. To Jesus, however, the youthful voices, raised in praise, were sweet music, reminding Him of the words of David, "Out of the mouth of babes and sucklings hast thou established strength" (Psalm 8:2, ASV). Our Lord used the Septuagint version (LXX), which suggests that the praises of children are the kind of material out of which God builds His stronghold of testimony.

"And he left them" (21:17). No doubt that is primarily a mere literal statement, but there is a moral connotation that could be matched with the solemn word of dereliction, "Behold, your house is being left to you desolate" (23:38). Although many ancient authorities omit the word *desolate* here, the fact remains that any man or institution abandoned by Christ is headed for desolation.

THE PARABLES OF LOST PRIVILEGE (21:23–22:14)

The withering of the fig tree is the only miracle of destruction performed by our Lord in the days of His flesh. It therefore calls for special attention. In the first place Mark tells us that it was not the season for figs. Why then did Jesus look for figs out of season? The answer lies in a phenomenon called firstripe fruit, which appears before the leaves break out. That fig tree, then, ought to have had some token of the harvest to come. The lush foliage was actually lying.

Of one thing we can be sure: Jesus did not act in a fit of temper arising out of personal frustration. There was meaning in what He did, and if we remember that He was now come to the crisis of two-way rejection, we shall expect that incident to have national significance. Even in Old Testament times God bemoaned the failure of His people Israel to bring forth the fruit of righteousness. Under the figure of a vineyard Isaiah depicts the failure and the judgment that was coming upon it (Isaiah 5:1-7). "He looked for judgment, but behold oppression; for righteousness, but behold a cry" (Isaiah 5:7). With what result? "I will lay it waste: it shall not be pruned, nor digged . . . I will also command the clouds that they rain no rain upon it" (Isaiah 5:6). In the light of such statements the so-called cursing of the fig tree does not seem so strange, but appears as an action parable of the state of Israel that was about to be visited with sore judgments.

Although the nation Israel is specifically in view here, we are surely justified in giving the incident a personal application. It is possible to have the lush foliage of Christian profession and be utterly lacking "the fruit of the Spirit"—to have the trappings without the reality. James warns us against such fruitless profession, summing up his admonition in the bald statement, "Faith without works is dead" (James 2:26).

All that is true, yet our Lord gave a different interpretation of His action. From it He drew a lesson on the power of faith. His pronouncement of barrenness upon the fig tree was an act of faith. Unbelief would have reasoned, "What if nothing happens? Then my authority and power and commission will be brought into question. I had better not go too far out on a limb." Instead, our Lord spoke the word of malediction with the same certainty that He manifested at the tomb of Lazarus when He said to the Father, "I thank thee that thou hast heard me. And I knew that thou hearest me always" (John 11:41-42). Now we would say that it takes a heap of faith to pronounce a curse on a barren fig tree, but the Lord affirms that faith no bigger than a mustard seed is capable of far greater accomplishments than that, even to the moving of mountains: and we remember that Jesus called the grain of mustard "the least of all seeds." Surely that tells us that the resources of faith are infinitely beyond anything we have as yet experienced.

Let us make no mistake here. Many there are who preach the virtues of faith, but when their faith is examined it turns out to be nothing more than a disposition of optimism, a feeling that things will turn out for the best. Biblical faith has a focus. "Have faith in God," says our Lord, whose own faith was focused on the Father (Mark 11:22). Ultimately, then, the power of faith is not in the faith itself, but in the One in whom our faith resides. That objective faith operates basically in the exercise of prayer. Notice the phrase, "ask in prayer, believing." There is an asking that is not prayer, and there is a praying that lacks believing. Prevailing prayer is both submissive and believing.

THE CONTROVERSIES OF THE KING (22:15-46)

Christ's vigorous purging of the Temple was not allowed to go unchallenged. It triggered a whole series of questions whose purpose was to bring an indictment against Jesus. In that controversy we can discern—

1. a question of authority (21:23-28)
2. a question of politics (22:15-22)
3. a question of doctrine (22:23-33)
4. a question of law (22:34-40).

All those were addressed to Jesus by various groups of leaders, after which He addressed a question to them, one that requires an answer from all men. We shall examine them in order.

We have already looked at the condition that Jesus attacked. Right well the rulers of the Temple knew that what they permitted and even sponsored was contrary to the holiness that becomes the house of God. They could not therefore condemn the action of Jesus itself. How, then, could they condemn Him? Their only resort was to challenge His authority. Since He was not a priest, nor a Levite, nor a member of the rabbinic order, by what right did He act in such drastic fashion? Why did He not leave disciplinary action to those whose prerogative was the care of the Temple? So their twofold question was the character and the source of the authority that Jesus claimed in acting as He did. His response was a counter question that had a twofold effect: it made clear that Jesus did not hold himself obligated to answer their question, and it threw them onto the horns of a dilemma from which their only escape was to plead ignorance. The issue was the rite of baptism as administered by John the Baptist. They could not affirm the divine commission of John without having to give account of their unbelief. To deny John's ordination would bring upon them the wrath of the people, who were convinced that he was indeed a prophet whose voice had broken the silence of four centuries. So they simply pleaded ignorance; "We don't know." Now a confession of ignorance can be noble and honorable, but in that case it was the answer of cowardice and escape. To reveal the secret of His strength and authority in such a situation would have been to cast His pearls before swine, a practice against which the Lord Himself had warned His disciples (7:6).

Yet Jesus did answer the question of the religious leaders, only in an unexpected way, by means of three parables that might be called the parables of forfeited privilege—the two sons (21:28-32), the wicked husbandmen (21:33-46), and the marriage supper (22:1-14).

In the parable of the two sons a general principle is laid down, followed by a special contemporary application. The principle concerns the nature of obedience. Stated simply, obedience consists of doing, not saying. Doubtless we have often used the phrase, "All say and no do." No matter how effusively we say yes to a command, that does not constitute obedience. The obedience comes in the doing. On the other hand, one's first response to a command may be negative, but if upon consideration he thinks better of it and carries out the order, the record will read, "Task accomplished. Obedient." When the Lord commissioned Moses to lead the emancipation of Israel from Egypt's bondage, Moses began multiplying reasons why he should not undertake such a task. That was quite an argument that took place by the burning bush. Yet what does the record say? "By faith (Moses) kept the Passover and the sprinkling of the blood . . . By faith they passed through the Red Sea" (Hebrews 11:28-29). A man who said no went out and by faith carried out the assigned task. Ananias was not too enthusiastic about his assignment to visit Saul of Tarsus, that tiger of a persecutor, but the no in his heart was changed to a yes of action, and he had the privilege of baptizing the great apostle.

Now Jesus applied His parable to two groups within Israel. There were those who lived contrary to the law, but who, on hearing the Word of God through the lips of John the Baptist, turned from their wicked ways to do the will of God. Their no became a yes. As for the religious leaders, whose carefulness to observe the minutiae of the law was an advertisement of their piety, they were unmoved by the preaching of the Baptist. They professed yes and practiced no. Our Lord's word to those religious professors was: "The publicans and the sinners go into the kingdom of God before you."

In the light of the following parables, we can hardly fail to discern a national aspect to that of the two sons. God chose Abraham and his seed as a peculiar treasure for Himself. They were the favored son. Theirs were the covenants, the law, the testimony, the Temple, the priesthood. All that professed a yes to the God who had chosen them. But action did not support profession. "I looked for righteousness," God said, "but behold, a cry!" (Isaiah 5:7). Now that situation persisted even in the days of our Lord's sojourn in the flesh, and in that parable He describes the favored people as a son who said yes but acted no. As for the other son, those were of the Gentile nations who would hear and receive the gospel and enter into the kingdom of God. The no of their heathenism would be changed to a yes of faith. Jesus reckoned that seeing the publicans and prostitutes entering the kingdom and enjoying its benefits should have stirred the religious leaders

to a holy jealousy making for repentance, even as Paul expected to
see that same holy jealousy aroused in his Jewish brethren in seeing
the conversion of the Gentiles (Romans 11:11).

We do not have to go far to see the thrust of the parable of the
wicked husbandmen. The chief priests and Pharisees perceived that
Jesus was speaking about them. Quite evidently the householder is
God; the vineyard is the kingdom of God; the husbandmen are the
Jewish nation, with special reference to the spiritual leaders and teachers; the servants sent to receive the fruit are the whole line of prophets
who persistently called the nation back to God, and were ill-treated
for their pains; the son is Jesus Himself, the well-beloved, who came
to seek and to save the lost, but was rejected by those who ought to
have welcomed Him with open arms and heart.

It is interesting to note that in both these parables Jesus draws from
the chief priests and Pharisees their own condemnation. "Which of
the two did the will of his father?" He asks, and their reply is a self-
indictment. Again the question, "What will he (the householder) do
unto those husbandmen?" (21:40) brings an answer which amounts
to passing sentence upon themselves. I rather think that the moment
they gave that reply they saw that they were trapped. No wonder
"they sought to lay hold on him"! But for the present their fear was
stronger than their hate. They would await a more propitious hour.

The reply of the priests and the Pharisees was not only self-con-
demnatory. It was prophetic. They have inadvertently listened to
their own history and have passed judgment upon it, not knowing
how literally that judgment would be fulfilled within forty years,
when the Roman legions would make rubble of their fair city, Jerusalem. But that is only part of their unconscious prophecy. The vineyard would not be given over to thorns and briers and thistles. Others
would occupy it, being given the place of privilege forfeited by the
rebellious husbandmen. Already the preparations were on foot for
the new occupants, the new people of God, the church. And if there
is any vagueness in the prophetic character of the self-imposed judgment, Christ dispels it with this unequivocal statement: "The kingdom of God shall be taken away from you, and given to a nation
bringing forth the fruits thereof" (21:43). That new nation knows

no ethnic nor political boundaries. It consists of people of every tribe and tongue.

By way of confirmation of the judgment just passed, Jesus appeals to Psalm 118:22-23. The figure is different, shifting from the vineyard to the building, but the truth is the same. Here is a stone that God has appointed to occupy the place of primacy and power in the eternal temple, "a chief corner stone, elect, precious" (1 Peter 2:6; Isaiah 28:16), but the builders, the religious experts, reject it. However, they cannot so easily get rid of the God-approved stone. It becomes a breaking stone to all who stumble over it, while those upon whom it falls are ground to powder, like the image of Nebuchadnezzar's dream upon whose feet the stone cut without hands fell (Daniel 2:31-35).

Again the scene changes, moving from the vineyard to the banquet hall. The story is told in four chapters. The first two tell of an invitation rejected; the third speaks of an invitation accepted; the fourth is the story of one who crashed the party.

It was no ordinary marriage. It was a royal feast to which the guests were invited. Actually they were doubly obligated to attend. For one thing, a royal invitation is a royal command. Do we remember that as we preach the gospel? Then it is evident that the invited ones had been apprised beforehand, so that they were committed to be in readiness for the call. When that call came, they simply ignored it. "They would not come" (22:3). That looks very much like our Lord's personal ministry in the days of His flesh, including the preaching tours of His disciples. Those who were "bidden" were "the lost sheep of the house of Israel," the chosen race, to whom Jesus primarily came. Despite the throngs that pressed in on Him, it must be acknowledged that "he came unto his own, and his own received him not" (John 1:11). That was specially true of the religious leaders, whom He was now addressing. Notice that that phase of the story ends with the simple statement, "They would not come." Nothing is said here about retribution—not yet.

The second phase is very much like the first in its beginning. The invitation was repeated to the same "bidden" ones, but by other servants, and with an addition to the former proclamation, calculated to press upon those invited the urgency of the case: "I have prepared my dinner . . . all things are ready" (22:4). What had happened in the meantime to make all things ready? The answer surely is the cross, represented by the slaying of the oxen and fatlings. It was a costly feast that the King had provided, adding greatly to the responsibility of the "bidden" ones to hasten to the banquet hall. But instead of receiving a ready response, the message of the cross aroused more enmity. Some treated it with scorn, some with bitter hatred, even to the maltreatment and murder of the King's servants. So it came to pass. The book of Acts certainly tells of great triumphs, but it is also a record of suffering for Christ's sake. Beatings, scourgings, imprisonments, even death were the lot of the servants of the King, the heralds of the cross. Does not Paul tell us that the preaching of the cross was "unto the Jews a stumblingblock"?

We have seen that the first refusal was not visited with punishment, but the second stirred the wrath of the king, so that he "sent his armies, and destroyed those murderers, and burned up their city" (22:7). We should remember that that second refusal was not only a rejection of the message of the cross, but also a repudiation of the testimony of the Holy Spirit who had come at Pentecost to support the witness of the church (Acts 5:32). So God used the Roman armies to avenge the rejection of His Son.

The third invitation is the same as the second in its message, but differs in its outreach. "They which were bidden were not worthy" (22:8), so they lost their place of privilege. It was now an open invitation. "The wedding was furnished with guests" gathered from the highways, "both bad and good" (22:10), for the invitation was not on the basis of merit, but by the King's grace. There we have a glimpse of the salvation of the Gentiles, a doctrine later expounded by the apostle Paul in his great epistle to the Romans.

The fourth phase of the story is not an invitation, but an expulsion. Among the guests was found "a man who had not on a wedding garment." Being challenged for this neglect, he had nothing to say in his own defense, so by the King's command he was cast "into the outer darkness." What does it all mean? For one thing, we see one who had some desire to enter the kingdom of heaven, but would enter on his own terms. That is unacceptable. There is no access but on the terms laid down by the King. Then, too, attire is used frequently in Scripture with reference to conduct and character. That is one of the apostle Paul's favorite figures. Even when he is speaking in terms of the old man and the new man, his verb forms are those which apply to dress. (See Ephesians 4:22-24 and Colossians 3:8-12). Behavior is the outward expression of inward condition. Here then was a man whose dress (behavior) gave no evidence of a changed heart, but shouted aloud his unfitness for a place among the true guests.

A third explanation is possible, and is frequently used in an evangelistic setting. There the wedding garment is regarded as the righteousness of Christ imputed to the believer on the ground of His having borne our sin. "Him who knew no sin he (God) made to be sin on our behalf; that we might become the righteousness of God in him" (2 Corinthians 5:21, ASV). Any other garment is "filthy rags," even our own righteousness (Isaiah 64:6). Thus without that gift—righteousness—here described as the wedding garment, we cannot enter the kingdom of heaven.

We have seen how three parables grew out of a question of authority. We look now at the other questions that marked this fierce controversy and see with what grace and wisdom Jesus answered His antagonists.

Next in line is a question of politics, hatched apparently by the Pharisees, the strictest of the Jewish sects. The first thing to observe is their dastardly purpose: "to ensnare him in his talk." If only they could press Him into saying something that they could use against Him, to break His hold on the people, or give grounds for indictment. Men are hard up for a case when they stoop to such tactics. But the Pharisees stooped still lower when they joined hands with the Herodians, their political opponents, the Quislings of their nation, in order to tighten the noose around Jesus' neck. It is noticeable, too, that the Pharisees appointed their disciples to the task of baiting Jesus, reasoning, no doubt, that if the tactic failed, the embarrassment would fall on the younger members of the sect rather than on the leaders.

The attack began with a bombardment of flattery. "We know that thou art true, and teachest the way of God in truth, neither carest thou for any man: for thou regardest not the person of men" (22:16). Now indeed, all that they said was true, but, unlike Nicodemus (John

3:2), they did not say it sincerely. Their complimentary remarks were the anaesthetic before the surgery, the bait to lure Him into their carefully prepared trap. Little did they know that the trap would spring on themselves.

Look at their question: "Is it lawful to give tribute unto Caesar, or not?" (22:17). We must keep in mind that the Holy Land and the Jewish nation were under the iron heel of Rome. What privileges they did enjoy were by the good graces of Rome and could be withdrawn at the whim of the emperor. Tribute was not only revenue for the Roman coffers, but a token of Jewish submission. Some in Israel bowed to the overlordship of the Caesar, while others resisted—if not openly, at least in attitude of mind. The Herodians belonged to the former group, the Pharisees to the latter. The question brought to Jesus put Him on the horns of a dilemma. If He said yes, He would be condemned for disloyalty to His own people. If He said no, He could be handed over to the Roman authorities and put on trial for sedition. His baiters were sure He could not escape that noose.

But truth is the answer to falsehood, and He who is the truth was ready with a great principle that would not only free Himself and embarrass His foes, but would also lay down a maxim for the guidance of all generations.

First, He asked to see a denarius, a Roman coin used in payment of tribute. Notice, He did not ask Judas, the treasurer of the apostolic band (John 12:6), for that piece of money. He asked His adversaries, and their possession and usage of the Roman money was in itself an admission of their vassalage. Then, as frequently, He posed a leading question, one that reversed the whole situation, putting His antagonists on the defensive. "Whose is this image and superscription?" He asked. Being a contemporary coin, it probably carried the head of Tiberius, with the superscription, "Son of Divine Augustus." Therefore, it was Caesar's money. The answer to the question of paying tribute was therefore clear and indisputable: "Render therefore unto Caesar the things that are Caesar's" (22:21). That, however, does not end our obligation. The universe about us bears the image and superscription of God. "In him we live, and move, and have our being" (Acts 17:28). "Render therefore . . . unto God the things that are God's." That amounts to much more than a Roman denarius. It calls for total commitment, and fulfilling our obligation to "the powers that be" is part of that total commitment. Two errors we must avoid: ignoring our duty to Caesar in the name of religion and neglecting our duty Godward through too much absorption in the kingdom of this world. It was a tragic word that Cardinal Wolsey spoke when he found himself rejected by an ungrateful monarch: "Had I but served my God as I have served my king, He would not have cast me off in my old age."

No fault could be found with that answer to the political question. Now the Sadducees brought a question of doctrine. They were the antisupernaturalists, who repudiated the doctrine of the resurrection, and angels, and spirits (Acts 23:8). Strangely enough, the high priesthood was in the hands of that sect, so their influence was great. Those, then, sent a delegation with a question that reflected their doctrinal stance, and, in their thinking, made the doctrine of the resurrection appear ludicrous. Cunningly they linked their question with a Mosaic ruling concerning marriage. If a man died childless, his brother (or nearest kinsman) was required to marry the widow. The firstborn of the marriage was considered the offspring of the deceased. It was that law of the kinsman-redeemer that Boaz followed when he married Ruth the Moabitess, whose Hebrew husband had died in Moab.

Was that a fabricated story, or were the Sadducees citing a known case? Whichever, it was intended to create a problem for the whole concept of resurrection. Their error was in thinking that resurrection meant a renewal of earthly relationships, so that husband and wife here would be husband and wife in the life beyond. If that were so, it would certainly be of interest to know how a woman would fare who had had seven husbands in sequence, all brothers. Would the first husband be her celestial husband, or the last one, or the one she loved most, or would she have all seven? If that all sounds trivial, then the trivialities grow out of their basic error. Jesus sensed the shallow character of the question and of those who put it forward, and there seems to be a touch of anger and disgust in His reaction: "Ye do err, not knowing the scriptures" (22:29). Those men ought to have known better. They had access to the law, the prophets, and the writings, which, had they bowed to their authority, would have enlightened them concerning the nature of the world to come.

"Not knowing . . . the power of God," Jesus added. If God could create a body for man with all the amenities of a sex life, does He not have power to recreate that body with all the amenities of immortality? Cannot He who created the angels impart to His redeemed people something of the angelic nature, free from the necessities of the mortal state?

The order of Christ's reply to the question of the Sadducees is remarkable. He first corrects their error concerning the nature of resurrection, then deals with the fact of the resurrection. His interrogators had quoted Moses as their authority. Now Jesus quotes a word from God to Moses to substantiate the fact of the resurrection. Out of the burning bush came the affirmation: "I am the God of Abraham, and the God of Isaac, and the God of Jacob" (Exodus 3:6). Notice the "I am." God is not speaking of a historic past when He was the God of Abraham, Isaac, and Jacob, but with the present. He is the God of men who died long since, yet live. The fact of the resurrection rests on the bigger fact that "God is not the God of the dead, but of the living." Given that, resurrection is no problem.

We have to turn elsewhere for our Lord's ultimate exposition of the doctrine of the resurrection, and when we find it, it is more astonishing than what He says here. That ultimate exposition is twofold. First, it is a declaration, and second a demonstration. The declaration relates it to Himself: "I am the resurrection and the life" (John 11:25). The second is His own resurrection, the guarantee of resurrection for all who believe on Him. "Because I live, ye shall live also" (John 14:19).

Now the discomfiture of the Sadducees was as honey to their rivals, the Pharisees. It helped to heal their own wound, and they decided to try again. That time, however, they would go it alone, since their experiment in joining forces with the Herodians had proven a disaster. Their specialty was the law. Many of their number were avid students of the Torah. The rabbinic school had test questions by which they would try those seeking the teaching office. Now Jesus held no diploma or license from the school of the rabbis. All things considered, it seemed reasonable to try one of their test questions on the unofficial, unlicensed, but popular rabbi, Jesus. So one of their legal scholars was appointed to pose the question, "Which is the great commandment in the law?"

One might argue that all laws are equal, all carrying like authority. Yet Jesus Himself admitted the superiority of two over all others. The two are one in this respect, that they both call for the exercise of love. The difference lies in the objects of our love. First, love God; then, love your neighbor (Deuteronomy 6:5; Leviticus 19:18). Loving God will embrace the first table of the Decalogue, while loving one's neighbor will care for the second. Duty to God and duty to man are fulfilled by love. Heart, soul, and mind must exercise their divers powers in the performance of one's sacred duty. However we may distinguish heart and soul and mind, they combine to make loving God a total act of worship, and when we so love God we shall not fail to love our fellows, created, like ourselves, in the image of God, and embraced, like ourselves, in the redeeming work of the Savior.

So the question of authority, the question of politics, the question of doctrine, and the question of law, all have been dealt with. Now, before allowing the Pharisees to disperse, Jesus puts a question to them. It is a question concerning the Messiah. We must be careful here. Jesus was not asking whether they regarded Him as the Christ, but rather what was their thinking regarding the Christ. Then He narrowed His question to the matter of ancestry. "Whose son is he?" Their reply was correct, but incomplete. The Messiah must come of David, progenitor of the royal line. That, however, does not tell the whole story. Son of David after the flesh, He carries another sonship by a triple begetting. He is Son of God by eternal begetting: He is Son of God by virtue of the miraculous conception in the womb of the Virgin (Luke 1:35); He is Son of God by the begetting of resurrection (Acts 13:32-33).

It was a higher sonship that Jesus brought to light, a sonship that David himself recognized and that moved him to call his son Lord, saying, "The LORD said unto my Lord: 'Sit at My right hand, until I make thine enemies thy footstool' " (Psalm 110:1). That first LORD, spelled in caps, is the equivalent of Jehovah. The second Lord, printed in lower case, represents Adonai and refers to David's Son and Lord, the Messiah. It was that twofold concept of the Messiah that the Pharisees lacked.

See what we learn from the incident. First, Jesus affirms the Davidic authorship of Psalm 110. Second, the dual relationship of the Messiah, Son of David and Son of God, was revealed to David by the Holy Spirit, a fact brought out clearly in the American Standard version, although somewhat obscured in the King James version. Third, if David, progenitor of the royal line, called his son Lord, how much more should we who have no such natural bond! It is noticeable that the Pharisees, for all their biblical knowledge, did not attempt a reply to Jesus' second question, nor did He offer an answer. They were in no mood to be enlightened, satisfied as they were with an academic knowledge of Messiah's genealogical link with David. Whereto do our thoughts of Christ lead us? To the point of calling Him Lord? And meaning it?

THE KING ADDRESSES FOUR GROUPS (23:1-39)

Jesus had effectually silenced the Pharisees and the scribes. Now He has something to say, first about them and then to them. See how He begins by recognizing their legitimate place in the religious life of the people. They "sit in Moses' seat." That is, they represented Moses as instructors of the people in the law of God. In this capacity they commanded recognition and obedience. But although their office called for respect, they themselves were unworthy of it, since there was a great gap between their teaching and their practice. "They say, and do not." They laid the whole burden of the law on the shoulders of the people, but seemed to consider themselves exempt from its obligations. Their chief concern was their own reputation. The King James translation of Philippians 2:7 says of Christ that He "made himself of no reputation," but here we have religious leaders whose objective was to build reputation for themselves. They had an insatiable lust for public acclaim that they sought to obtain by means of the externals of religion, including enlarged phylacteries and lengthened tassels. The phylacteries were small leather cubes containing appropriate Scriptures, worn on the left arm and the forehead as reminders of their covenant with God. The "borders" here mentioned may refer to the strings of the phylacteries or to tassels on the hem of their robes. They had become objects of display. At public functions the scribes made straight for the places of honor, whether it were a festive table or a religious service. They expected obsequious greetings and to be addressed with titles of respect. They were indeed puffed up, and the religion that ought to have humbled them before God became a means of exalting them before men.

Having given that damaging description of the scribes and Pharisees, Jesus turned it into a warning to His followers. "Don't you be like them," He said in effect and pressed the lesson in the area of titles. Let the titles be reserved for the One who alone is worthy to carry them. The brotherhood of Christ knows no exalting of one above the others as the authoritative teacher. We may not therefore covet a title that would indicate such superiority. Quite evidently the prohibition to call any man our father does not refer to the natural relationship, but rather speaks of *father* in a religious sense. Malachi exclaims, "Have we not all one father?" (Malachi 2:10). And the apostle Paul, in his address on Mars Hill, quotes approvingly from contemporary literature, "We also are his offspring." In this one Father "we live and move and have our being." We can have no intermediary here, nor can we ascribe to any man the stream of life that comes from God alone, nor give him a title that would set him in the place of God.

Another title that Christ forbids us to seek is "Master," which signifies a guide. I have known Christians who cast a spell upon other believers, assuming a control over their lives that robbed them of the power to think and act for themselves. Their "guide" dictated the will of God. The only one to be trusted with such control is Christ. So we learn from our Lord that what the Pharisees and the scribes sought for themselves we are to avoid. Rather we must covet the place of a servant, even as "the Son of man came not to be ministered unto, but to minister" (20:28). In the kingdom of God we climb by stooping.

Having drawn the portrait of the scribes and Pharisees, Jesus now pronounces sentence upon them. Early in His ministry He had portrayed the character that becomes the kingdom of heaven. The Beatitudes carry that picture. Now Jesus faces the rulers of the people, men who had rejected the message of the kingdom, refusing to be conformed to the righteousness set forth therein. The Beatitudes are therefore exchanged for woes. There are nine beatitudes, and if we count the final lament over Jerusalem, nine woes. The attempt to relate them, each to each, meets with some difficulties. For instance, the ASV omits verse 14 as not appearing in many ancient authorities, while others insert it immediately after verse 12. If we follow the order of the KJV that difficulty is in part surmounted. This we can say, that the woes answer to the Beatitudes as opposites, and the woes are the inevitable fruit of rejected Beatitudes. Let a man reject "the kingdom of God and his righteousness," and he ends up as "a son of Gehenna."

We cannot but be impressed with the severity of our Lord's language here, which is in striking contrast to the last verses of chapter 11: "Come unto me, all ye that labour and are heavy laden, and I will give you rest. Take my yoke upon you, and learn of me; for I am meek and lowly in heart: and ye shall find rest unto your souls. For my yoke is easy, and my burden is light" (11:28-30). Over against that gracious invitation we have the seven times repeated indictment: Hypocrites! Here were men whose practices belied their profession. Professing to be agents of the kingdom of heaven, they were stumbling blocks in the way of those whose hearts would incline them to enter. They made a theatrical show of prayer while engaged in the nefarious practice of evicting and dispossessing widows who lacked the means of fighting a court battle. Their proselytizing zeal was boundless, but they trained their converts in the "fine art" of deception. They were scrupulous in weighing out the tithes of the lesser grains, while neglecting the major duties. As Christ so vividly stated it, they "strain at a gnat, and swallow a camel" (23:24). They were punctilious about ceremonial cleanness but were corrupt in their hearts.

Now the Pharisees were engaged in a task in which they took great pride, hoping to secure merit from it. They were building tombs and erecting memorials for prophets and righteous men whom their forefathers had killed. In doing so they were attempting to dissociate themselves from their fathers' deeds. Boastfully they declared, "If we had been in the days of our fathers, we would not have been partakers with them in the blood of the prophets." And they regarded the tombs that they built and decorated as a witness to their piety. They forgot the law of entail that made them a part of their fathers' actions. On the good side we read of Levi that he "payed tithes in Abraham. For he was yet in the loins of his father, when Melchisedec met him"

(Hebrews 7:9-10). Here was the other side of the coin. By that same law the Pharisees were involved in the slaying of the prophets "from the blood of righteous Abel to the blood of Zechariah, the son of Berechiah" (23:35, NASB), and their sepulcher building, far from absolving them, stood as mute witness to the fact that they were the sons of the slayers, and therefore bound with them.

There is also a moral use of the term *son*. How often in Scripture the phrase "son of" signifies likeness in character! So it is here. Those Pharisees and scribes were made of the same stuff as those who killed the prophets, and Jesus indicated that theirs was the generation that would bring the long trail of blood to an issue. He was referring to His own death; to accomplish it they would use the Roman power. That would be "filling up the measure of your fathers."

The death of Christ would not be the end of the bloodshed. Christ's sent ones, prophets, wise men, and scribes would go forth with the gospel, only to experience the same persecution that would bring the day of judgment upon Jerusalem. Now the tone changes. With the rulers Jesus' vocabulary was that of severity: hypocrites, sons of gehenna, vipers, serpents, the damnation of hell (gehenna). But facing the holy city, it is a great cry, a sob, a lament. The sin is almost forgotten in the sorrow, and the sun breaks through at last. "Ye shall say, Blessed is he that cometh in the name of the Lord" (23:39). True, in the meantime there is the long desolation of the house, and the long absence of the King, but "he that shall come will come, and will not tarry" (Hebrews 10:37). Then shall the children of Jerusalem be gathered and sheltered under His wings, and "thy people shall be willing in the day of thy power" (Psalm 110:3).

PREDICTIONS CONCERNING ISRAEL, THE CHURCH, AND THE NATIONS
(24:1—25:46)

We come to the distinctly predictive portion of our Lord's teaching, generally referred to as the Olivet discourse. Admittedly there are almost as many interpretations as there are interpreters. It behooves us to tread softly and maintain a spirit of charity toward those who differ from us. It will help us in our understanding of that amazing passage if we keep in mind how it came about.

Jesus had just castigated the religious leaders, the scribes and the

Pharisees, for their hypocrisy, and ended His diatribe with a great groan for the coming desolation of Jerusalem and its Temple. "My house of prayer" had become "your house of desolation." The disciples could not take it in. Surely such magnificence could not be brought to desolation. So, as they were leaving the Temple they called His attention to the beauty and grandeur of the structure as if to say, "This crumble to dust?" "Yes," He replied. "There shall not be left here one stone upon another, that shall not be thrown down" (24:2). And it is a matter of history that that took place in A.D. 70 when the Roman legions under Titus sacked the city, destroyed the Temple, and scattered the populace.

It was a silent walk down the Kidron valley and up the slopes of Olivet where Jesus sat down, surrounded by that little group of perplexed disciples. He had spoken of desolation, but also of an appearing that would be greeted with acclaim: "Blessed is he that cometh in the name of the Lord." It all seemed to suggest finality, as if the present structure of things were to come to an end. So three big thoughts filled their minds, not in any clear order, but with some confusion: "these things," focusing on the desolation; "Thy coming" to be seen and acclaimed; the "consummation of the age," leading into the expected era of the kingdom of heaven. Their disturbed thoughts found expression in two questions, the time question and the sign question. Doubtless, their *when* embraced the whole spectrum of future events, and in their thinking, *these things,* the *coming* and the *end* were all of a piece, so one sign would herald the "one far-off divine event to which the whole creation moves." Whatever distinctions and sequences we may recognize do not come from this one passage, but from an assembling and analyzing of the whole range of prophecy. Therefore we do not attempt a detailed chronology here, but rather seek out the marks of the age, the marks of the end, and the marks of the coming, as those appear in our Lord's preview of events.

What sort of an age is it, whose consummation is anticipated here? First of all, it is an age of deception. "Take heed that no man deceive you. For many shall come in my name, saying, I am Christ; and shall deceive many" (24:4-5). And how easily we are led astray, like silly sheep, failing to "try the spirits whether they are of God" (1 John 4:1).

Second, it is an age of conflict. "Ye shall hear of wars and rumours of wars" (24:6-7), but that must not disturb us, since they play an integral role in the purposes of God. The rise and fall of kingdoms and empires is part of the process to bring about the alignment of nations for the final conflict.

Third, it is an age of disaster. "There shall be famines, and pestilences, and earthquakes, in divers places" (24:7). It would seem that as the age advances, those terrifying events increase, and today we have to add airquakes to the earthquakes. Bringing together two phrases from verses 6 and 8, we have: "not the end, but the beginning," surely warning us to expect a crescendo of disasters as the end approaches.

Fourth, it is an age of affliction. "Then shall they deliver you up to be afflicted" (24:9-10). It is a special kind of affliction. Since it is for Christ's sake, it takes on the character of martyrdom. We shall recall that one of the Beatitudes, given near the beginning of our Lord's ministry, reads like this: "Blessed are ye, when men shall revile you, and persecute you . . . for my sake" (5:11). Here at the close of His ministry He exhorts us to expect such opposition to our witness, wherever we carry it.

Fifth, it is an age of falling away. "The love of many shall wax cold" (24:12). How strange that the gospel of love should stir hate. We have already seen that the age was to be tormented with false Christs. Here now are their supporters, false prophets, helping along the work of deception. So by the pressures of false teaching and persecution many are induced to turn away from the truth and to abandon their love for Christ. That combination of false Christs and false prophets appears in Revelation 13 under the figure of the two beasts, bringing an age-long trend to its climax.

Sixth, it is an age of evangelism. "This gospel of the kingdom shall be preached in all the world . . . and then shall the end come" (24:14). The statement would seem to have a double thrust. For one thing, the entire age introduced by the death and resurrection of Christ is to be marked by an ever widening preaching of the gospel; and the completion of that task will herald the consummation. That is the sunshine that breaks through all the gloom of this age, with its deception, its conflicts, its catastrophies, its persecutions, its apostasies; and it would seem that while the darkness deepens, the light shines brighter and farther. False Christs and false prophets abound; men talk peace and prepare for war; persecution has so increased that the twentieth century has been well called "the century of the martyrs." But for all that, there has never been such a world-encircling preaching of the gospel as this generation has witnessed. God has put new tools in the hands of His church, and while those tools are used by the world for the corruption of men's minds, they are God's instruments for the hastening of His purposes. So whatever special application those marks of the age had to the brief period between Pentecost and the sacking of Jerusalem, we must recognize their relevance to the entire era. That brings us to consider the marks of the end.

The end is marked by the revelation of "the abomination of desolation, spoken of by Daniel the prophet" (24:15). See how our Lord sets His seal on the prophetic ministry of Daniel and incorporates it into His own declaration concerning the end time. But the question may be asked, "What end is in view?" If we turn to Daniel 12:11 we shall observe that the "abomination" is related to the taking away of the daily sacrifice, which actually was accomplished when the Roman armies both desecrated and destroyed the temple in A.D. 70. With the passing of the Temple went the ritual of the Temple, including the sacrifices. So the destruction of Jerusalem did mark an end, and a very significant end at that, but can we call it *the* end? Will there be another Titus who will lead the forces of Antichrist against the Holy City in the final battle of Armageddon? Many believe so.

Related to the abomination is tribulation that our Lord describes as "great . . . such as was not since the beginning of the world to this time, no, nor ever shall be" (24:21). Quite evidently this grows out of the "abomination of desolation," and the necessity of flight from Jerusalem makes it the more difficult for pregnant women and suckling mothers. It is a matter of history that many, heeding those warnings of Jesus, saved their lives by flight to the mountains at the approach of the Roman army. So that tribulation marks the same historic end as did the abomination. We are informed of another tribulation, described as "the great one" (Revelation 7:14), but that belongs to the end of the church era, not to the end of a Jewish era. At any rate, intense tribulation is one of the marks of the end, whichever end is in view.

Days of pressure seem to invite deception. Charlatans make prey of puzzled people. So our Lord warns that those end times, with their abominations and tribulations, will witness the rise of false Christs with false prophets to support them, and "great signs and wonders" calculated to convince, but actually deceiving. For many regard anything supernatural as divine, whereas there is a supernatural kingdom of evil, capable of imitating the divine, "insomuch that, if it were possible, they shall deceive the very elect" (24:24). How thankful we can be for that "if it were possible"!

We seem to have been gradually moving away from the events of the first century of our era, till now we are clearly engaged with events still future. The tribulation now before us is not that connected with the fall of Jerusalem, but that related to the end of the age in which we live. Note the word *immediately* (24:29). One would think that the precursor of our Lord's return would be a great brightening of the heavens. Instead, the sign is a darkening—a blackout, accompanied by great confusion in the heavenly bodies. We have had little tastes of blackouts through the failure of human ingenuity, but there is something terrifying in the thought of the failure of the solar system, even for a few moments or hours. Add to that the break up of the stellar order, and we have a situation that baffles the imagination.

"And then." Do not miss the order here: "tribulation, such as was not from the beginning"; immediately after, signs in the heavens; and then, the coming. That marks the terminus of the age.

> Lo, He comes, with clouds descending,
>   Once for favored sinners slain;
> Thousand thousand saints attending
>   Swell the triumph of His train:
> Alleluiah! alleluiah!
>   God appears on earth to reign.
>
> CHARLES WESLEY
> ("Lo, He Comes with Clouds Descending")

It is now for us to search out the marks of the coming. Our Lord Himself has given us four analogies. The first is to combat the idea of a secret coming, reported by false messengers who say, "Lo, here is Christ, or there . . . Behold, he is in the desert . . . Behold, he is in the secret chamber." All such furtive reports are to be repudiated. The coming will be as the lightning (24:27). From east to west the flash of His glory will be seen. "Every eye shall see him" (Revelation 1:7).

The second analogy is more difficult to understand: "For wheresoever the carcass is, there will the eagles be gathered together" (24:28). How do carcasses and vultures (as some translate it) fit in with the coming of the Lord? What about it? As vultures are drawn by long ranging sight and keen smell to a carcass, so the saints will be irresistibly drawn to Christ when He descends in the clouds, heralded by trumpet sound, accompanied by a host of angels. Perhaps to us the analogy seems inappropriate, and certain features both of the carcass and of the vultures we shall have to ignore. Our Lord is not carrion, neither are the saints birds of prey, but at least we have a picture of the drawing power of the descending Lord upon His waiting church, "caught up . . . to meet the Lord in the air" (1 Thessalonians 4:17).

The third analogy, also from nature, concerns the seasons. Spring is the harbinger of summer. So "all these things" cry aloud, "He is near, even at the doors" (24:33). Then to emphasize the nearness Jesus adds, "Verily I say unto you, This generation shall not pass, till all these things be fulfilled" (24:34). But how are we going to interpret that statement? One interpreter affirms that it revolves around the meaning of "all these things." Since the destruction of Jerusalem is clearly alluded to in the passage and actually did take place within the lifetime of many then alive, the conclusion is that our Lord is here referring to that event. Another school of thought holds that the interpretation depends on the meaning of the word *generation*. Although it ordinarily refers to those living within a stated period of time, it is also used in the sense of race—in this case, the Hebrew race. What Christ is saying, therefore, according to this thinking, is that the Jewish people would survive all eventualities and still be a distinct people when "all these things," right to the consummation of the age, became history. And certainly the Jews have been miraculously preserved to this day.

A third interpretation sees "all these things" as referring to the last time, and "this generation" as those living in that last time. To state it simply "all these things" pertaining to the end will be compacted within the space of one generation, so that the generation that sees the beginning of the end will see the end.

Scofield holds strongly to the second interpretation in the original edition of his notes, viewing "this generation" as the Hebrew race that would be preserved to the end; but the revised issue allows two and three as alternatives. That is surely significant in the history of interpretation. I recall the time when evangelist John Linton began to promote the view that the generation referred to was the end time generation who, seeing "all these things" beginning, would witness their consumation. He endured considerable criticism at the time, but the view has won much acceptance since. Mr. Linton inclined to the belief that we were that generation. Perhaps that was going out on a limb, but we shall admit that many of today's developments would seem to say that the end is near. "Though it tarry, wait for it; because it will surely come, it will not tarry" (Habakkuk 2:3).

The fourth analogy is drawn from history. "As the days of Noe were, so shall also the coming of the Son of man be" (24:37). We are not left to figure out the analogy for ourselves. It is done for us: "As in the days that were before the flood they were eating and drinking, marrying and giving in marriage, until the day that Noe entered into the ark . . . so shall also the coming of the Son of man be" (24:38-39). Now those were not illicit practices in themselves. However, in the light of the record in Genesis 6:1-13 we may well believe that much of the eating was gluttony, much of the drinking drunkenness, and much of the giving in marriage a swapping of wives, as some have suggested. But the analogy here seems to be in the area of total unawareness of impending disaster, despite Noah's preaching over a period of a hundred and twenty years. (See 2 Peter 2:5; Genesis 6:3.) They were walking in a stupor, so that their surprise was complete. The coming of the Son of man will be of like order. The routines of this life, whether legitimate or illicit, will so absorb men's attention that they will have no place in their consciousness for the most solemn warnings.

A short time ago I was engaged in a telephone conversation with a Chinese brother, whose broken English called for close attention. We were discussing the meanings of certain words in the Greek New Testament—an absorbing subject. So wrapped up was I in our conversation that I was completely oblivious to the activities of a thief who had secured entrance to our apartment by means of a stolen key and was going from room to room seeking cash. A less worthy oblivion characterized the people of Noah's day, and a like hypnotic state seems to be abroad today. Are we afflicted with such blindness, or do we see God's movements in our restless world?

There is a secret attached to the coming, concerning the time of it. "Of that day and hour knoweth no man, no, not the angels of heaven, but my Father only" (24:36). Here we are dealing with highly classified material. That rules out all attempts to set dates for the coming of the Lord.

Mark's record carries a phrase that has been the basis of much controversy: "Neither the Son." Here Jesus is affirming that He, the Son of God, shared the ignorance of men and angels concerning the time of His coming again. From that many have denied the omniscience of Christ; and with the omniscience go the omnipotence and the omnipresence; and with the attributes of deity goes deity itself. We cannot allow an ignorance that has such consequence. The "ignorance" of the Son of God must be a sovereign ignorance, a deliberate putting out of His mind, for purposes of redemption, such items of knowledge as would not serve the theanthropic personality.

Christ sovereignly limited Himself to such knowledge as the Father imparted to Him. He Himself said: "As my Father hath taught me, I speak these things" (John 8:28). There is, I believe, an analogy between that situation and God's determinative, sovereign forgetting of our sins, which is part of the new covenant defined by Jeremiah (Jeremiah 31:34) and quoted for us in Hebrews (Hebrews 8:12; 10:17). So Jesus chose not to know the hour and day of His coming again, but concerning the fact, He had absolute certainty and passed that certainty on to His disciples and to us.

That secrecy regarding the time of the coming, coupled with the certainty of it, becomes the ground of solemn exhortation. "Watch, therefore: for ye know not what hour your Lord doth come" (24:42); and again: "Therefore be ye also ready: for in such an hour as ye think not the Son of man cometh" (24:44). And the rest of the Olivet discourse, including the parables of chapter 25, rings the changes on these two thoughts—watchfulness and readiness.

A strange and awesome separation will mark the Lord's coming. "Then shall two be in the field; the one shall be taken, and the other left. Two women shall be grinding at the mill; the one shall be taken, and the other left" (24:40-41). That is in keeping with our Lord's promise to His disciples, and to us through them: "I will come again, and receive you unto myself" (John 14:3). The form of the promise suggests a great division, and the apostle Paul, writing by the Spirit, expands the teaching, indicating very clearly that it is "they that are Christ's" who rise "at his coming" (1 Corinthians 15:23).

By this time it is clear that in the Olivet discourse our Lord is not giving us a prophetic timetable. Quite evidently it is a panoramic view embracing several events that can well carry the common title, "The coming of the Lord." How those events are related is a study of considerable magnitude, covering the whole field of prophecy. Our present portion teaches us that the "coming" is a day of reckoning. It means promotion for the faithful servant, but retribution for the hypocrite who used his position in the house of God for his own ends.

The twenty-fifth chapter continues the theme of the Lord's coming. It is depicted there as the arrival of the Bridegroom, the homecoming of the Householder, and the enthronement of the King. The persons involved, therefore, are the virgins who wait upon the Bridegroom, the servants entrusted with the Householder's goods, and the subjects under the rule of the King. In each case there is a cleavage. The ten virgins are divided into two groups, the wise and the unwise; the servants are divided into the faithful and the slothful; the subjects are divided into merciful and unmerciful. Those characteristics appear in relation to the kingdom of God. The foolish virgins were unready when the Bridegroom arrived; the slothful servant had nothing to show for the trust committed to him during his Master's absence; the cursed subjects were those who failed to minister to the King's brethren, and therefore to the King Himself. In every case the Lord's arrival heralded the hour of reckoning. For the unwise maidens there was rejection, and no entrance to the marriage feast; for the slothful servant who refused to do business with his Master's talent, the "outer darkness," which surely means completely shut out from the light; for the uncharitable subjects who had no heart for the needs of the King and His kinsfolk, the "everlasting fire, prepared for the devil and his angels" (25:41).

Although exercising due caution against overinterpretation, we should not miss the practical lessons wrapped up in the parables. Take the ten virgins. Five of them had a supply of oil that kept their lamps burning even through the hours of sleep. The other five had something that gave their lamps the appearance of burning till the crucial hour arrived; when it failed, they cried, "Our lamps are going out!" So there are substitutes for the true oil that give one an outward appearance of Christian profession, but will be found wanting in the day of testing. Good works, religious forms, church affiliation, and the like are external marks of Christian profession, but unless they spring from a living faith, they will be met by the words of rejection, "I know you not." Since oil is one of the symbols of the Holy Spirit, we could somewhat change the metaphor and say that what the foolish virgins lacked was the seal of the Holy Spirit that identifies the children of God. Refuse all substitutes. They will fail you at the last.

Many practical lessons could be drawn from the parable of the talents, but let this suffice: a man is responsible for what he has, not for what he has not. Although the talent here spoken of was an amount of money, it may well stand for anything one has by which he may serve God, whether money, ability, power, position, or gift. To turn those to our own account or to allow them to atrophy will bring sure condemnation. God does not require equal return from all His servants, but He expects return commensurate with the gift. Failure to put to use what is entrusted to us amounts to a maligning of the character of God. Notice the complaint of the one talent servant: "I knew thee that thou art an hard man" (25:24). We are apt to excuse ourselves on the ground that God did not give us more to work with. It is a lame excuse that will be met with appropriate judgment, "Cast him out!"

Is the judgment of the nations, as here described, a parable? Or is it a literal declaration? Perhaps we have here a bit of both. Some things are clear. For one thing, our treatment of Christ's "brethren" is reckoned as our treatment of Christ. But who are His "brethren"? He Himself has told us. "Whosoever shall do the will of my Father which is in heaven, the same is my brother, and sister, and mother" (12:46-50). In face of such a statement I cannot confine the "brethren" of our present passage to the Jews. Although they occupy a special place in the economy of God, we can hardly say that judgment rests solely upon our treatment of the Jews. The deeper lesson here is the identity of the King with His loyal subjects, so that good done to His people is good done to Him, and evil perpetrated against His people is evil perpetrated against Him. It is that identity that demands such rich reward, on the one hand, and such sore judgment on the other hand.

Other items are beyond dispute: Jesus is coming again; Jesus is coming again as King; His coming will be accompanied by hosts of angels; He will sit on the throne of His glory; all nations will be subdued under Him; the judgment that is effected at His coming will therefore embrace all the nations of earth; the recompense and the condemnation are both "everlasting," for judgments passed at the beginning of the millennial age will hardly be reversed at the end of it.

Some there are who identify the judgment with that described for us in Revelation 20:11-15, generally called the great white throne judgment. The differences, however, are too many and too great to admit of such identification. Others think of the judgment of the nations, not in terms of an event which introduces the messianic age, but as an ongoing activity through the whole millennial period. We shall have to admit that righteous judgment will be a feature of the King's reign from the throne of David. "Righteousness shall be the girdle of his loins, and faithfulness the girdle of his reins" (Isaiah 11:5). One thing is sure—we shall not then be vexed with corruption in high places as we are in the present economy.

17

ENDURING HIS PASSION

(26:1–27:66)

THE SHADOW OF THE CROSS lay upon Jesus all His earthly days, ever deepening. Now we see the King moving quickly, but unhurriedly, to the climactic event, the cross itself. "After two days," said Jesus to His disciples, "is the feast of the passover, and the Son of man is betrayed to be crucified" (26:2). Note the time element. That is important, for the leaders of Israel had their own meeting in the court of the high priest's residence. There they passed three resolutions: Jesus must die; His death must be skillfully planned; it must not be on the feast day. Jesus said the feast day; the Sanhedrin said not the feast day. Whose word prevailed? Jesus was master even of His own death. Every previous attempt to arrest Him had been frustrated, but His hour was now come, and He would sovereignly give Himself into the hands of His foes and just as sovereignly die, even though through the instrumentality of His enemies. Listen to His own claim in this regard: "I lay down my life . . . no man taketh it from me, but I lay it down of myself" (John 10:17-18).

The chief priests found support for their nefarious purpose from an unexpected source—from the inner band of Jesus' followers. One of the twelve had been chosen treasurer for the group, doubtless because he had more business experience than some of the others; or perhaps he had wormed himself into the position of trust. But according to John, Judas was a pilferer. I am sure that the "bag" was not often overstocked, but covetousness is still covetousness whether it leads to petty thievery or grand larceny.

TWO CONFERENCES AND TWO SUPPERS (26:1-30)

An incident occurred in the home of Simon of Bethany that stirred the covetous spirit of Judas to the boiling point. Mary, sister of Martha and Lazarus, was moved by a strong impulse to express her love and gratitude to Jesus for all He had done for them as a family. Her cruse of liquid nard was probably her richest, rarest material treasure. Breaking the alabaster cruse, she poured the content on His head and feet as He reclined at supper. "Waste!" cried Judas. There was at least three hundred denarii down the drain that could have been distributed among the poor—or used to swell his personal account. The latter, of course, he whispered to himself. But he won the support of the apostolic band in his criticism of that beautiful expression of love and devotion. A sensitive soul like Mary must have been cut to the quick by their brutal criticism, but Jesus Himself came to her rescue. He gave that anointing a meaning that perhaps Mary herself had not fully realized. "For my burial," He said, and with that He established a memorial to Mary that would last as long as the testimony of the gospel itself. It still endures after nearly two thousand years and will still endure when time has run its course.

That incident seems to have been the last straw in Judas's alienation from Jesus. Seeing three hundred pieces of silver run through his fingers was more than he could take. So, summoning up all his impatience, all his frustration, all his disappointed ambition, he went to the chief priests with his offer to play the traitor—for a price. Now the value which Judas placed upon Mary's ointment was over three hundred denarii, that is, three hundred days' wages. He accepted thirty pieces of silver (of uncertain value) as the price for selling the Son of God.

There are two opposing views of Judas, both of which I reject. One affirms that Judas intended no ill to Jesus; that he fully believed in the messiahship of Jesus, but grew impatient with His tactics and sought to force Him into action by establishing a crisis situation in which Jesus would announce His kingship and rally the nation to His standard. The turn of events took Judas by surprise. The failure of his scheme and the realization that, instead of spurring Jesus to action he had brought about His death, so wrought upon his mind that he went out and hanged himself. According to that view Judas did not purposely betray Jesus but actually sought to help Him to the throne. His action, then, was not so much criminal as just a big mistake. We can only answer that Jesus did not so regard the man and his deed. The man, according to the judgment of Jesus, was "a son of perdition," and his deed, base treachery. We are not prepared to call him "Saint Judas."

The other opposite view is that Judas was not a normal human being, but actually a devil, brought into the world supernaturally for the very purpose of committing a crime, the enormity of which would put it beyond the range of human wickedness. Our Lord's reference to Judas as "the son of perdition" (John 17:12) is sometimes used to strengthen that view. That is reading too much into the text. When Jesus said to the religious leaders of Israel, "Ye are of your father the devil" (John 8:44), He did not infer that they were literally begotten of Satan. Nor am I persuaded that there is any sin of which men are incapable. Certainly we shall not say that Judas committed his supercrime unaided. We read in John's record that Jesus identified the traitor by giving to him the "sop" that is said to have been the token of friendship, "and after the sop Satan entered into him" (John 13:27). That he was a Satan-inspired man we shall admit, but still a man we must hold. Jesus Himself referred to him as "that man" (26:24).

The supper in Bethany was of a social nature, marked by the establishment of a memorial. Jesus there ordained that Mary's lovely act of devotion should be part of the gospel story. We see Him now in that borrowed "upper room," this time at a religious supper—the Passover. And there He establishes another memorial—His own. Lifting two of the simplest items of the Passover feast, He enriches them with new meaning. Of the bread He says, "This is my body" (26:26), and of the cup, "This is my blood of the new testament" (26:28). Then He adds, "This do in remembrance of me" (Luke 22:19). We recall that when Peter confessed Jesus as "the Christ, the Son of the living God," Jesus forbade the apostles to advertise it. Attached to the identity must be the mission. He will not be acclaimed the Christ apart from the cross. So here His appointed memorial celebrates His death in its redemptive power. It is "for the remission of sins" (26:28).

Let us sum up the differences in the two suppers. One was social, the other ritual. At Bethany a woman (Mary) anointed His head and His feet, while in the upper room He washed the feet of the disciples. At the former He established Mary's memorial, while at the latter He ordained His own memorial. In the home of Simon He was the object of loving gratitude, while the presence of the traitor polluted the atmosphere of the upper room until the Lord dismissed him.

GETHSEMANE (26:31-56)

The next conversation evidently took place on the way from the upper room to Gethsemane. Since Judas had already been dismissed (John 13:27-30), only the eleven were accompanying Jesus. In the light of what He had said about one of the twelve betraying Him, followed by Judas's hasty exit and continued absence, some suspicion that he was the guilty party must have formulated in their minds. But Jesus turned their thoughts upon themselves. Judas may betray Him, but they would not be altogether blameless. All of them would be offended at Him, seeing Him humiliated even to the shame and anguish of the cross. That is a harsh word—offended. The Greek gives us our word *scandalize* but carries the sense of stumbling, physically or morally. Here Jesus affirms that all eleven are going to be guilty of moral stumbling, deserting Him in the hour of crisis. The desertion would come as no surprise to Jesus, who understood the hearts of men and knew also how it was written of Him in the prophets, "Awake, O sword, against my shepherd, and against the man that is my fellow, saith the LORD of hosts: smite the shepherd, and the sheep shall be scattered" (Zechariah 13:7).

Of course the eleven did not believe themselves capable of such dastardly disloyalty. As for Peter, he repudiated the very suggestion that he would act the coward and, in good Petrine style, expressed confidence in his superior strength. Others may . . . but not I! That was the theme of his boast. To a man so sure of himself our Lord's next statement must have been devastating indeed: "This night, before the cock crow, thou shalt deny me thrice" (26:34). Remember, it was already night (John 13:30), and Peter's denial of Jesus was to be "before the cock crow," that is, before the first streak of dawn. How close is boasting to downfall! Notice, too, how the Lord's warning, instead of humbling Peter, made him more wildly vocal till the

others, not to be outdone, joined him in his boast, "Though I should
die with thee, yet will I not deny thee" (26:35).

It makes sad reading. Note three phrases: in verse 21, "one of
you"; in verse 31, "all ye"; in verse 34, "thou." Together they form
a dark picture. The first spells betrayal; the second, flight; the third,
denial. Truly, "it was night."

Gethsemane! How often the Lord had come there with His disciples for rest and refreshing! (See John 18:2.) Tonight it became
the scene of spiritual conflict.

Although He knew that within hours those men would fail Him,
He still wanted them near Him in that struggle. He craved the support of their presence. But surely it was for their sakes also that He
invited them to come within sight of the scene of His battle, with the
three privileged ones only a stone's throw away. Was He thinking
especially of Peter, who sorely needed this fellowship in the Master's
suffering to rid him of his boasting? But instead of "watching unto
prayer," and instead of supporting his Master in those strong wres-
tlings, he joined the others in sleep. First boasting, then sleeping.

Consider the Gethsemane prayer: "My Father, if it be possible, let
this cup pass from me: nevertheless not as I will, but as thou wilt"
(26:39). Traditionally the "cup" has been regarded as referring to
the cross, with all involved in it; so that the prayer expressed Jesus'
shrinking from that awful ordeal, the bearing of a world's sin. But
with the shrinking came the submission. He would have the Father's
will, even to the death of the cross. Some, however, find that view
repugnant. They ask, Would Jesus, who came into the world for the
express purpose of making the great atoning sacrifice, seek to turn
away from it at the last hour? Would He suggest a cancellation of
the appointment made in the counsels of eternity? In place of it they
offer another meaning to the cup. We learn from Luke's record that
"his sweat became as it were great drops of blood falling down upon
the ground" (Luke 22:44, ASV). Such a condition, we are told,
would soon end in death. If, then, Jesus died under that great pressure, there would be no cross. It was that possible failure to reach the
cross that greatly disturbed Jesus and drew from Him the cry, "Let
this cup pass away from me," the cup being the bloody sweat that

threatened the completion of His mission. But even for that He was prepared if it should be the Father's will.

Although I appreciate the devotion that inspires that interpretation, I cannot accept it. If the cup is the bloody sweat, then the prayer, "Nevertheless not as I will, but as thou wilt," presupposes the possibility of a change of plan on God's part, so that what was predetermined in the eternal counsels is suddenly scrapped and a death from natural causes is substituted for the long-predicted death of the cross.

In addition, the times that our Lord used the figure of the cup in relation to His sacrificial death would call for a like meaning to be attached to the word here. Jesus and His disciples had just come from the upper room, where He had instituted the memorial supper in which the cup certainly points to the blood of His cross. And when Peter wielded a faulty sword in behalf of His Master, Jesus rebuked him, saying, "The cup which my Father hath given me, shall I not drink it?" (John 18:11). That was said after the conflict of Gethsemane, so quite evidently the cup was not Gethsemane. But rather than make so sacred a thing a matter of controversy, let us be profoundly thankful that He did not turn away from the cup, bitter as it was.

Jesus went voluntarily out to meet those who had come to arrest Him. His "time" having come, there was no more walking through the midst of them and so passing on (Luke 4:30).

There was something ludicrous about the arrest of Jesus. Can you imagine "a great multitude with swords and staves" sent to arrest one defenseless man? Perhaps they remembered those occasions when He eluded the multitudes. Perhaps they expected His disciples to put up a fight. Perhaps Judas had warned them to be prepared for the unexpected. In Mark's record Judas adds the warning note, "Lead him away safely" (Mark 14:44).

Two incidents highlight the arrest—the kiss and the sword. That kiss established Judas's place in the world's hall of infamy and gave a title to the lowest form of perfidy—a Judas kiss. One identifying kiss would have been despicable enough, but according to the Greek text, with its prefix to the verb, Judas kissed Him much, or, to use an old English phrase, "smothered Him with kisses," and every kiss was a poisoned stab at the heart. One cringes at the thought. Nor can Judas be excused on the ground that he was predestined to perpetrate this atrocity. God's predestinations are indeed sure, but they are not necessitarian. By his own will and action Judas is the supreme traitor of all time. As one of our Scottish divines has stated it, "Judas was the worst of men, because he was a traitor to the best of men." And that "best of men" was the Son of God.

There is considerable difficulty in understanding Jesus' rebuke of Judas, rendered in the ASV, "Friend, do that for which thou art come" (26:50). My suggestion is that we link it with the much kissing. The purpose of the coming of Judas was to identify Jesus to His enemies. The first kiss accomplished the purpose, and when Judas made to continue Jesus said, "Enough! Do what you came to do, and be satisfied with that, not adding insult to injury!"

Then came Peter. He had boasted; then he had slept. Now, thoroughly aroused, he determined to make good his boast, and with a touch of drama. But what was Peter doing with a sword? Was it in response to a too literal obedience to our Lord's dictum given in Luke 22:36, where Jesus abrogates a previous command? "But now . . . he that hath no sword, let him sell his garment, and buy one." Or it may have been a small, swordlike instrument used to slit open fish, and useful for other purposes. Perhaps self-defense? Whichever it was, Peter was not skilled in the more offensive use of the weapon, and, missing the blow to the head, cut off the ear of the high priest's servant, Malchus, a member of the arresting party. Jesus rejected that carnal and futile support, reminding Peter of three great truths: first, that more than seventy-two thousand angels were at His disposal for the asking; second, that what was now taking place was in fulfillment of the Scriptures; third, that this was the "cup" that the Father had given Him, and He would not turn away from drinking it (John 18:11). "Then all the disciples forsook him, and fled" (26:56) in keeping with the Lord's prediction (26:31).

THE JEWISH TRIAL (26:57—27:2)

Matthew does not recount all six stages of the trial of Jesus, but it may be profitable to gather them together.

I. The Jewish trial:

(a) The preliminary hearing before Annas (John 18:12-24). Since Annas had been the official high priest, the dignity of the office remained with him, so it was not unusual for matters of importance to be referred to him for counsel. Note that Annas questioned Jesus before any charge was laid.

(b) The official hearing before Caiaphas (Matthew 26:57-66). Several points emerge here. Death was determined before the trial began. The prosecution actually sought false witness. The high priest put Jesus under oath and incriminated Him on what He said. No defense was sought or allowed. Since it was a trial for life, conducting it by night was illegal.

(c) The hasty morning gathering of the chief priests and elders to confirm their nocturnal sentence and to give it a semblance of legality (27:1).

THE ROMAN TRIAL (27:3-26)

II. The Roman trial:

(a) The first hearing before Pilate (Luke 23:1-7). The Jewish leaders condemned Jesus on religious grounds, but they sought judgment from Pilate on political grounds, accusing Jesus of stirring up rebellion against Rome.

(b) The hearing before Herod (Luke 23:8-12). Pilate was happy to shift the responsibility of the case to other shoulders, and Herod welcomed the possibility of seeing that miracle Man perform! Both were disappointed. Not only did Jesus not act for Herod Antipas, the murderer of John the Baptist, but He spoke not a word to him. As for Pilate, he was not so easily relieved of the task of sitting as judge on that most amazing case.

(c) The final hearing before Pilate, described in our chapter. Pilate tried to appease the priests and elders of Israel by compromise, suggesting a beating and release. But why a beating for one in whom neither he nor Herod found any wrongdoing? Then he tried cunning. The release of a prisoner of the people's choice at the Passover season had become traditional. Pilate reduced the options to two, one a notorious criminal, and one the Man in whom they could find no fault. Surely the people would go for the good Man! But they were too well brainwashed. Soon the Praetorium was ringing with the cry, "Away with him! Crucify him! Give us Barabbas!" And out of the shouting emerged a threat: "If thou let this man go, thou art not Caesar's friend" (John 19:12). Pilate could not fail to see in that a report to Rome that would be far from advantageous to him. It could mean impeachment, disgrace, and the end of his political career. So finally self-interest proved stronger than the boasted Roman justice. Then, to allay his conscience, Pilate used a theatrical gesture to dissociate himself from the murder of the Christ. Washing his hands he exclaimed, "I am innocent of the blood of this righteous man." But was he?

However, there is a potent detergent for the removal of sin's stain.

> What can wash away my sin?
> Nothing but the blood of Jesus.
>
> ROBERT LOWRY
> ("Nothing But the Blood of Jesus")

Two incidents are interwoven with the trials of Jesus. One concerns Peter and took place in the court of the high priest's house; the other concerns Judas and his pitiful end.

Peter had boasted when he should have sought "grace to help in time of need"; he had slept when he ought to have been praying; he wielded a sword in a futile attempt to defend his Master. Three rebukes he had suffered, till his inward strength was sapped, and now, while he followed the crowd to the high priest's residence and obtained entrance by the good offices of John, he was in poor condition to meet temptation. Three times he was identified as one of Christ's followers, and three times he denied any acquaintance with Jesus, the third time with oaths and curses. His speech certainly did betray him that day. It revealed what kind of man he had been before Jesus found him—a rough, cursing braggart. But never mind, recovery is just around the corner, and those bitter tears (26:75) were a good preparation for that recovery. If Judas had shed tears, he might not have had to shed his own blood.

And that brings us to the second incident—the end of Judas. Those thirty pieces of silver—they were as thirty ovens, all burning his soul with remorse. Did Judas repent? Our text tells us that he "repented himself." But the Greek word used here is not that used with regard to true gospel repentance. Judas's "repentance" was only a change of feeling, based on the unexpected turn of events. True repentance is a complete change of mind, not just of feeling, and exactly that was the difference between Peter and Judas. As for the disposing of the money, it fulfilled a somewhat obscure prophecy in Zechariah 11:12-13 in which the thirty pieces of silver, the house of the Lord, the potter, and the field were all involved. Did you notice the callousness of the priests toward tormented Judas and their punctiliousness in not putting blood money into the temple treasury? Whited sepulchers indeed, as Jesus truly called them.

The Roman army was noted for its discipline. But they were disciplined in cruelty. Then, too, the Pax Romana reduced the life of a soldier to a dead monotony, with no great heroic campaigns. So a crucifixion was at least a break in that monotony, and here was a specially interesting case—an itinerant Jewish rabbi defying the might of Rome, like a fly attacking an elephant. Here was an occasion for merriment. So they staged a mock coronation. The scarlet robe was doubtless a cast-off officer's garment; the thorns that were used for the mock crown could have been any one of several species of thorny shrubs that now carry the name of Christ, such as the *Zizyphus spina-christi;* the mock scepter was probably the familiar cattail reed. In mockery they bowed to Him and beat Him in turn until their sadistic tempers were satiated. Then they prepared Him for the via dolorosa from Gabbatha to Golgotha. On the way the soldiers pressed Simon, the father of Alexander and Rufus (see Mark 15:21) to carry the cross. Most of us have sung the hymn, "Must Jesus bear the cross alone,/and all the world go free?" (Thomas Shepherd, "Must Jesus Bear the Cross Alone?"). It may be of interest to know that the original version runs, "Must Simon bear the cross alone, and all the rest go free?" For it was written for St. Simon's day to commemorate his carrying the cross after Jesus.

The Crucifixion (27:27-56)

Several incidents are connected with the actual crucifixion. Those recorded by Matthew are: the mixture of vinegar and gall, provided, we are told, by benevolent women to ease the pain of crucifixion, but refused by Jesus (see Psalm 69:21), who would not have His senses dulled while He accomplished the great work of redemption; the parting of the garments, a practice permitted to the quaternion of soldiers who carried out the execution, but complicated in this instance by the seamless robe, calling for a casting of dice; the controversy about the superscription ordered by Pilate over the objection of the Jewish leaders as a sop to his conscience for his betrayal of justice; the jeering of the passersby, the religious leaders, and His cosufferers, the two thieves. Some of those call for special comment.

The seamless robe (perhaps more of a tunic) has been regarded by many expositors as typifying the perfect righteousness of Christ, made over to us upon acceptance of Him as Lord and Savior. He exchanged His perfection for our sin, that we might exchange our sin for His perfection. To use the words of the apostle Paul, He was made "sin for us, who knew no sin, that we might be made the righteousness of God in him" (2 Corinthians 5:21).

What was inscribed above a gallows for crucifixion was generally a statement of the crime being expiated by death. The superscription in this case, apparently ordered by Pilate himself, did not read like an accusation, but rather like an affirmation, and on that he stood fast against the clamor of the priests and elders. He was personally convinced of the innocence of Jesus, so that, while not acknowledging any political right, he saw in Jesus the moral grandeur of true kingship. "The King of the Jews" indeed, one day to be acclaimed "King of kings and Lord of lords."

In the jeering hurled at Jesus, two phrases stand out by repetition: "If thou be the Son of God," and, "Come down from the cross." So both His person and His mission were brought under attack. It was no new thing. The temptation in the wilderness focused upon those two issues. Throughout His ministry they surfaced again and again, the divine sonship being rejected by His enemies, and the cross being rejected by His friends. We recall Peter's blunt declaration, "This shall not be unto thee" (16:22).

Would the chief priests have believed on Him, as they affirmed, if He had come down from the cross? I doubt it. Unbelief is not easily overthrown. In the story of the rich man and Lazarus (Luke 16:19-31), Dives begs Abraham to send Lazarus on an errand of mercy, to warn his (Dives's) five brothers of the fate that awaits the unrepentant sinner. His argument is, "If one went to them from the dead, they will repent" (Luke 16:30). In other words, they would respond to evidence. Abraham replies, "If they hear not Moses and the prophets (that is), the Word of God, neither will they be persuaded, though one rose from the dead" (Luke 16:31). Well, One did rise from the dead, and gave "many infallible proofs" of the reality of His resurrection, to which they replied by ignoring the evidence. For unbelief is a moral condition, not an intellectual state amenable to argument and appraisal. Take, for instance, the statement of Hastings Rashdall, a European critic, concerning the resurrection of Christ: "Were the testimony fifty times stronger than it is, any hypothesis would be more possible than that." Would coming down from the cross have secured any better response?

Of the "seven last words" spoken from the cross, only one is recorded by Matthew: "My God, my God, why hast thou forsaken me?" (27:46). Those, of course, are the opening words of Psalm 22, a psalm that the evangelical world unanimously regards as prophetic and messianic. The psalm begins with that cry of anguish and ends with a shout of triumph that is quite the equivalent of "It is finished." Thus our Lord made the sustained sob of Psalm 22:1-21 His own and embraced the latter part of the psalm (vv. 22-31) as His own paean of victory.

There on the cross Jesus was the great derelict. Bearing the sin of the world, He must know the horror of darkness, typified by that shroud of darkness that fell upon the earth during those three terrible hours. He was there taking the sinner's place, experiencing what it means to be cast out from the presence of God that He might bring us to God. Draw the contrast between the upper room prayer in John 17, where the address is consistently to the Father, and that cry of dereliction, addressed to God as God. But there is faith even in this great sob. God is still "My God," and that becomes the groundwork for the shout of victory.

Bishop Nicholson wrote a little gem of a book on "The Miracles of the Cross." Three of those are given brief mention in Matthew's account. We have already looked at one of them—the supernatural darkness. The second was the rending of the great veil of the Temple that hung before the Most Holy Place, giving access to the high priest alone, and that only on the annual Day of Atonement. So long as it hung there it bore mute testimony to the inability of the Levitical system to give access to God. Its rending in that hour of our Lord's atoning work proclaimed the opening of a "new and living way" into the presence of God for all who come by way of Jesus Christ. Instead of "No Admittance" the sign now reads, "Let us . . . come boldly unto the throne of grace, that we may obtain mercy, and find grace to help in time of need" (Hebrews 4:16). It is surely not without significance that the rending was "from the top to the bottom," suggestive of an act of God rather than a work of vandals who normally would proceed in the other direction. Nor am I convinced that the rending of the veil was the result of the earthquake, although the two are mentioned together. An earthquake would more readily pull down stones and timbers than tear a curtain. But what matter? It was the Lord's doing, conveying a great truth to our hearts.

The earthquake is more likely to be associated with the opening of the graves, giving exit to the "bodies of the saints" who rose from the dead after His resurrection and appeared to many in Jerusalem. Admittedly that is a strange and difficult passage, simply ignored by many expositors. Is it one of the doubtful passages, like John 8:1-11? Or are we just afraid to take it at face value? Personally, I see no reason why they should not be in the same category as Lazarus, the son of the widow, and the daughter of Jairus—restored to mortal life for a season, only to taste of death a second time. Only those post-resurrection risings carry a special message. They are related to His resurrection, as much as to say, "In His resurrection He bestows resurrection life upon His saints." Some day we shall meet those saints and learn more of the mystery.

There was an occasion when Jesus bluntly affirmed, "I am not sent but unto the lost sheep of the house of Israel" (15:24). Yet it almost appears as if the first fruit of the cross was Gentile. The centurion in charge of the crucifixion was deeply moved by the supernatural occurrences, and especially by what he saw in Jesus till he said, with deep emotion, "Truly this was the Son of God" (27:54). Now we do not know what all that Roman soldier meant by "Son of God," but tradition has it that he, Longinus, came to faith, became a faithful witness, and sealed his testimony with his blood. As for those who were with him that day, we know nothing about them.

From the moment that Jesus cried, "It is finished," no inimical hand touched his body. The Jews would not "defile" themselves by touching a dead body at the Passover season. The Roman soldiers had done their job and had no responsibility for the disposing of the body.

THE BURIAL (27:57-66)

Crisis brings out both the worst and the best in men. In the case of Joseph of Arimathea, it brought out the best. John tells us that up to that point Joseph's discipleship had been secret. But with the arrest of Jesus his secrecy was abandoned in favor of a full devotion. To begin with, he refused to go along with the Sanhedrin in its condemnation of Jesus. Then, on the death of Jesus, he assumed guardianship of the dead body, providing honorable burial for his beloved Master, and in so doing fulfilled the Scripture which says, "He made his grave with the wicked, and with the rich in his death" (Isaiah 53:9). Appointed to death as a criminal, He would have filled a felon's grave had not Joseph stepped into the picture and given "his own new tomb, which he had hewn out in the rock" (27:60). Of course he could not do that without Roman permission, so we see the secret disciple boldly facing Pilate with his request. Matthew leaves it up to John to tell us about the part that Nicodemus played in the sacred burial. He does, however, take note of the sorrowing women who watched the crucifixion from a distance, then followed Joseph to the place of entombment.

But the chief priests and Pharisees were just as afraid of Jesus dead as alive. Had He not predicted that He would rise again the third day? Strangely enough, the enemies of Jesus had taken it to heart more than His friends, so they sought Pilate's help to guard against such rumors. By that time Pilate was tired of the whole affair and brusquely dismissed the Jews with "Have what you want, but get out of my sight," or words to that effect. So the tomb of Jesus was secured with a Roman guard and a Roman seal.

PART FOUR

The King in His Power

(28:1-20)

18

TRUMPHANT IN GLORY

(28:1-20)

WE HAVE FOLLOWED THE KING in His preparations, His procedures, and His passion. His adversaries are sure that they have effectually disposed of "this deceiver," as they bitterly call Him. They have even provided against a possible theft of the body and a rumor of resurrection. The Roman guard and the Roman seal are guarantee of permanent entombment. So they reasoned. But now we see the King in His power. True, He appears still in humble guise so that Mary Magdalene mistakes Him for a gardener. Nevertheless He is the conqueror of death, and there is a majesty in His person that calls for worship.

THE EMPTY TOMB (28:1-7)

The earth shook when Jesus died. It shuddered at the awful crime of man. Then again the earth shook when Jesus rose from the dead. It trembled with the excitement of victory, in response to the opening of the tomb by angelic hands. We shall remember what has been well stated by many, that the angel did not roll away the stone to give Jesus exit from the sepulcher, but to give the disciples entrance and to display the empty tomb. That stone was no more a barrier to the risen King than was the door of the upper room (John 20:19).

I think the visiting angel took on more radiance that day, out of very joy at the triumph of his Lord, so that we read, "His countenance was like lightning, and his raiment white as snow." In the presence of such heavenly radiance the guards were overwhelmed with fear, and it is noticeable that the angel made no attempt to allay their fears, but he did say to the women, "Fear not *ye*," with emphasis on the *ye*. For the enemies of the King have cause to fear, but His friends, those who seek Him, have nothing to fear. They may, like Longinus, die for

225

their faith, but ultimately that is nothing to fear. "Fear not them which kill the body," said Jesus on another occasion, "but are not able to kill the soul" (10:28), for "absent from the body" means "present with the Lord."

An angel announced the birth of the Lord Jesus to a small company of shepherds "keeping watch over their flock by night" (Luke 2:8-12); an angel announced the resurrection of Christ to a small group of women keeping watch over the tomb where the body lay. In each case the angelic message was prefaced with "Fear not," then reason was given for the dismissal of fear, in the first case the Savior born, in the second the Lord risen.

Let us analyze the angel's message to the women.

First, *commendation.* "I know that ye seek Jesus" (28:5). How better could they be engaged? Their understanding may have been defective, but there was nothing wrong with their occupation.

Second, *declaration.* "He is risen" (28:6). The humiliation was over; the glorification had begun, to be consummated at "the right hand of the throne of the Majesty in the heavens" (Heb. 8:1).

Third, *invitation.* "Come, see the place where the Lord lay" (28:6). We of the nonconformist order are not much given to "sacred places." At least we profess so, and yet there is something in us that responds to the sanctity of the past. For instance, when I preached in St. Stephen's Church in Dundee, Scotland, I could not but sense a hallowed atmosphere coming down from the long past ministry of godly Murray McCheyne. What, then, can we say of "the place where the Lord lay"? We shall remember that the angelic invitation to see was for the purpose of demonstrating that the tomb was empty, because He was risen. It is the past tense that counts here—not "the Lord lies," but "the Lord lay." It was an invitation to accumulated evidence.

Fourth, *direction.* "Go quickly, and tell his disciples" (28:7). Now we know why the women were the first to receive the good news. They were there to receive it. Where were Peter and John? They were in that upper room nursing their grief, and not till the women burst in on them with their unbelievable tidings did they bestir themselves to find out for themselves. But since the women were the first to be informed and to see the risen Lord Himself, they must also be the first to bear the good news to the apostolic band. Come, see; go, tell. That is the order. If we have obeyed the first duo, the second presses heavily upon us.

Fifth, *anticipation*. "Galilee . . . there shall ye see him." Galilee saw the beginnings of our Lord's earthly ministry. It was appropriate that He should pay a post-resurrection visit to the scene of so many of His labors. It is to be observed that the promise of seeing Him was given to believers only. Indeed, so far as the record goes, none but believers saw Him during the forty days between the resurrection and the ascension. Some might think that that would weaken the testimony, for the witness would be biased. We can only answer that Jesus "took that risk." His strategy was to assure His own disciples "by many infallible proofs," and send them forth in the power of the Holy Spirit to convince others. So the angel promised the women, and the apostles through them, that they would see Him in the familiar region of Galilee.

THE RISEN LORD (28:8-10)

Wonderful as it was for those devoted women to receive an angelic messenger, that falls far short of a meeting with the Lord Himself, and it is indeed significant that while they went about obeying the instructions of the angel, "Jesus met them." From that we may learn that obedience to present light is the pathway to deeper and fuller communion. Perhaps one reason that angelic ministries are so largely invisible and inaudible is that seeing and hearing them would become an end in itself, till we should fail to seek His face. The good can be a hindrance to the best.

"All hail," said Jesus to the women as He met them on their way to the apostles. And right good reason He had to use this greeting, which had become the Greek form ever since Pheidippides had burst into the senate chambers in Athens with news of the victory of the Greek army over the Persians at Marathon. *"Chairete nikomen!"* was his cry (Rejoice, we conquer!), as he fell exhausted from the Marathon race. Well might Jesus use that joyous greeting, for He had just come from a far greater triumph than Marathon. That victory had indeed cost Him His life, but He had overcome death itself and stood before the amazed women as the Living One.

"They came and held him by the feet, and worshipped him" (28:9). There is no word here of His forbidding them, yet when He met Mary Magdalene alone and she went to hold Him by the feet, He forbade her. Two words would seem to explain the discrepancy. "Rabboni!" cried Mary as she fell before Him to grasp His feet. But Rabboni, for all its tenderness, suggested the old, pre-crucifixion, pre-resurrection relationship of Teacher. But when the women, coming from the meeting with the angel, held Him by the feet, it was as an act of worship. They recognized the new relationship, the new lordship.

Look again! He who accepts worship, claims worship, demands worship, calls His people "my brethren." Such intimacy must come from His side. From us must come reverence.

THE FUTILE LIE (28:11-15)

While all that blessed reunion was being effected, the enemies of Jesus were not idle. The Roman guard, lent to the chief priests for the securing of the tomb, were bound to report to their temporary Jewish masters. Their report was far from welcome news. Rejecting all evidence for the resurrection, the rulers were prepared to admit that all their precautions had been of no avail, and to affirm what they knew well could not have been accomplished, that the disciples of Jesus had stolen the body while the guards slept. Death was the penalty for sleeping on duty, yet the chief priests offered big enough bribes to the soldiers to induce them to take the risk of such a false report, on the assurance that the priests would take care of Pilate. Once more we see the obduracy of unbelief.

Matthew tells us that the story of the stolen corpse was still being propagated by the Jews when he was writing his gospel. Actually there has been a revival of that fallacy many times during these intervening years, as critics have tried to discredit the resurrection, that Luthardt of Leipsic rightly called "the foundation of Christianity." However, the proponents of the stolen body theory are unable to agree as to the perpetrator of the theft. The contemporary charge was laid against the disciples, but Joseph of Arimathea, Pilate, even the Sanhedrin have come under suspicion. It seems so foolish, for it certainly would not have required a Sherlock Holmes to solve the mystery had there been such a theft. Instead, only a few days later "a great company of the priests were obedient to the faith" (Acts 6:7).

THE ROYAL DECREE (28:16-20)

The last scene, so far as Matthew's account carries us, was in Galilee, on a mountain previously appointed. That appointment seems to have been forgotten by the disciples until reminded of it by the women. I suppose we could entitle this paragraph, "The King Gives Marching Orders." We generally call it the Great Commission. In it we observe the King's power, the King's precept, and the King's pledge.

"All power is given unto me," said the King (28:18). Power is of various sorts. Here it is the power of authority. Elsewhere (John 5:22-23) our Lord tells us that the Father has committed all judgment to Him. That also is power, but this is even broader than "all judgment," judgment being but one area in which the "all authority" is wielded. The extent of the authority vested in Christ is indicated in the phrase, "in heaven and on earth" (28:18, ASV), and in Bible parlance that embraces everything. We note, too, that the risen Lord did not claim that universal authority as something pertaining to Him naturally, though He might have done so, but as a bestowal from the Father.

Authority carries with it the right of command, and it is here that the Great Commission proper is introduced. It will help us if we examine the grammar of the passage. There is one verb in the indicative mode that makes it the chief action verb—"make disciples." The other verbs are participial in form. Chart it like this:

> Going . . . .
> Make disciples . . .
> Baptizing
> Teaching

Let us see what that grammatical structure is trying to say to us.

First, the church of Jesus Christ is a *going* institution. It is on the move. It is caught up in the mighty movement of the kingdom of God. And what is true of the church as a body is true (or ought to be) of the individual. That passage contemplates an "on the go" people.

Second, what activity is to characterize our going? We are told, and that with strong emphasis: Make disciples. That is the main verb of the passage and therefore must have prominence in all our thinking and doing.

But now, third, the steps in the discipling process are presented. They are: baptizing and teaching. The baptizing indicates a crisis of submission, a confession of faith, an identification with Christ, a beginning of the new life. It is a trinitarian ordinance in which the young believer is baptized "into the name of the Father, and of the Son, and of the Holy Spirit." It is one name, but triune.

That beginning is followed up with teaching, and practical teaching at that. The Christian must be taught obedience. There is theological teaching that is doubtless inspiring and edifying, but teaching that falls short of obedience is defective. So disciple making has two stages. It begins with the call to an initial step of faith and continues with a process of instruction that, to change the figure, leads from apprenticeship in the things of God to the status of master craftsman.

It is a big task, bigger than we could handle in our own resources. So our risen King and the Lord has pledged Himself to our support, not from a distance, but in personal presence, in continuity, and unto the consummation when, the purpose of the age completed, He will call us to Himself and be glorified in "a glorious church, not having spot, or wrinkle, or any such thing" (Ephesians 5:27). So the King is presented in His power, not only by His rising from the dead, but in the full accomplishment of that for which He came into the world.

"And he hath on his vesture and on his thigh a name written, KING OF KINGS, AND LORD OF LORDS" (Revelation 19:16).